D1236727

Libertines

Libertines

American Political Sex Scandals from Alexander Hamilton to Donald Trump

J. Michael Martinez

ROWMAN & LITTLEFIELD
Lanham • Boulder • New York • London

Published by Rowman & Littlefield
An imprint of The Rowman & Littlefield Publishing Group, Inc.
4501 Forbes Boulevard, Suite 200, Lanham, Maryland 20706
www.rowman.com

86-90 Paul Street, London EC2A 4NE

British Library Cataloguing in Publication Information Available

Library of Congress Cataloging-in-Publication Data

Names: Martinez, J. Michael, author.
Title: Libertines : American political sex scandals from Alexander Hamilton to
    Donald Trump / J. Michael Martinez.
Description: Lanham : Rowman & Littlefield, [2022] | Includes bibliographical
    references. | Summary: "Historian Michael Martinez surveys political sex
    scandals in American history, from the earliest years of the Republic to today, to
    explore how these events impacted the politics of the day and the legacy they
    left for future generations of American leaders"— Provided by publisher.
Identifiers: LCCN 2021051872 (print) | LCCN 2021051873 (ebook) | ISBN
    9781538167533 (cloth) | ISBN 9781538167540 (ebook)
Subjects: LCSH: Sex scandals—United States—History. | Politicians—Sexual
    behavior—United States. | Politicians—United States—Conduct of life. |
    United States—Politics and government.
Classification: LCC HQ18.U5 M3635 2022 (print) | LCC HQ18.U5 (ebook) |
    DDC 306.770973—dc23/eng/20211022
LC record available at https://lccn.loc.gov/2021051872
LC ebook record available at https://lccn.loc.gov/2021051873

For Chuck Redmon, a longtime friend and colleague

I have no objection to anyone's sex life as long as they don't practice it in the street and frighten the horses.

—attributed to Oscar Wilde

Contents

List of Photos

Introduction and Acknowledgments

Sexual desire is so obviously a part of the human condition that the assertion needs no debate. It is not surprising, therefore, that individuals seek to gratify that desire, usually in private, but occasionally in ways that spill into public life. This book seeks to understand why public figures sometimes take extraordinary risks, sullying their good names, humiliating their families, placing themselves in legal jeopardy, and potentially destroying their political careers as they seek to gratify their sexual desires.

During the early years of the republic, voters cared deeply about the moral rectitude of their elected officials. A public man was entrusted with public business, and so he must be a man of high moral character. It meant that he controlled his sexual desires. Good character required a man of integrity to conduct himself privately exactly as he would in the public square. Anyone who would cavort with women of easy virtue or cheat on his wife presumably would feel emboldened to compromise the public's business, or so the conventional wisdom dictated. Consequently, candidates for high office were subjected to exacting standards of moral purity and sexual chastity. Even the whiff of scandal was enough to imperil a successful public man's reputation and success. (As late as the 1970s, political operatives wondered whether Ronald Reagan's previous divorce disqualified him from serious consideration as a presidential candidate.)

Alexander Hamilton and Thomas Jefferson, the two earliest figures profiled in this book, faced withering scrutiny for their transgressions. Hamilton's tryst with Maria Reynolds might have destroyed his public career, but it came to light after he had left his position as secretary of the treasury. He offered a classic defense of "I did it, but so what?" Hamilton admitted that he had slept with Maria Reynolds, revealing the facts of the sordid episode in excruciating detail, but he vehemently denied that he had compromised the public's business. It was the classic libertine's explanation: You must

1

separate my private and public conduct. I may be a reprobate behind closed doors, but in public I am a faithful steward of the government's business. The defense succeeded—to a degree. Hamilton's subsequent presidential ambitions were derailed owing to several factors—the Reynolds affair was not the sole reason—but clearly evidence of his poor judgment did not aid his cause.

Jefferson's relationship with his slave Sally Hemings is far more problematic than Hamilton's affair with Maria Reynolds. Unlike Hamilton, Jefferson never addressed the issue directly, and he certainly never penned a chronology of his relationship with his slave. Moreover, Sally Hemings did not possess the autonomy that Maria Reynolds enjoyed. As a married white woman, Reynolds could come and go as she chose, interacting with whomever she pleased. She instigated the affair with Hamilton of her own volition, although historians might quibble as to whether her opportunistic husband coerced her into it. The point is, however, that she was a free white adult.

Denied free agency, Sally Hemings lived in the shadows. Her voice is muted in history. What is known of her relationship with Jefferson comes from her children, and they spoke of the connection decades after the events allegedly occurred. The chronology must be pieced together with incomplete, perhaps tainted information.

The nature of the Jefferson-Hemings liaison is unclear as well. It may have begun when Sally was 14, 15, or 16 years old. Jefferson was thirty years her senior. Aside from the salaciousness of the tale, it goes to the heart of consent in a sexual relationship. Can a child consent to a sexual relationship with a much older man? Could a slave consent to having sex with her master? Does it rob Sally Hemings of her free agency to conclude that she could not love Jefferson and must have been coerced, or does it recognize her untenable position as human property?

The stories first emerged even before Jefferson campaigned for the presidency in 1800. His political enemies circulated tales of "Mr. Jefferson's Congo Harem" cloistered together in the wilds of Monticello. It was titillating stuff, but true or untrue, it was over the top, straining credulity for all but the most partisan anti-Jeffersonian. Later, the scandalmongering pamphleteer James Callender flung charges at Jefferson, as he had at Hamilton, about the great man's weakness for the flesh, notably his taste for his "dusky Sally."

Jefferson understood that he must not answer such scurrilous charges. Callender was hardly a reputable source. After all, Jefferson had employed the man to dig up dirt on his political enemies precisely because Callender represented the dark side of American politics. To acknowledge the incendiary rumors was to risk creating an enduring story that would not die. It was best to leave it alone, unaddressed, to languish in the shadows. The lack of an evidentiary record left the public, along with historians, scratching their heads over the facts of the case. It was not until the era of DNA in the 1990s that the presumption changed against Jefferson's innocence.

Hamilton's and Jefferson's scandals presented a straightforward narrative of desire and gratification, but Andrew Jackson's sex scandal was one of the strangest episodes in American political history. Still reeling from the death of his beloved wife, who had been tainted by her marriage to Jackson before her divorce from her first husband was finalized, the incoming president defended the virtue of a young woman who had married his secretary of war. That a president of the United States would stoop to notice the ostracism of a cabinet member's wife is bizarre enough, but that he would also reorganize his administration, at least in part, owing to his advisers' treatment of the woman is perverse. To modern audiences, the so-called "Petticoat Affair" is absurd, a reminder that the mores and lifestyles of men and women who lived long ago often are alien to later generations.

At least Daniel Sickles's motives and actions appear comprehensible, as highlighted in chapter 4. A jealous husband killing his wife's lover is a familiar fact pattern, a type of action that is as old as mankind itself. The legal proceedings that followed the homicide, however, introduced a novel concept into the American lexicon: temporary insanity. To argue that a man cannot be held liable for his actions when he is temporarily blinded by rage troubles citizens today, exactly as it troubled them when Sickles and his lawyers asserted the defense in 1859.

Apart from the question of temporary insanity, observers fell into two camps. One camp thought that Daniel Sickles had gotten away with murder. He shot his wife's lover in broad daylight in full view of eyewitnesses, and he escaped the legal consequences of his actions. The other camp viewed his wife's paramour as a rapscallion who received his just desserts for alienating the affections of another man's wife.

Chapters 5 and 6 discuss Henry Ward Beecher's scandalous affair as well as Grover Cleveland's illegitimate son, respectively. The formula for the garden-variety sex scandal involving a prominent American political figure was established with these cases. A famous man with a sterling reputation is alleged to have taken advantage of a woman to satisfy his base desires. Initially, the allegations sound dubious, but subsequent facts support the charges. The powerful man salvages his career, but his reputation is sullied and makes him an object of undying ridicule.

A famous Civil War–era minister and political activist, Beecher reputedly was a serial womanizer who hid stories of his sexual escapades until a close friend and colleague alleged that the great man had seduced the friend's wife. The sensational allegations led to a widely publicized trial that forever damaged Beecher's public reputation. He remained a powerful, renowned figure in some quarters, but his critics laughed at the minister's well-established hypocrisy. He condemned free love even as he failed to practice what he preached.

Similarly, New York governor Grover Cleveland, a man nicknamed "Grover the Good" for his resistance to political corruption, faced a summer surprise during his campaign for the presidency in 1884. A woman alleged that Cleveland was the father of her illegitimate child. Even worse, she claimed that he had sexually assaulted her a decade earlier, which led to the child's conception. Cleveland admitted that he had engaged in sexual intercourse with the woman, but he insisted that it was consensual. He survived the scandal by portraying himself as a Good Samaritan, providing financial support for the child despite the possibility that the woman was lying or mistaken in her paternity claims. The sexual assault charge, never proven or disproven, failed to prevent Cleveland's electoral victory. Nonetheless, Grover the Good was shown to be a deeply flawed character. His reputation never completely recovered.

By the time Warren G. Harding became a serious presidential candidate in 1920, as discussed in chapter 7, standards for reporting on the sex lives of public figures had changed. Scholars have debated the reasons for this shift in the national mood. Some researchers have suggested that the professionalization of the press corps led to an emphasis on a public figure's policies and professional life with less desire to report on private indiscretions. Sexual dalliances no longer seemed newsworthy. It is difficult to envision in the twenty-first-century era of "Gotcha" journalism and instant social media posts, but many reporters knew of Warren G. Harding's, Franklin D. Roosevelt's, and John F. Kennedy's affairs but did not print stories until after these men had died.

Other scholars have suggested that the changing attitudes on the legitimacy of political power also changed attitudes on the appropriate scope of public revelations about politically prominent figures. According to the historian John H. Summers, beginning after the 1880s and extending well into the latter half of the twentieth century, the need to increase faith in consolidated government—always a controversial proposition, especially in the early days of the republic—required the creation of a mystique about elites occupying positions of power. "In a democratic republic whose citizens still harbored suspicions of concentrated power, that sense of the state demanded cultural as well as legal justification," Summers observed in his article "What Happened to Sex Scandals? Politics and Peccadilloes, Jefferson to Kennedy." "That is, transforming elitist ideas about power into legitimate authority meant that officials and quasi officials presented a new cultural frame through which Americans were encouraged to view the federal government, and reticence about reprehensible sexual matters contributed to that project by bestowing prestige upon powerful politicians." Later in the same article, Summers observed that the "preservation of the moral integrity of twentieth-century political elites, one element in this scheme, aspired to unify the nation around the federal state. By adopting reticence, the guideposts of mass communications implied that between the polity and the state lay sacredness and mystification, a symbolic distance. To many, political authority now appeared not immediate and corporeal, but abstract and intangible, increasingly shrouded in the office of the presidency and other protected images that together functioned as a bulwark against dissent."[1]

Whatever the reasons for a changing ethos, Harding benefited from the press corps's reluctance to divulge his many sexual indiscretions. Immediately following his death, however, lurid stories circulated about a secret love child. Harding's former mistress published a tell-all book about their affair while protectors of Harding's legacy, including his wife, attacked the veracity and character of the author. It was only decades later, thanks to DNA evidence, that the mistress's account was confirmed.

Political sensibilities and social mores changed again. By the 1970s, when Wilbur Mills was stopped by police during a late-night joyride in Washington, DC, with a stripper who threw herself into the Tidal Basin, reporting on a public official's peccadilloes was no longer out of bounds. As discussed in chapter 8, snickering at the antics of the aged congressman and the much younger "Argentine firecracker" became a national pastime.

The Mills case and the other examples in this book illustrate a recurring theme in sex scandals. As John H. Summers argued, powerful public figures seem removed from normal human society, aloof from the concerns and temptations of mere mortals. Alexander Hamilton and Thomas Jefferson are men of granite, distant historical figures memorialized in books and on monuments. They appear supernatural. Henry Ward Beecher was one of the most famous public figures in nineteenth-century America, a member of a prominent family that included Harriet Beecher Stowe, author of the influential anti-slavery novel *Uncle Tom's Cabin*. Bill Clinton was a two-term president of the United States. Even lesser lights such as Daniel Sickles, Wilbur Mills, Bob Packwood, Gary Condit, and Anthony Weiner were members of Congress—not legends, but powerful and influential men who had carved out public careers, overcoming numerous obstacles in their rise from obscurity.

Sex scandals humanize public figures but not necessarily in a positive light. Scandals demonstrate that even elites seek sexual gratification and are driven to act in perverse ways. Often the public figures appear silly, as when Congressman Mills's stripper girlfriend jumped into the Tidal Basin. Anthony Weiner's multiple episodes of sexting made him the butt of many a late-night talk-show host and numerous comedians who could not resist riffing on the man's surname. Bill Clinton will forever be linked to Monica Lewinsky's semen-stained blue dress.

In a similar vein, when Colorado senator Gary Hart, campaigning for the Democratic presidential nomination in 1987, was photographed with a young actress-model sitting on his lap while they each held a drink and he wore a T-shirt bearing the words "Monkey Business Crew," the name of a luxury yacht, his momentum ground to an abrupt halt. In an era of sensationalistic journalism, when reporters and political opponents combed the written and digital record in search of damaging material, a public figure had to be squeaky clean—or at least offer a plausible explanation—if he or she hoped to rehabilitate a sullied reputation. Gary Hart was a serious man with serious ideas, but he became a national joke owing to his presumed affair with a young actress-model. His story is discussed in chapter 9.

Bob Packwood's case, detailed in chapter 10, demonstrates how much the standards applied to powerful figures changed over the years. Packwood entered the United States Senate in 1969. During the ensuing years, he took advantage of a Washington culture that allowed men of power to harass their underlings with impunity. Packwood became infamous on Capitol Hill as a man who made unwanted sexual advances to vulnerable women. Believing that he was somebody important and they were nobodies, the women thought they would risk their careers if they alerted authorities to his actions. They may have been correct.

By the 1990s the day of reckoning had come. A slew of women came forward alleging that the senator had assaulted them over many years. Packwood sought to deflect and evade responsibility, but when all was said and done, he was forced to resign from the Senate in humiliation. The culture of Washington, DC, had undergone a sea change in the decades since he had come to power. Some famous men still eluded responsibility for their sexual misdeeds—President Donald J. Trump immediately springs to mind— but a powerful political figure could no longer count on his colleagues and the public to turn a blind eye to the figure's transgressions.

Arguably the most infamous and consequential sexual scandal in American history involved President Bill Clinton and White House intern Monica Lewinsky. Clinton had a long history of sexual misconduct before he entered the White House. As recounted in chapter 11, his association with Monica Lewinsky was especially difficult to fathom. He was locked in a series of bitter political fights with Republicans anxious to bring him down. He was also facing numerous investigations as well as a sexual harassment lawsuit by a civil servant, Paula Jones, who claimed that Clinton had exposed his penis to her in a hotel when he was governor of Arkansas. To engage in a sexual affair with a young intern more than a quarter century his junior inside the White House while his private life was under a microscope was beyond risky. It was self-destructive. Afterward, to lie about the affair under oath in a deposition invited impeachment, which is exactly what happened.

Clinton survived the legal proceedings, but his reputation was irreparably damaged. He also undermined faith in political figures as cynical Americans concluded, "there goes another lying politician, misbehaving and taking advantage of his exalted position to escape justice." Expressing deep remorse and finally accepting responsibility when he could no longer credibly lie about his actions, Clinton became a symbol of the flawed public servant who cares more about satisfying his own urges than about upholding the public trust.

Clinton's political foes also overplayed their hand. As horrible as his conduct was—an older, powerful man taking advantage of a much younger, impressionable woman—he was not the threat to the republic that his most vehement detractors charged. In fact, his approval ratings improved after the unsuccessful impeachment, demonstrating that many Americans believed the punishment was disproportionate to the transgression.

The cases of sexual impropriety addressed in chapters 12 and 13 of *Libertines* are unusual, but for different reasons. Chapter 12 recalls the story of Gary Condit, a US congressman from California, who engaged in an affair with a Capitol Hill intern, Chandra Levy, in the year 2000. Aside from the obvious fact that a congressman does not have the same public profile as a president of the United States, Condit's affair resembled Clinton's relationship with Monica Lewinsky. Like Clinton, Condit was a powerful married man who enjoyed risky sex with a much younger woman. Condit's affair ended differently, however, when Chandra Levy disappeared. No one knew what had happened to her, but her family suspected that Gary Condit knew.

After Levy's dead body turned up in a park, some observers, including the DC police, initially suspected that Congressman Condit was involved, perhaps killing her or hiring someone to kill her to cover up the affair. No evidence linked Condit to the crime, but his involvement in her disappearance and death was plausible. The case took a bizarre turn when an illegal immigrant, Ingmar Guandique, was arrested, tried, and convicted of her murder. Later, Guandique was granted a new trial after evidence emerged that a key witness against him had lied. Recognizing that they could not prove their case, prosecutors dropped the charges, and immigration authorities deported Guandique. As of this writing, the Chandra Levy murder case remains unsolved, although some skeptics still insist that Gary Condit is somehow implicated.

Chapter 13 discusses Anthony Weiner, an up-and-coming congressman from New York who single-handedly, and inexplicably, destroyed his own political career. Although rude, abrasive, and overbearing, Weiner was a rising star in the Democratic Party. Married to Huma Abedin, a top aide to Hillary Clinton, and campaigning for mayor of New York City, Weiner sabotaged his own political career by sending sexually explicit photographs of himself to several women, including an underage girl, in a series of incidents stretching across several years. He was initially caught in this social media debacle and expressed the appropriate measure of contrition.

A public figure might escape a singular act of misconduct if he or she can demonstrate that it was a mistake caused by undue pressure, a prescription medication problem, or an isolated lapse in judgment. But Weiner continued his pattern of behavior even after the initial incident. He destroyed his electoral viability, caused a permanent rift with his wife, and may have changed the course of presidential history. When the US Federal Bureau of Investigation (FBI) seized Weiner's laptop computer, searching for evidence of criminal behavior late in the 2016 election season, agents discovered emails related to Hillary Clinton's time as secretary of state. Clinton, the Democratic presidential nominee, was locked in a tight race with Donald J. Trump for the presidency in 2016. The FBI's announcement that it was reopening an investigation of whether Clinton improperly transmitted classified information on her personal computer (with her emails appearing on Weiner's laptop) may have cost her crucial votes, which thereby may have cost her the presidency. Although the electoral consequences of the FBI's seizure of Weiner's laptop is open to debate, the absurdity of his own self-destructive behavior is assured.

The final chapter in *Libertines* covers Donald J. Trump's affairs and alleged sexual assaults. In addition to the most prominent cases of consensual sexual encounters outside his marriage—notably with *Playboy* model Karen McDougal and pornographic film actress Stormy Daniels—the chapter delves into allegations of sexual assault lodged against the man who became the forty-fifth president of the United States. As of this writing, Trump has escaped serious repercussions for his behavior. Indeed, throughout his long career in business and television, he has eluded responsibility for his numerous failures and scandals.

Trump's singular talent for escaping relatively unscathed from numerous poor decisions and scandals is based on his utter shamelessness. For many people, a sense of shame and fear of public humiliation serve as a check on their behavior. If sunlight is the best disinfectant, as the adage suggests, public figures struggle to act in ways that ensure popular support, at least when their behavior undergoes media scrutiny. Sometimes facts cannot be avoided. When they are caught in an uncompromising position, many public figures reluctantly accept responsibility. Alexander Hamilton wrote a pamphlet admitting to an affair but assured the public that he never looted the federal treasury. Wilbur Mills blamed alcohol for his antics with a stripper. After repeatedly denying an affair with a White House intern, Bill Clinton eventually acknowledged his shortcomings and sought forgiveness.

Donald Trump's take-no-prisoners approach to public life will never allow him to apologize or accept responsibility. Facts are not facts for him. His mantra is to deny, deny, deny, regardless of how compelling the evidence might be. Faced with numerous charges of affairs and sexual assaults on the eve of the 2016 presidential election, Trump was unrepentant. "Nothing ever happened with any of these women," he claimed in a tweet he sent on October 15, 2016. "Totally made up nonsense to steal the election. Nobody has more respect for women than me!" Whether Trump's shameless lying is a shrewd method of surviving a sex scandal—a winning playbook for Trumpian libertines—or a unique technique applicable only to Trump is a point of no small debate.[2]

My college roommate during my sophomore year decried the propensity of a young male to think with his groin rather than his brain. Setting aside the crude expression, the point is well taken. The observation need not be limited to males, however, but to anyone who allows their passions and sexual attractions to overtake their rational judgment about long-term self-interest. Each of the cases of sexual misconduct described in this book shows the seamy side of political life. What all sexual scandals share is the existence of an urge, an intense and sometimes irresistible desire, to satisfy a basic human need. Calculations about covering up the deed or portraying it in a favorable light typically occur after the fact.

Speaking of after the fact, this is where I need to thank the kind folks who helped me research and write this book during the two years it took to complete the project. Many folks freely gave of their talents while others provided encouragement and emotional support. Thanks especially to Jon Sisk, vice president and senior executive editor at Rowman & Littlefield. Jon and I worked together on several previous books. He is always a supportive editor. Thanks also to Elaine McGarraugh and Sarah Sichina at Rowman & Littlefield.

Evan Sapio, Charlotte Jackson, and Princess Pratt at Alamy provided invaluable assistance in searching for the photographs included in chapters 9 and 12. As always, I appreciated assistance from the staffers at the Horace W. Sturgis Library at Kennesaw State University (KSU), who provided guidance with the interlibrary loan process. KSU has been my academic home since 1998.

Many professional colleagues provided support and assistance, notably Dr. William D. Richardson, a distinguished professor emeritus at the University of South Dakota. The late Dr. Jeffrey L. Brudney, formerly the Betty and Dan Cameron Family Distinguished Professor of Innovation in the Nonprofit Sector at the University of North Carolina Wilmington, was a treasured resource. I miss him immensely. Dr. Bradley Wright, a professor of public administration in the Department of Public Administration and Policy within the School of Public and International Affairs at the University of Georgia, provided encouragement and moral support during the research and writing process. A longtime friend and confidant, Dr. Thomas Rotnem, a professor in the School of Government and International Affairs at Kennesaw State University, encouraged me as well. W. Clifton Wilkinson, a senior lecturer in political science and public administration at Georgia College & State University, was incredibly supportive.

I deeply appreciated the support and encouragement of my friends Keith W. Smith and Chuck Redmon. Chuck and I met in 1992, and he has been a wonderful cheerleader. This book is dedicated to Chuck. Thanks also to Shirley Hardrick, housekeeper and babysitter extraordinaire, and Gabriel Botet, part-time babysitter and full-time creative spirit.

Finally, I appreciate the encouragement from family members who are fellow writers: Walter Russell Mead (cousin), Christopher A. Mead (cousin), Robert Sidney Mellette (cousin), William W. Mellette (uncle), and Jim Wise (cousin). They have inspired and continue to inspire me.

—Monroe, Georgia
August 2021

NOTES

1. John H. Summers, "What Happened to Sex Scandals? Politics and Peccadilloes, Jefferson to Kennedy," *Journal of American History* 87, no. 3 (December 2000): 850.

2. The tweet is quoted in Barry Levine and Monique El-Faizy, *All the President's Women: Donald Trump and the Making of a Predator* (New York: Hachette Books, 2019), 259.

CHAPTER 1

"My Real Crime Is an Amorous Connection with His Wife"

Alexander Hamilton and Maria Reynolds

Secretary of the Treasury Alexander Hamilton was at the height of his political power and influence in June 1791 when a comely 23-year-old woman arrived at his home at 79 South Street in Philadelphia and asked to speak with him privately. He might have ignored the entreaties of a stranger who appeared unannounced at his door. After all, he was a busy man handling weighty affairs of state. He did not have time to speak with every stranger who happened off the street seeking an audience. Nonetheless, when he was informed that a female visitor had come calling, he stepped away from his duties and "attended to her in a room apart from the family."

As Hamilton later described the encounter, she told a tale of woe with "a seeming air of affliction" about a husband who had treated her cruelly and deserted her, leaving her financially destitute. She appealed to Hamilton, "knowing that I was a citizen of New York." Apparently believing him to be a generous man, she "had taken the liberty to apply to my humanity for assistance." In short, she needed a loan.[1]

Hamilton was in his mid-thirties in 1791, and he cut a dashing figure. He was not tall, but he was thin and well proportioned. By all accounts, he was the sort of charismatic man who commanded attention whenever he entered a room. People noticed him, and they gravitated to him naturally. He was accustomed to both men and women seeking his counsel.

Even more than his physical attractiveness, however, was his manner. He carried himself with uncommon poise and grace. He was brilliant, condescending, and confident to the point of arrogance. As the consummate self-made man, he was an astute, skilled practitioner of bare-knuckle politics. He had been born a "bastard brat of a Scottish peddler" and risen from his humble beginnings to become one of America's most revered Founding Fathers, an extraordinary metamorphosis that puzzled and enchanted contemporaries and subsequent historians alike. After rendering distinguished service in the Continental Army during the Revolutionary War, he had pursued a storied career in law and politics. A principal figure at the Constitutional Convention of 1787 and coauthor of *The Federalist Papers*, a series of essays ruminating on the nature of democratic governance, Hamilton could rightly claim to be a leading citizen of the nation, arguably the most influential figure in President George Washington's cabinet.[2]

Hamilton should have been suspicious that a young woman he had never met would approach him asking for money. Why she came to him as opposed to some other gentleman of means was not clear. Like many men of power, however, Hamilton understood that a young woman seeking refuge from a heartless world might seek out a public figure of his position. He saw himself as chivalrous and upstanding, a white knight who would not hesitate to assist a fellow New Yorker in her hour of peril. Appealing to his manly virtue, this maiden in distress surely knew that she would find a willing champion in Hamilton. Moreover, his wife was not living in Philadelphia at the time. Eliza Hamilton would eventually return, but it was common for wives of politicians to take up residence back home while their husbands conducted business in the capital. Perhaps Hamilton's vanity, coupled with loneliness and a strong sense of adventure, caused him to ignore his normally canny political sense and entertain the woman's pleas.[3]

The petitioner's name was Maria Reynolds. Little is known of her background or early life. She was born Mary Lewis in Dutchess County, New York, in 1768. At age 15, she married James Reynolds. She gave birth to a daughter, Susan, two years later. She also began calling herself "Maria." Beyond that, few facts can be confirmed.

Contemporaries later recalled her as a chameleon, a malleable personality who molded herself into whatever was required to accomplish her immediate goals. To some observers she appeared as intelligent, sensitive, and genteel. To others she was a mercurial character, prone to wild mood swings and often hostile toward men. She and her loutish husband engaged in a tumultuous on-again, off-again relationship. Maria seems to have worked for a time as a prostitute, a profession tolerated by her husband because it provided sufficient funding for their lifestyle.

Whatever the facts, she was hardly the demure, vulnerable, desperate creature she presented to Hamilton that June day in 1791. Although she wore the face of an ingénue, beneath the carefully constructed facade, she was a conniving, manipulative, blackmailing hustler—a woman of "easy virtue," as wags euphemistically described an adulteress in that age. Almost certainly she presented herself to Hamilton in the hopes of luring him into a sexual relationship that would lead to blackmail.

If his wife was the proverbial Jezebel, James Reynolds was her Ahab. He was no king, of course, but he aspired to be a man of means. By most accounts James was a well-known liar and cheat. He had defrauded Continental soldiers or their widows and orphans of back pay in a well-known escapade. Hamilton may have known of the man's sordid reputation. If so, his wife's story rang true. To the uninitiated, Maria was another hapless victim of this dastardly scoundrel who had left behind a frantic woman in need of pecuniary relief. The fact that she was physically attractive and morally flexible suggested a means for acquiring the relief she sought.[4]

Hamilton did not have any funds on the premises, but he vowed to visit his bank and bring money to her later in the day. This was an extraordinary promise to make to someone he had just met. Had anyone other than an attractive young woman appeared at his house, he probably would have sent the petitioner packing in short order. In this case he agreed to accommodate a lady in distress.

Maria told him the address of the boarding house where she was staying. True to his word, he appeared that evening at 154 South Fourth Street with a thirty-dollar bank bill, equivalent to $400 today. While Hamilton's state of mind is unknowable, it is difficult to cast his behavior in a positive light. Stepping away from his pressing public duties to deliver funds to an attractive young woman at her boarding house after meeting her only once suggests that Hamilton either was extremely gullible or he understood what might happen with a pretty, estranged wife in his debt. He may not have resolved to act on his impulses, but he certainly must have entertained illicit intentions before he appeared at her residence, money in hand. She had asked for a hero, and he had agreed to play the part.

When he arrived at the boarding house, according to Hamilton's account, "I inquired for Mrs. Reynolds and was shown upstairs, at the head of which she met me and conducted me into a bed room." He handed her the bank bill, and they spoke briefly. Standing in this young woman's bedroom after fulfilling her request, the incident came to a predictable conclusion. Hamilton recognized that "it was quickly apparent that other than pecuniary consolation would be acceptable." They fell into her bed.[5]

"After this," Hamilton admitted later, "I had frequent meetings with her, most of them at my own house; Mrs. Hamilton with her children being absent on a visit to her father." The on-again, off-again affair lasted approximately a year. Even after his wife returned to Philadelphia, Hamilton found time to sneak away to see Maria.

"In the course of a short time," Hamilton recalled, "she mentioned to me that her husband had solicited a reconciliation and affected to consult me about it. I advised to it, and was soon after informed by her that it had taken place." Perhaps Hamilton had come to see his position as precarious. If so, the reunification of husband and wife provided him with a convenient rationale for breaking off the affair. It is also possible that he did not encourage reconciliation, and he merely wrote about the possibility to cast himself in a more favorable light.[6]

This purported "reconciliation" begs the question of whether Maria and James were estranged in the first place. During the year that the treasury secretary and his lover met for their assignations, her husband knew of the affair. The standards of the time suggested that a cuckold could demand satisfaction from his wife's paramour on the dueling ground. Such a confrontation, aside from the promise of physical violence, frequently became public, and Hamilton was anxious to keep the trysts secret. James Reynolds knew this, of course, and he resolved to use it to his advantage.

As the affair continued, Maria intimated to Hamilton that her husband had profited from speculation in government securities and had even used insider information from a source in the Treasury Department. When he heard that someone in the department might compromise Hamilton's good work, he sent for James Reynolds. It is ironic that in fearing for the reputation of the Treasury Department owing to the work of a scoundrel, Hamilton failed to see, or he ignored, the strong possibility that he himself was acting as a scoundrel.[7]

In any event, James Reynolds appeared before him and claimed that William Duer was the source of his information. Duer had already left the department at the time the disclosure reputedly occurred, and so Hamilton decided that "this discovery, if it had been true, was not very important—yet it was the interest of my passions to appear to set value to it, and to continue the expectation of friendship and good offices." The remark is telling. Hamilton recognized that James Reynolds might be lying, and yet the affair with Maria remained "the interest of my passions."[8]

On the surface this initial meeting was amicable, but danger lurked for Hamilton. He must have known that he had left himself vulnerable to blackmail. If he didn't know it, he would soon learn. During the initial meeting, however, the parties acted as though they were the best of friends. Maria told her husband that Hamilton had aided her when she needed it. James feigned gratitude. The only overtly sour note came at the conclusion. According to Hamilton, "Mr. Reynolds told me he was going to Virginia, and on his return would point out something in which I could serve him. I do not know but he said something about employment in a public office." No firm offers were tendered.

Reynolds returned from his travels and, as he had promised, he asked for a job in the Treasury Department. In the man's absence Hamilton had discovered the sort of fellow he was, assuming he had not known beforehand. The secretary refused, explaining that no openings existed in his office. Subordinate officers made employment decisions in other offices within the Treasury Department, but Hamilton would not intervene to install a clerk of his choosing. He could not accommodate the gentleman.

Reynolds was dissatisfied with this excuse. He believed that during their initial meeting, Hamilton had agreed to provide a job. "The situation with the wife would naturally incline me to conciliate this man," Hamilton candidly admitted. "It is possible I may have uttered vague expressions which ratified expectation, but the more I learned of the person, the more inadmissible his employment in a public office became."[9]

He now knew that he faced stark choices. During the fall of 1791, Hamilton attempted to break off contact with Maria. She wrote him copious letters filled with misspelling and atrocious grammar, but her intentions were plain enough. She loved Hamilton. She could not bear to part with him. Maria told her paramour that James approved of Hamilton's visits with Maria "as a friend," suggesting that her husband did not suspect the sexual nature of the visits.

Although no overt threats had been uttered, Hamilton knew that he was in an untenable position. He dreaded public disclosure for fear of how his wife, Eliza, would react, to say nothing of the effect on his public career. The wisest course of action would have been to cease all contact, but he seemed unwilling or unable to cut ties with the Reynolds duo. Hamilton remained locked in the destructive relationship. He labeled his vacillation between breaking off the affair and continuing the visits a "state of irresolution."[10]

Matters came to a head on Thursday, December 15, 1791. On that date Hamilton received letters from both Maria and James Reynolds. The former wrote, she said, to warn that her husband had discovered their sexual affair and might blackmail the secretary. "It was a matter of doubt with me whether there had been really a discovery by accident, or whether the time for the catastrophe of the plot was arrived," Hamilton later mused.[11]

In his letter James Reynolds played the role of the affronted husband, outraged that Hamilton had "acted the part of the most Cruelist man in existence," and, in so doing, "you have made my whole family miserable." Reynolds promised that "I am [determined] to have satisfaction." Recognizing that he could not ignore the implied threat, Hamilton summoned the aggrieved man to his office that afternoon.

Reynolds arrived to find a wary adversary. Hamilton could not be sure how much Reynolds knew or whether the man possessed incriminating evidence. Resolving not to worsen an already terrible situation, Hamilton listened as James changed his demands from seeking employment to requesting a "loan." It was a depressingly typical extortion scheme. The extortionist spoke of compensation in exchange for a vow of silence. Hamilton understood the risks, but he thought that he had no choice but to comply.[12]

During a second meeting a few days later, Reynolds said that he would consider $1,000 an adequate sum to restore his "wounded honor." Hamilton agreed, paying one installment on December 22, and a second on January 3. Finally coming to his senses, he sought to end the affair.[13]

James Reynolds demonstrated his venality beyond any doubt, as if such a demonstration were needed, when he responded to Hamilton's decision to terminate all contact with Maria. The wounded spouse, staggering from the blow to his pride and upset at the cruel man who had alienated his wife's affection, suddenly wrote a letter to Hamilton explaining that Maria was inconsolable. She missed Hamilton so much that she had broken down. Out of a selfless concern for her welfare, James invited Hamilton to consider Maria a "friend" and renew his visits.

After having exercised a modicum of wise judgment, Hamilton threw caution to the wind and continued seeing Maria long past the point when he should have walked away. The sexual obsession would not be denied. Not surprisingly, James Reynolds remained involved, expressing concern for his wife and seeking additional payments from her lover. He also ran hot and cold, occasionally telling Hamilton to stay away from his wife and other times encouraging their visits. By the time all was said and done, the pimp-turned-blackmailer had received $1,300, a princely amount.[14]

What started as a private failing of a public man became a sensational scandal owing to a confluence of events in 1792. It began with Jacob Clingman, a former clerk to Frederick Muhlenberg, speaker of the Pennsylvania House of Representatives. Clingman knew James and Maria Reynolds, and he was visiting them when he spied Alexander Hamilton leaving the premises. The odd spectacle of seeing one of the nation's most famous men at the Reynolds residence occurred again several days later, when Clingman saw Hamilton enter a room, pass a message to Maria, and hastily leave. When Clingman asked what was going on, Maria told him that Hamilton had paid her husband more than $1,100. James said that Hamilton had given him money for speculation. Initially skeptical, Clingman changed his mind when he accompanied James Reynolds on a visit to see Hamilton. While Clingman waited outside, Reynolds went in to see Hamilton, and he emerged from the meeting with one hundred dollars.[15]

A political opponent of the treasury secretary, Clingman was convinced that Hamilton was skimming money from the US Treasury to engage in financial speculation, an illegal breach of the public trust. The extravagant payments to James Reynolds only confirmed his suspicions. Still, he sat on his suspicions until he was arrested, along with James Reynolds, for defrauding the US government after posing as executors of a deceased war veteran's estate to procure payment for money owed to the man for his military service.[16]

Because the Treasury Department prosecuted the case, Reynolds believed that Hamilton had engineered the charges to ensure his silence. Reynolds and Clingman were hauled off to jail. Reynolds wrote to Hamilton twice asking for assistance. When he did not receive a response, he loudly complained to anyone who would listen that he possessed damaging information and could "make disclosures injurious to the character of some head of a department." When Hamilton learned of the threats, he instructed his men to keep Reynolds locked away until such time as the man was prose-cuted.[17]

Clingman, however, secured his release on bail. He immediately ran to his former boss, Frederick Muhlenberg, then serving as a US congressman. After hearing about the possibility of financial misconduct, Muhlenberg agreed to assist Clingman, although he carefully distanced himself from the "scoundrel" James Reynolds. Accompanied by New York senator Aaron Burr, Muhlenberg met with Hamilton and arranged a compromise. Clingman agreed to refund the stolen money, turn over a purloined list of soldiers who were owed money by the government, and provide the name of the Treasury Department official who had leaked the list. In exchange, the Treasury Department would drop the charges against Reynolds and Clingman.[18]

Rather than expressing his gratitude to Hamilton for arranging a compro-mise, Clingman confided in Muhlenberg that the secretary had engaged in improper speculation with Reynolds, suggesting that Treasury Department funds were used to enrich Hamilton and his friends. Muhlenberg was ini-tially skeptical, but James Reynolds insisted that he possessed information that would "hang" Hamilton. Muhlenberg eventually decided that he could not keep the information to himself. The nature of the claims would have to be investigated.

Muhlenberg approached two Virginia men, Senator James Monroe and Congressman Abraham B. Venable, and told them of his suspicions. Clingman had provided Muhlenberg with unsigned notes from Hamilton to James Reynolds, which lent an air of authenticity to the claims. The Virginians were Hamilton's political adversaries and anxious to expose any information that would present the treasury secretary in a poor light. They hastened to James Reynolds's jail cell. The prisoner was as circumspect as ever, but he alluded to the misconduct of a person of high office. Monroe and Venable knew that Reynolds was speaking of Hamilton, but Reynolds would not say his name.[19]

These behind-the-scenes machinations among Clingman, Muhlenberg, Monroe, and Venable revolved around a muddled claim of financial im-propriety. No one in the circle yet knew of the sexual liaison at the heart of the mystery. Still unsure of what they were investigating, Muhlenberg and Monroe visited Maria Reynolds on the evening of December 12, 1792. She furnished them with additional information about payments, but she did not mention an affair. She had confided in Pennsylvania governor Thomas Mifflin about the Hamilton trysts, but she chose not to inform the members of Congress now delving into the matter.[20]

In the meantime James Reynolds, newly released from prison, ran off to God-knows-where, leaving the three members of Congress more suspicious than ever that Hamilton must be engaged in a massive financial scandal.

The trio drafted a letter to President Washington, but they needed to perform one last act of due diligence. They requested an audience with Hamilton to outline what they knew and seek his response.

On December 15, 1792, Messrs. Muhlenberg, Monroe, and Venable filed into Hamilton's office and confronted him about the "very improper connection" with James Reynolds. Angered by the accusation, Hamilton demanded to know plainly what they were insinuating. The men were taken aback. They assured the secretary that they had no concrete evidence, but they felt duty-bound to inform the president of what they did know. They produced the handwritten notes from Hamilton to Reynolds, which changed Hamilton's demeanor instantly. His anger evaporated. Requesting time to prepare his case, he asked the men to join him at his home that evening and he would lay bare all the facts necessary to explain his connection with James Reynolds.

The men appeared at Hamilton's door at the allotted time expecting to hear a defense of his financial transactions. They were stunned at what he told them. Having decided that he should provide all the facts in excruciating detail, Hamilton laid bare the circumstances of the affair from beginning to end. He produced letters to show the sequence of events. It was clear that his interlocutors were uncomfortable by this running narrative, but Hamilton was determined to supply an exhaustive explanation for his conduct.

It is possible that the affair never occurred, and the lengthy narrative was an elaborate ruse to disguise financial improprieties. If that was the case, Hamilton gave a virtuoso performance that evening. His audience never doubted him for a moment. The level of detail and Hamilton's obvious embarrassment at having been duped by the unscrupulous couple convinced Muhlenberg, Monroe, and Venable that a scandal involving marital infidelity was a private matter. They departed with promises to keep the matter confidential. They never sent the draft letter to Washington.

Regardless of their politics, Muhlenberg and Venable were sympathetic to Hamilton. James Monroe, however, was too much of a partisan to allow such matters to remain buried indefinitely. Hamilton subsequently asked for copies of the correspondence that the three men had shown him. They readily agreed, but they also retained copies. One set wound up in the hands of John Beckley, clerk of the House of Representatives and a devoted friend of Hamilton's archenemy, Thomas Jefferson. Monroe may have shared copies with Jefferson as well. Even as he battled his political enemies in a public arena, Hamilton knew that they retained damaging information that might destroy his political career.[21]

For four and a half years, despite "dark whispers" that circulated among his Republican opponents, Hamilton conducted his public business without having to answer for the Reynolds affair. He left the Treasury Department in 1795. Always spoken of as a potential presidential candidate, he never formally pursued the ultimate prize, although it's doubtless he coveted the position. Perhaps he knew the affair would come to light if he threw his hat into the ring.

Enter one James Thomson Callender, a Scottish-born political operative who had fashioned himself into a scandalmonger. Callender had carved out a career as a purveyor of rumor and innuendo in service of political causes, mostly on behalf of Jefferson's Republican Party. His charges usually appeared in pamphlets to boost sales, similar to the yellow journalism and tabloid fodder of a later era. In this case Callender advertised a publication titled *The History of the United States for 1796*, which promised to expose information about the Hamilton-Reynolds episode in 1791–92. The gist of the argument was that when he was secretary of the treasury, Hamilton had engaged in official misconduct, and the payments to James Reynolds were proof. As part of his string of allegations, Callender referred to Hamilton's adultery.

The timing of the Callender missive was not accidental. The previous year Hamilton had alluded to improprieties in Jefferson's private life, a not-so-subtle reference to rumors about the master of Monticello and his slave Sally Hemings. Callender was often in the Republicans' employ, and so his revelations may have been payback for Hamilton's indelicate remarks about the Sage of Monticello.

Hamilton was furious when he read *The History of the United States for 1796* and saw copies of the documents that Muhlenberg, Monroe, and Venable had had in their possession in December 1792. After sifting through the documents, Hamilton understood that he had been betrayed. He thought he knew the source of the leak, too: James Monroe. He and Hamilton were political enemies, and it was certainly plausible to assume that Monroe had provided the documents to Callender. When Hamilton confronted Monroe, however, the latter denied his involvement. The two men exchanged words, and they came perilously close to engaging in a duel. Ironically, it was only through the intervention of Aaron Burr—who killed Hamilton in a duel seven years later—that the potential combatants agreed to stand down.[22]

Faced with public disclosure of his conduct when he held high office, Hamilton might have ignored the slurs and innuendo, explaining to anyone who inquired that it was beneath his dignity to respond to salacious gossip. Many a public man might have adopted the adage that discretion is the better part of valor. Hamilton, however, treasured his public reputation as beyond reproach. He could not or would not let the charges pass without comment.

And so, he did what he did best. An energetic, prolific writer, he relied on his literary prowess to extricate himself from a difficult situation. Hamilton put pen to paper and produced a lengthy essay thoroughly refuting the charges. Although he might have been brief in his defense, Hamilton decided to lay out his case in the full context of the controversy rather than allow his detractors to misinterpret his words. The result was one of the most astonishing public letters ever written by an American politician. Published on August 25, 1797, and titled *Observations on Certain Documents Contained in No. V & VI of "The History of the United States for the Year 1796," In which the Charge of Speculation Against Alexander Hamilton, Late Secretary of the Treasury, is Fully Refuted, Written by Himself*, it is usually known as *The Reynolds Pamphlet*. Just as he had done with Muhlenberg, Monroe, and Venable years earlier, Hamilton exhaustively reviewed the facts, providing copies of letters and referring to his critics' charges head-on. The crux of his argument was that the scandal was sexual, not financial: "The charge against me is a connection with one James Reynolds for purposes of improper pecuniary speculation. My real crime is an amorous connection with his wife, for a considerable time with his privity and connivance, if not originally brought on by a combination between the husband and wife with the design to extort money from me."[23]

In one sense *The Reynolds Pamphlet* achieved Hamilton's goal. He ably defended his public reputation by sacrificing his private life. His argument—yes, I misbehaved by straying from my marriage, but I never abused my public office by stealing from the Treasury—was strong and convincing. In laying out such unflattering information about himself, complete with copies of pertinent correspondence, he left little room for his critics to add much to the story. His candor and willingness to confront the scandal without waffling or deflecting blame demonstrated his ability to make hard choices and persevere, come what may. Yet he also diminished his reputation immeasurably. Republicans chortled that the man long viewed as a low-class bastard from the West Indies had been revealed as the unprincipled libertine they knew him to be. He humiliated his wife and family as well. Hamilton's well-wishers remained adamantly at his side—George Washington sent him a warm letter with a gift of wine coolers—but he may have destroyed his chances to capture the presidency.[24]

In virtually every tale of a powerful man engaging in risky behavior, critics shake their heads and ask, "what was he thinking?" Surely, Hamilton knew or should have known that the affair would become public. Great men with famous faces and an array of political enemies must realize that, sooner or later, sexual peccadilloes will become fodder for newspapers and political opponents. Yet time and again, these men engage in affairs that damage their reputations, their family lives, their political careers, and their historical legacy.

Armchair psychologists no doubt can pontificate on the personality traits of philandering politicians and their penchant for engaging in risky behav-

Figure 1.1. This idealized portrait of Alexander Hamilton by the celebrated artist John Trumbull dates from 1806, two years after Hamilton's death. Courtesy of the Library of Congress.

ior. Much ink has already been spilled on the subject. In the final analysis, perhaps the best that can be said is that public figures who rise to the top of a tough, competitive field are by their very nature risk takers. They are accustomed to deciding what they want and pursuing it with unbridled zeal. The normal rules of behavior that constrain the average person do not seem to apply to them.

Alexander Hamilton was a nobody who came from nowhere. He was a bastard born in the West Indies, the wrong side of the tracks if ever they existed. Yet he defied the odds and rose to become one of the most powerful men in government. His genius was apparent to all. Even his enemies recognized his intelligence and industry, although they believed he was overly ambitious and might tear the republic to pieces. Because he had so often taken enormous risks, most of which had paid off handsomely, he might have thought that here was another risk he could afford to take. It is not impossible to attribute to him, as to so many strong, capable political figures, a desire to take what he wanted, and the consequences be damned.

The sexual impulse is so alluring, too, that he may have been willing to ignore his usually astute, crafty decision-making process. Hamilton could be shrewd and calculating, a Machiavellian figure of the first order. When it came to sex, however, he may simply have surrendered to passion without worrying about logic and reason. That explanation certainly goes far in explaining why he and so many others have behaved recklessly when they were presented with the temptations of a sexual affair.[25]

NOTES

1. Alexander Hamilton, *Observations on Certain Documents Contained in No. V & VI of "The History of the United States for the Year 1796," In which the Charge of Speculation Against Alexander Hamilton, Late Secretary of the Treasury, is Fully Refuted, Written by Himself* (Philadelphia, PA: Printed for John Fenno, by John Bioren, 1797), 17; Richard Brookhiser, *Alexander Hamilton: American* (New York: The Free Press, 1999), 97-98; Ron Chernow, *Alexander Hamilton* (New York: The Penguin Press, 2004), 364; Jacob Katz Cogan, "The Reynolds Affair and the Politics of Character," *Journal of the Early Republic* 16, no. 3 (Autumn 1996): 389; Willard Sterne Randall, *Alexander Hamilton: A Life* (New York: Harper Perennial Political Classics, 2014 [2003]), 405.

2. Brookhiser, *Alexander Hamilton*, 1-6; Bruce Chadwick, *Triumvirate: The Story of the Unlikely Alliance That Saved the Constitution and United the Nation* (New York: Fall Rover Press, 2009), 30-36.

3. Chernow, *Alexander Hamilton*, 364; Randall, *Alexander Hamilton*, 405-7.

4. Cogan, "The Reynolds Affair and the Politics of Character," 390; Randall, *Alexander Hamilton*, 405-7.

5. Hamilton, *Observations on Certain Documents*, 18. See also Brookhiser, *Alexander Hamilton*, 98; Chernow, *Alexander Hamilton*, 364; Cogan, "The Reynolds Affair and the Politics of Character," 390; Randall, *Alexander Hamilton*, 406.

6. Hamilton, *Observations on Certain Documents*, 18. See also Cogan, "The Reynolds Affair and the Politics of Character," 392; Randall, *Alexander Hamilton*, 407.

7. Brookhiser, *Alexander Hamilton*, 98; Randall, *Alexander Hamilton*, 407-8.

8. Hamilton, *Observations on Certain Documents*, 19. See also Chernow, *Alexander Hamilton*, 365; Randall, *Alexander Hamilton*, 408-9.

9. Hamilton, *Observations on Certain Documents*, 19. See also Cogan, "The Reynolds Affair and the Politics of Character," 392-93; Kim Long, *The Almanac of Political Corruption, Scandals & Dirty Politics* (New York: Delta Paperbacks, 2007), 10.

10. Hamilton, *Observations on Certain Documents*, 20. See also Chernow, *Alexander Hamilton*, 365-67; Randall, *Alexander Hamilton*, 408-9.

11. Hamilton, *Observations on Certain Documents*, 20.

12. Reynolds is quoted in Chernow, *Alexander Hamilton*, 365. See also Brookhiser, *Alexander Hamilton*, 99; Chernow, *Alexander Hamilton*, 367-68, 369-70.

13. Chernow, *Alexander Hamilton*, 369.

14. Hamilton, *Observations on Certain Documents*, 22.

15. Chernow, *Alexander Hamilton*, 409-10; Cogan, "The Reynolds Affair and the Politics of Character," 392-93.

16. Hamilton, *Observations on Certain Documents*, 12-13; Chernow, *Alexander Hamilton*, 413.

17. The quote is found in Chernow, *Alexander Hamilton*, 413. See also Hamilton, *Observations on Certain Documents*, 12-13; Cogan, "The Reynolds Affair and the Politics of Character," 393, 394; Randall, *Alexander Hamilton*, 413.

18. Chernow, *Alexander Hamilton*, 413-14; Cogan, "The Reynolds Affair and the Politics of Character," 395.

19. Chernow, *Alexander Hamilton*, 413-15; Cogan, "The Reynolds Affair and the Politics of Character," 394.

20. Chernow, *Alexander Hamilton*, 414-15.

21. Hamilton, *Observations on Certain Documents*, 25-27; Brookhiser, *Alexander Hamilton*, 110-11; Cogan, "The Reynolds Affair and the Politics of Character," 394; Long, *The Almanac of Political Corruption, Scandals & Dirty Politics*, 10; Randall, *Alexander Hamilton*, 413-14.

22. Callender's work was published as James Thomson Callender, *The History of the United States for 1796; Including a Variety of Interesting Particulars Relative to the Federal Government Previous to That Period* (Philadelphia, PA: Snowden & McCorkle, 1797). The Hamilton allegations can be found especially on pages 204-31. The story of the trio's attempts to investigate the matter has been reported in many sources. See, for example, Brookhiser, *Alexander Hamilton*, 110-11, 133; Chernow, *Alexander Hamilton*, 414-16; Cogan, "The Reynolds Affair and the Politics of Character," 396-98; Randall, *Alexander Hamilton*, 420.

23. Hamilton, *Observations on Certain Documents*, 9. See also Chernow, *Alexander Hamilton*, 528-38; Cogan, "The Reynolds Affair and the Politics of Character," 398-404; Long, *The Almanac of Political Corruption, Scandals & Dirty Politics*, 10.

24. Brookhiser, *Alexander Hamilton*, 187; Chernow, *Alexander Hamilton*, 535-45; Chernow, *Washington*, 781; Cogan, "The Reynolds Affair and the Politics of Character," 406-9. To be fair, Hamilton's chances to win the presidency were always remote. He was a man of proven talents and industry, but he had amassed legions of political enemies during his career.

25. Cogan, "The Reynolds Affair and the Politics of Character," 411-17.

CHAPTER 2

"Dreams of Freedom in His Slave's Embrace"

Thomas Jefferson and Sally Hemings

Thomas Jefferson—the Sage of Monticello, principal author of the Declaration of Independence, founder of the University of Virginia, and third president of the United States—was one of the most venerated statesmen in American history. Yet for all his political prowess, he is revered for more than his accomplishments in government service. His soaring, eloquent prose, his idealistic philosophical ruminations, and his abiding interest in a wide array of scientific pursuits transformed him into the quintessential Renaissance man of the Founding generation. During a 1962 dinner honoring Nobel Prize winners, President John F. Kennedy remarked, "I think this is the most extraordinary collection of talent, of human knowledge, that has ever been gathered together at the White House, with the possible exception of when Thomas Jefferson dined alone. Someone once said that Thomas Jefferson was a gentleman of 32 who could calculate an eclipse, survey an estate, tie an artery, plan an edifice, try a cause, break a horse, and dance the minuet."[1]

Despite the litany of achievements for which Jefferson is rightly celebrated, he also represents a dark chapter in the nation's history. He lived in the eighteenth and nineteenth centuries during an era when it was permissible for one group of human beings to own another. As a slaveowner who never repudiated the peculiar institution, Jefferson's views on race and master-slave relations were complex. He was not a man who could profess ignorance of the slave's plight. He knew all too well from both personal experience and his studies that slavery was an abomination. At times he condemned the institution in uncompromising terms. "The whole commerce between master and slave is a perpetual exercise of the most boisterous passions, the most unremitting despotism on the one part, and degrading submissions on the other," he wrote in Query XVIII of his only book, *Notes on the State of Virginia*. Later in that same essay, he explained, "I tremble for my country when I reflect that God is just: that his justice cannot sleep for ever: that considering numbers, nature and natural means only, a revolution of the wheel of fortune, an exchange of situation, is among possible events."[2]

Yet Jefferson did not free his slaves, nor did he disavow the brutal institution. He also may have had a sexual relationship with his slave Sally Hemings, who possibly bore him at least one and perhaps as many as six children. The likelihood that Jefferson may have fathered one or more mulatto children with his slave has been a vexing question for more than two hundred years. In the era before DNA testing was possible, historians wrestling with the question had to examine records of when the Hemings children were conceived and track Jefferson's whereabouts near those dates. They also debated whether it was out of character for this thoughtful, venerable leader to have engaged in such behavior.[3]

In 1998 scientist Eugene Foster published the results of a DNA test in the journal *Nature* indicating that the Sage of Monticello may have fathered at least one of Sally Hemings's offspring. The study required researchers to gather samples from descendants of Thomas Jefferson and Sally Hemings. Foster and his colleagues discovered a match in the Y chromosome DNA—material passed from father to son—between descendants of Field Jefferson, Thomas's paternal uncle, and Eston Hemings, Sally's last child. Foster could not rule out other Jefferson men as the father, but circumstantial evidence suggested that Thomas, owing to his proximity to Sally Hemings on crucial dates, was the most likely parent. Sally gave birth to four children between 1795 and 1808, and Thomas was present during the times the children were conceived.[4]

The inability to state a definitive conclusion for or against Jefferson's paternity complicated the statesman's legacy. His defenders insisted that Jefferson was shy and seldom preoccupied with mundane matters of sex and bodily functions following the death of his wife. She died in 1782, when Jefferson was 39 years old. He lived another forty-four years. Having promised her that he would never remarry, Jefferson honored his pledge and remained a celibate widower, spending his time and energy on loftier matters of philosophy, science, and governance. Had he engaged in a sexual liaison with Sally Hemings, which supporters of the Jefferson-Hemings coupling contend probably began while they both lived in France in 1789, the young woman would have been 16 years old while her master was 46. The disparity in age, wealth, and social status is off-putting for Jeffersonian enthusiasts who cannot envision the great man taking a slave mistress.[5]

For others the DNA test, although not definitive, strongly suggested that Thomas Jefferson was the father of Sally Hemings's children. The master had made the slave his lover. Jefferson's paternity fit in with a larger narrative on master-slave relations. It was a dirty little open secret on many a southern homestead that the slave children bore an uncanny resemblance to the slave master or his male relatives. Wives and daughters were forced to turn a blind eye to the stepchildren and half-siblings who came and went on the plantation grounds. The Jefferson-Hemings union was further evidence of the depraved relations that flowed from a monstrous institution. The only difference was that Jefferson was a prominent public figure; his story was replayed innumerable times on plantations scattered across the South.

Another troubling question concerned the matter of consent. If Thomas Jefferson and Sally Hemings engaged in a sexual relationship, what was the nature of that relationship? Were they genuinely in love, did Jefferson force himself on her, or was it some odd mixture of the two—a Stockholm syndrome whereby the slave girl came to identify with her oppressor? Of course, the issue can never be resolved to everyone's satisfaction. The two people who know the answers are long gone. Nonetheless, speculation continues. Moreover, the question of whether a slave could ever consent to anything gives way to objections: To assume that Sally Hemings had no choice is to objectify her as a victim with no will of her own. Yet to argue that she consented is to ignore the fundamental precepts of the master-slave relationship. On and on the queries extend into the murky past.[6]

The story's questionable provenance did not help matters. First reported in the press in 1802, the tale originated with James Callender, an unscrupulous "scandalmonger" who had written unsavory pamphlets in service of Jefferson's Democratic-Republicans until the two men had a falling out. With the gloves off, Callender wasted no time in repeating rumors about President Jefferson cavorting with his slave woman. As the *Richmond Reporter* observed, "It is well known that the man, whom it delighteth the people to honor, keeps, and for many years has kept, as his concubine, one of his own slaves. Her name is SALLY." It was not enough to cite the name of the mistress. Evidence, however circumspect, must be presented to lend the scurrilous reports an air of legitimacy. "The name of her eldest son is TOM. His features are said to bear a striking, although sable resemblance to those of the President himself."[7]

It was the sort of ugly, salacious rumor that surfaced whenever political foes faced off in the race for public office. The president's supporters scoffed at the story while his critics predictably raised an eyebrow and mulled over the veracity of the tale. Because it emanated from questionable sources and appeared to be an over-the-top accusation, the story gained little traction and never seriously imperiled Jefferson's reelection chances in the 1804 contest.

Figure 2.1. James Akin's caricature *The Philosophic Cock* depicts Thomas Jefferson as a preening rooster with Sally Hemings as a hen. Courtesy of James Akin, 1804.

Although it did not erupt into a full-fledged scandal during Jefferson's lifetime, the rumor occasionally elicited wry comments, such as this ditty from the Irish poet Thomas Moore:

> The weary statesman for repose hath fled
> From halls of council to his neighbor's shed,
> Where blest he woos some black Aspasia's grace,
> And dreams of freedom in his slave's embrace![8]

Although Jefferson never publicly commented on the tale, Sally Hemings's descendants believed that he was an ancestor. Oral history passed down through generations noted that Sally Hemings was Jefferson's mistress and that she exercised a degree of autonomy that would have been difficult to fathom were she not his concubine. As Madison Hemings, her son, remarked in a two-thousand-word interview published in a partisan Republican newspaper in Ohio in 1873, the two became lovers while Jefferson was in France. When it came time for him to return to the United States, Sally Hemings initially resisted.

"He desired to bring my mother back to Virginia with him but she demurred," the son recalled. "She was just beginning to understand the French language well, and in France she was free, while if she returned to Virginia, she would be reenslaved. So she refused to return with him." It is difficult to know how forceful the much younger slave would have been with the esteemed master, but Madison Hemings's account is not completely unbelievable. If Sally Hemings meant something to Jefferson, it is plausible that he would have accepted a measure of defiance without objection. According to Madison Hemings, Jefferson promised her "extraordinary privileges" if she would cross the Atlantic to America. Her children, he said, would be free at age 21. "In consequence of this promise, on which she implicitly relied, she returned with him to Virginia."[9]

Given the sensitive issue of miscegenation in southern society, Jefferson's heirs possessed a strong incentive to deny paternity. Thomas Jefferson Randolph, the president's eldest grandson, surmised that Peter Carr, Jefferson's nephew, was the father. Samuel Carr, another nephew, was mentioned as a viable candidate as well. To the extent that mainstream historians addressed the controversy at all, they typically credited the Carr story as the answer to the mystery and seldom inquired further. For many historians, the facts were so heavily disputed and the documentary evidence so scant that the matter was ignored for the remainder of the nineteenth century and most of the twentieth century.[10]

The undisputed facts are that Sally Heming returned to Virginia and lived out her life there. She bore a total of six children. Beyond those bare statistics, almost everything else is mired in controversy. Madison Hemings's oral history was never afforded much weight among scholars, who typically dismissed his assertions as tainted by his family's desire to affiliate themselves with a major historical figure. Moreover, some scholars suggested that Madison Hemings never actually granted the 1873 interview; it was the ghostwritten work of an anti-Jeffersonian hack intent on besmirching the dead president's legacy.[11]

Twentieth-century historians struggled to make sense of the story, but their findings failed to satisfy anyone. Merrill D. Peterson, a renowned historian of the early American republic, dismissed the Hemings rumor as "malicious barbs of political satirists" in his book *The Jefferson Image in the American Mind*. In discussing the evolution of Jefferson's public image over time, Peterson noted that anti-Jeffersonian partisans were especially interested in using the rumor to slander the former president's reputation.

Federalists gleefully repeated Callender's slander as a means of securing electoral advantage. Later in the nineteenth century, abolitionists raised the claim as evidence that the peculiar institution corrupted all men, great and small.[12]

Dumas Malone, the author of a magisterial six-volume Jefferson biography, joined the chorus of apologists who cast doubt on the tale owing to the great man's character.[13] A decade later Joel Williamson's book *New People: Miscegenation and Mulattoes in the United States* concluded that the circumstantial evidence was close, but Jefferson probably was not the father. Williamson found that Sally Hemings might have been sexually promiscuous—a standard conclusion about mixed-race slave women—and therefore any analysis of paternity would be suspect. It was a conclusion that failed to resolve the issue, and it infuriated partisans on both sides of the question.[14] In his book *American Sphinx: The Character of Thomas Jefferson*, Joseph J. Ellis, a Pulitzer Prize–winning historian of the founding period, expressed doubts that Jefferson fathered the Hemings children, although he was not as zealous as many of his predecessors.[15]

Not everyone who examined the evidence reached the same conclusion. Fawn Brodie, a prominent scholar who authored a 1974 book on Jefferson, concluded that he probably did father Sally Hemings's children. Some historians criticized Brodie's reliance on psychological analysis to assess the actions and motives of long-dead figures, but her suppositions were no more or less likely than any others.[16]

Harvard Law School professor Annette Gordon-Reed, an expert on the legal history of the early republic, is the most prominent scholar to insist that Jefferson fathered Sally Hemings's children. Her major works, *Thomas Jefferson and Sally Hemings: An American Controversy* and the Pulitzer Prize–winning *The Hemingses of Monticello: An American Family*, argued that white scholars' beliefs that Jefferson was a moral exemplar who would not have engaged in sex with a slave portray the man as a staid, sexless caricature. He only comes alive when he is viewed as a flesh-and-blood man who succumbed to the human temptations of the flesh. Historians who dismiss the Hemings family's voices by referring to Jefferson's exemplary character are naïve about the realities of slaves' lives and deliberately blind to the sources of information, such as oral histories, that augment white people's letters, diaries, and self-serving memoirs.[17]

Gordon-Reed's analysis places the Jefferson-Hemings controversy into a broader context. The implication is that when skeptics deny the coupling occurred, blacks are once again portrayed as silent victims of slavery. If the paternity story is accepted as fact, blacks take their rightful place in the family of Americans. While some historians have accepted the view, conservative critics reject this kind of scholarship as mythology. The prominent historian Herman Belz referred to the "legend of Sally Hemings" in assessing the issue.[18]

Before the latter half of the twentieth century, the consensus seemed to be that Jefferson was not the father of the Hemings children. The standard narrative gradually evolved as the controversy entered popular culture. In 1979 Barbara Chase-Riboud published a novel, *Sally Hemings*, that envisioned what the "forbidden love" between Hemings and Jefferson must have been like. The 1995 film *Jefferson in Paris* portrayed Jefferson as a man who preferred "heart over head" when it came to romance.[19]

The DNA results in 1998 did more than anything else to shift the mainstream discussion. Shortly after the results were published, the Thomas Jefferson Foundation commissioned a study to sift through the available data, such as the DNA evidence, oral histories, letters, and statistical calculations on the likelihood of someone with Jefferson's DNA makeup (other than Jefferson himself) being present during the time that Sally Hemings conceived her children. In January 2000 the committee announced that a high probability existed that Thomas Jefferson fathered Eston Hemings as well as some or all of the other children. The foundation concluded that "the issue is a settled historical matter." Although the evidence was not definitive, it was persuasive: Jefferson was the father.[20]

Most historians fell in line with this assessment, but not everyone agreed. The Thomas Jefferson Heritage Society examined the same evidence but reached a different conclusion. This group suggested that Sally Hemings was a peripheral figure in Thomas Jefferson's life. Randolph Jefferson, Thomas's younger brother, was more likely the father of at least some of the Hemings children, according to this source.[21] In his book *The Jefferson Lies: Exposing the Myths You've Always Believed About Thomas Jefferson*, David Barton concluded that, based on the DNA evidence, ten men of the Jefferson line possibly fathered one or more of the Hemings children. The rush to judgment ensured that Thomas Jefferson's good name would be smeared in the pages of history.[22]

Before the 1998 DNA results, the weight of the evidence suggested that Jefferson probably was not the father. After the testing, the weight of the evidence shifted. The reality is that no one will ever know the nature and extent of the Jefferson-Hemings relationship. The scandal was little more than a vicious rumor circulated by unscrupulous partisans during Jefferson's lifetime. It was only centuries later that it became a major source of contention among historians and persons interested in the legacy of the nation's third president.

NOTES

1. The JFK quote can be found in many sources. See, for example, David Barton, *The Jefferson Lies: Exposing the Myths You've Always Believed About Thomas Jefferson* (Nashville, TN: Thomas Nelson, 2012), xii–xiii.

2. Thomas Jefferson, *Notes on the State of Virginia* (New York: Penguin, 1999 [1785]), 168, 169.

3. Kim Long, *The Almanac of Political Corruption, Scandals & Dirty Politics* (New York: Delta Paperbacks, 2007), 14–15; Suzette Spencer, "Historical Memory, Romantic Narrative, and Sally Hemings," *African American Review* 40, no. 3 (Fall 2006): 507.

4. Mia Bay, "In Search of Sally Hemings in the Post-DNA Era," *Reviews in American History* 34, no. 4 (2006): 408; Venetria K. Patton and Ronald Jemal Stevens, "Narrating Competing Truths in the Thomas Jefferson-Sally Hemings Paternity Debate," *The Black Scholar* 29, no. 4 (Winter 1999): 8; Spencer, "Historical Memory, Romantic Narrative, and Sally Hemings," 507–8.

5. Patton and Stevens, "Narrating Competing Truths," 9.

6. Patton and Stevens, "Narrating Competing Truths," 11–15; Spencer, "Historical Memory," 509–10.

7. The quote is found in Jon Meacham, *Thomas Jefferson: The Art of Power* (New York: Random House, 2012), 378. See also Bay, "In Search of Sally Hemings," 407; Patton and Stevens, "Narrating Competing Truths," 8.

8. Moore is quoted in Meacham, *Thomas Jefferson*, 380.

9. Hemings is quoted in Patton and Stevens, "Narrating Competing Truths," 9. See also Meacham, *Thomas Jefferson*, 217–18.

10. The DNA evidence excluded the Carrs from the pool of possible fathers. Meacham, *Thomas Jefferson*, 455; Patton and Stevens, "Narrating Competing Truths," 9.

11. Herman Belz, "The Legend of Sally Hemings," *Academic Questions* 25, no. 2 (June 2012): 221.

12. Merrill D. Peterson, *The Jefferson Image in the American Mind* (Charlottesville: The University of Virginia Press, 1998 [1960]).

13. Dumas Malone, *Jefferson the President: First Term, 1801–1805* (Boston: Little, Brown, 1970).

14. Joel Williamson, *New People: Miscegenation and Mulattoes in the United States* (New York: Free Press, 1980).

15. Joseph J. Ellis, *American Sphinx: The Character of Thomas Jefferson* (New York: Vintage, 1998).

16. Fawn M. Brodie, *Thomas Jefferson: An Intimate History* (New York: W. W. Norton, 2010 [1974]).

17. Annette Gordon-Reed, *Thomas Jefferson and Sally Hemings: An American Controversy* (Charlottesville: University of Virginia Press, 1998); Annette Gordon-Reed, *The Hemingses of Monticello: An American Family* (New York: W. W. Norton, 2009).

18. Belz, "The Legend of Sally Hemings," 218–27.

19. Bay, "In Search of Sally Hemings," 407; Barbara Chase-Riboud, *Sally Hemings* (New York: Avon Books, 1980 [1979]).

20. "Monticello Affirms Thomas Jefferson Fathered Children with Sally Hemings: A Statement by the Thomas Jefferson Foundation," the Thomas Jefferson Foundation, www.monticello.org/thomas-jefferson/jefferson-slavery/thomas-jefferson-and-sally-hemings-a-brief-account/monticello-affirms-thomas-jefferson-fathered-children-with-sally-hemings/, accessed January 31, 2020.

21. "Hemings," the Thomas Jefferson Heritage Society, www.tjheritage.org/hemings, accessed February 5, 2020.

22. Barton, *The Jefferson Lies*, 7–16.

CHAPTER 3

"She Is as Chaste as a Virgin"

Andrew Jackson and the Petticoat Affair

Andrew Jackson entered the American presidency in 1829 as a new kind of public figure. He was a frontiersman, uneducated, rough around the edges, and determined to govern without assistance from political elites. His would be a populist administration anchored in genuine participatory democracy. Despite his predecessors' claims to employ only the "best men," Jackson would appoint loyal public servants to do his bidding. He intended to ignore the effete aristocracy that had directed the executive department before his accession.[1]

To the victor belong the spoils, he insisted. He had clawed his way to the top, and he felt justified in rewarding supporters who had aided his efforts. Jackson's ascent had been painstaking and fraught with obstacles. During his initial bid for the presidency in 1824, he had endured all manner of insults and humiliation. He was an uneducated bumpkin, a blasphemer, a fraudulent land speculator, and even a murderer. As horrible as these charges were for him, the slander against his wife's name was infinitely worse. Jackson had lost his heart to a woman whose reputation was suspect, and her supposedly tainted past became a potent political issue.[2]

During the acrimonious 1824 contest, Rachel Jackson was labeled an adulteress and a bigamist. It was a simple insult, while the truth was complicated. She had married a Kentucky businessman, Lewis Robards, in 1785. After five years the jealous Robards believed that his wife had been unfaithful, and he sought a divorce. Rachel thought the divorce was final. In 1791 she married a promising young attorney, Andrew Jackson, whom she had met at her mother's Nashville boardinghouse. It was only two years later that she learned that the divorce had not been finalized. Much to her dismay, she and the man she thought was her second husband had been living in sin. The Jacksons hastily renewed their vows.

Jackson's opponents wasted no time in attacking his relationship with Rachel, gleefully circulating all manner of invective to slander the woman's good name. The personal attacks took their toll. The 1824 election was close, although Jackson initially appeared to have won. Undaunted, his political enemies engaged in a series of seemingly unending machinations. When all was said and done, Jackson narrowly lost to John Quincy Adams after the election was thrown into the House of Representatives. Bitter at what he believed was a fraudulent election, Old Hickory vowed to return four years later to avenge his loss. He knew that his enemies would assail his marriage to Rachel if he ran a second time, but he would not relent. Andrew Jackson was never a man to run from a fight.

Predictably, the blistering attacks recommenced as the 1828 election drew near. John Quincy Adams did not escape unscathed. His enemies charged that he had procured a woman for Czar Alexander I while Adams served as minister to Russia. Opponents questioned the money he had spent to redecorate the president's mansion, implying that Adams was profligate and could not be trusted with the public purse.[3]

The attacks on Adams could not compare to the slander lodged against Jackson, though. Partisans decried the general's propensity to engage in duels. He was a hothead who did not possess the judgment and temperament to serve as the chief magistrate of the nation. The atrocities he had perpetrated against the British, the Spanish, and Native Americans when he had served as a general officer in the army were trotted out as evidence of the man's viciousness. Even his female relations did not escape notice. His mother was a whore, critics alleged. As for Rachel, the old charges reappeared, this time with a harder edge. One anti-Jacksonian newspaper did not mince words. "Ought a convicted adulteress and her paramour husband to be placed in the highest offices of this free and Christian land?"[4]

Although he had known what he would face, Jackson nonetheless lamented that the women in his life were subjected to such slander. "Even Mrs. J. is not spared, and my pious Mother, nearly fifty years in the tomb, and who, from her cradle to her death had not a speck upon her character, has been dragged forth . . . and held to public scorn as a prostitute who intermarried with a Negro, and my eldest brother sold as a slave in Carolina," the old general confided to a friend.[5]

Jackson was enraged by the assaults on his wife's virtue, but his rage soon turned to grief, for Rachel did not share her husband's intestinal fortitude. The harsh words wounded her deeply, and she visibly showed her apprehension. "The enemies of the General have dipped their arrows in wormwood and gall and sped them at me," she said during the bitter campaign season. "Almighty God, was there ever anything equal to it?"[6]

After Jackson won the election, she shared her husband's joy, but she was also filled with misgivings. She enjoyed a comfortable life at their home, the Hermitage, near Nashville. The move to Washington, DC, promised to be new and exciting but also a test of strength and endurance she was not certain she possessed. She dreaded the prospect of departing.

On December 17, 1828, as President-Elect Jackson sat outside the house handling his correspondence, Rachel collapsed in her sitting room, screaming in pain. When Jackson learned of her collapse, he rushed to her side. She lived for five days before she died from the effects of an apparent heart attack on December 22, three days before Christmas. In what should have been a celebratory season—the holiday after his victory in the hard-fought presidential election—Jackson was immersed in grief. He had loved Rachel for almost four decades, and he could not imagine a life without her. Although they had been separated for long periods during his military campaigns, he had been secure in the knowledge that she waited patiently for him at home. Now she was gone as Andrew Jackson prepared to shoulder the responsibilities of high office without a trusted partner at his side.[7]

He arrived in Washington with relatives in tow, ensuring that he was not alone. Yet he never forgot—or forgave—Rachel's loss. He was not a man who avoided conflict, but now, more than ever, he was combative. He would not allow Rachel's death to go unpunished. His political enemies must be vanquished.[8]

Still grieving his dead wife, Jackson experienced the so-called "Petticoat Affair," a sexual scandal that threatened to derail his presidency. It involved a charming young woman: dark-haired, blue-eyed Margaret "Peggy" O'Neill (sometimes spelled "O'Neale" or "O'Neal") Eaton, who became the wife of the new president's secretary of war. Under ordinary circumstances Peggy Eaton's plight would have escaped a president's notice. These were hardly ordinary circumstances, for Rachel's death was still too fresh. Rachel's demise, Jackson believed, was hastened by scurrilous rumors; wagging tongues and heartless snubs had killed his true love. Watching similar rumors swirl around Peggy Eaton, Jackson dug in his heels. He was hell-bent on saving a good and noble woman who reminded him of his Rachel.[9]

Jackson viewed political attacks as personal attacks, and with good reason. Sometimes an incoming president can separate attacks on his administration's policies from attacks on his character, but few people knew much about Jackson's plans. As a candidate in 1828, he had kept his policy goals obscure, leaving his supporters free to promise whatever a local audience needed to hear to support the popular general. He campaigned on the strength of his personality and his military record. Observers looked to his cabinet nominations for clues about his administration's agenda. Aside from the undistinguished nature of the men he selected—except, perhaps, for his secretary-of-state designee, Martin Van Buren—their eclectic views raised more questions than they answered.[10]

Jackson's choice for secretary of war was especially questionable. John Henry Eaton, a US senator from Tennessee, had established a "late unfortunate connection" with Peggy O'Neill, a woman viewed by many society dames as immoral. Her humble origins were not the issue. Her outspoken nature and audacious actions were the source of her—and, as it turned out, Andrew Jackson's—woe.[11]

She was born in 1799. Her father, William O'Neale, an Irish immigrant, owned a prosperous boardinghouse and tavern, the Franklin House, in Washington, DC. The oldest of six children, young Peggy came of age among the politicians who frequented her father's establishment. She heard riveting tales of legislative debates, international intrigue, and societal gossip that were the currency of the ruling classes. Beautiful and vivacious, the girl quickly learned to navigate among the powerful men who could not resist her charms. "I was always a pet," she would recall from those formative years.

In an era when women were expected to be demure appendages of their fathers or husbands, seldom uttering an unsolicited opinion, Peggy was an aberration. She had long inhabited the coarse world of men, reveling in their ribald tales and bawdy reminiscences, real and imagined. She felt free to join in the conversation when it suited her. To counterbalance this rude upbringing and instill a sense of propriety in their daughter, her parents sent her to an excellent school in the capital. There she acquired a first-rate education, studying English and French grammar. She also excelled at dance and piano playing. On one notable occasion, twelve-year-old Peggy O'Neill performed for First Lady Dolley Madison.

As she grew to maturity, this high-spirited woman who seemed afraid of nothing, including rumors about her reputation, invited attention from every man who encountered her. Perhaps she knew her virtue would always be called into question, regardless of the choices she made, for no woman of fine breeding would labor in a tavern, even if her father were the proprietor. The social mores of the era placed her in an awkward position. She knew many congressmen and senators by name, but the taint of her upbringing ensured that she would have an exceedingly difficult time parlaying her connections into a respectable position in high society.[12]

Everywhere she went, Peggy O'Neill attracted attention. One contemporary described her as "very handsome" and bright, with "perfect proportions," a "perfect nose," and "dark hair, very abundant, clustered in curls about her broad, expressive forehead." She was a favorite among the many well-connected "uncles" who resided under her father's roof when Congress was in session. The historian Jon Meacham observed that she "seems to have had few impulses on which she did not act, few opinions that she did not offer, few women whom she did not offend—and few men, it appears, whom she could not charm if she had the chance to work on them away from their wives."[13]

The stories of this unconventional young woman were delightful in their salaciousness. In most versions Peggy was an enchantress, virtually impossible to resist. One infatuated young man, when rebuffed by the object of his amorous advances, was thought to have ingested poison, preferring the afterlife to a world without his love. The son of President Jefferson's treasury secretary, Albert Gallatin, reputedly enjoyed frequent visits with the young woman. Peggy's father supposedly dragged her back into the house when she was climbing out of her bedroom window to elope with an aide to General Winfield Scott. These tales, true or not, portrayed Peggy as a wanton free spirit, unencumbered by middle-class mores.[14]

Andrew Jackson met the young woman in December 1823, half a decade before he entered the presidency. As a junior senator from Tennessee, he boarded at the Franklin House. The accommodations had been recommended by the state's senior US senator, John Henry Eaton. Jackson found that he liked his hosts, especially their 23-year-old daughter. By this time Peggy O'Neill had married a navy purser, John Bowie Timberlake. She eventually bore him three children, two of whom survived infancy. Jackson described Peggy as the "smartest little woman in America," a sentiment echoed by the general's wife, Rachel, when she accompanied him to Washington in 1824. Jackson did not pursue Peggy Eaton as a lover. Instead, he saw her as a spirited "niece" who flattered him. It was little wonder that he enjoyed her company.[15]

John Eaton met Peggy in 1818, and he heard the stories of her uninhibited behavior. He also came to know her husband, John Timberlake. In fact, Eaton unsuccessfully lobbied his Senate colleagues to reimburse the desperate purser for losses he suffered while he was away at sea. Peggy Timberlake told one and all that Senator Eaton was "my husband's friend," and "he was a pure, honest, and faithful gentleman." The words might have been taken at face value but for the rumors that circulated among the close-knit Washington community. John Timberlake, they said, constantly sailed away from home to escape both financial setbacks and knowledge of his wife's infidelity. Spotted in the widower Eaton's company on numerous occasions while her husband was absent, Peggy Timberlake was thought to be the senator's lover.[16]

John Timberlake conveniently died of "pulmonary disease" while serving aboard a ship, the USS *Constitution*, in April 1828. The timing of his death and the vague circumstances left tongues wagging. Perhaps the seaman had not succumbed to disease after all. Perhaps he could no longer close his eyes to his wife's dalliances. More than a few Washingtonians surmised that John Timberlake had killed himself to avoid his creditors or because he could no longer endure tales of his wife's infidelity. Whatever the reason, the man's disappearance from the scene cleared the way for Senator Eaton, the "pure, honest, and faithful gentleman," to declare his love for the widow.

John Eaton and Peggy Timberlake's close association while her husband was alive thrilled Washington gossipers, but it might have been written off as nothing more than coincidence. They were seen together repeatedly, but their meetings might have been explained as something other than a sexual escapade. After the purser's death, however, the association became even more frequent and potentially scandalous. Eaton's willingness to embrace a small woman with a large reputation might have been the kiss of death for an ambitious politician under different circumstances. Fortunately for the senior senator from Tennessee, he was friendly with the state's junior senator. Andrew Jackson was a man who valued political friendship and loyalty, especially with a colleague who shared a similar background.[17]

Jackson rewarded his friend by appointing Eaton to serve as his secretary of war in the incoming presidential administration. Shortly before he assumed his new duties, Eaton married Peggy O'Neill Timberlake. She had been a widow for only nine months, but Eaton was anxious to bring her fully into his life. When he informed the president-elect of his plans, Jackson, perhaps thinking of his own marriage to Rachel, assured his friend and colleague that a speedy marriage was fine. "If you love Peggy Timberlake," Jackson counseled the man, "go and marry her at once and shut their mouths." The people whose mouths Jackson wished to shut were the gossipers who could not or would not stop talking about the scandalous relations between the incoming secretary of war and the flirtatious widow.[18]

If Jackson thought that John Eaton's marriage would conclude the matter, he was sadly mistaken. Soon after the wedding occurred on New Year's Day 1829, the sniping began. Louis McLane, a well-known Maryland politician who would later serve as a cabinet officer during Jackson's second administration, snidely commented that Eaton "just married his mistress—and the mistress of 11-doz. others." He was not the only person of consequence to snub the couple. Floride Calhoun, the wife of Jackson's vice president, John C. Calhoun, became the most prominent critic of the Eatons and their marriage.[19]

As a new cabinet officer, Eaton, accompanied by his bride, expected to receive a slew of invitations to social events in and around Washington City. The capital was still a small, southern town in the 1820s. Elected officials and their wives were tight-knit, sharing friendships and social camaraderie despite partisan wrangling over affairs of state. Yet so great was the stain on Peggy Eaton's reputation that the society dames of Washington blacklisted her from most events.

It started at Jackson's inauguration, when "virtuous and distinguished" attendees scampered away from the couple to avoid engaging in conversation. Some women, upon learning that Jackson's "little friend Peg" would attend a specific inaugural ball, boycotted the event. Even in Jackson's family, Peggy Eaton became a *persona non grata*. Emily Donelson, the president's niece and official hostess following the death of Rachel Jackson, reluctantly consented to visit with Peggy Eaton once, but she emphatically refused to meet with the woman again. Donelson said she was "so much disgusted with what I have seen of her that I shall not visit her again."[20]

A few discourtesies might be ignored, but it became evident that Peggy Eaton was to be shunned indefinitely. When the Eatons paid a call on the vice president's wife, she accepted the call. According to the etiquette of the time, the Calhouns were expected to reciprocate, but Floride steadfastly refused to perform her duty. The vice president could not dissuade his wife from her plan, leaving him to muse over the difficulties he would encounter with the president, who was not a Calhoun ally.[21]

Upset at the indignities, the president resolved to lay the matter to rest. On September 10, 1829, he invited everyone in the cabinet, save for John Eaton, to the executive mansion to lay out the evidence showing that his war secretary's wife had been viciously maligned. John C. Calhoun was out of town, and his absence, Jackson hoped, would help smooth over relations. Two priests, Reverend John N. Campbell and Reverend Ezra Stiles Ely, were present as well. Jackson laid out affidavits attesting to Peggy Eaton's good conduct. He would brook no dissent about the evidence. When one minister objected, Jackson overrode him. "She is as chaste as a virgin," he exclaimed. As the mother of two surviving children, the woman was less sexually innocent than the president claimed, but his point was that he wished to close off debate.[22]

Believing that he had proven his point, Jackson scheduled an overdue cabinet dinner in November 1829. The event passed without major disruptions or snide comments, but it was clear that the guests were uncomfortable. Cabinet members and their spouses choked down their food and departed as quickly as possible lest they find themselves speaking to the Eatons, who were seated next to Jackson in a place of honor. At the next party cabinet members arrived without their spouses, each of whom invented an excuse to stay away.[23]

Observers wondered why the president was so obsessed with protecting Peggy Eaton. Perhaps, Democrats surmised, she was the power behind the throne. If so, she might be distributing patronage on Jackson's behest. A picture emerged of a vengeful young woman manipulating the ailing 62-year-old president to do her bidding.[24]

Anyone who knew Andrew Jackson understood that he would not be manipulated by anyone for long. He agreed with his detractors that his "deplorable infatuation" with Peggy Eaton's social position involved more than the plight of a tavern keeper's daughter. From his perspective, the issue wasn't even the resemblance between Peggy Eaton and Rachel Jackson. The president believed that his political opponents, especially the crafty Whig Henry Clay, had manufactured the crisis to present the administration with "troubles, vexations, and difficulties." He also found it curious that the cabinet members most opposed to the Eatons were politically aligned with Vice President Calhoun.[25]

Calhoun and Jackson enjoyed an uneasy relationship. The South Carolinian had helped to elect Jackson, but everyone knew that Calhoun was politically ambitious and was quick to change positions and loyalties if he believed a change would advance his interests. Floride Calhoun had led the opposition to Peggy Eaton, and Jackson could not believe that she had acted without her husband's tacit approval.[26]

If anyone benefited from the imbroglio, it was the secretary of state, Martin Van Buren. Calhoun, in his second term as vice president—he had served under John Quincy Adams during the preceding administration—had been Jackson's heir apparent before the Eaton affair arose. As he became suspicious that his vice president was disloyal, Jackson looked to Van Buren as a potential successor. The former New York governor was sometimes known as the "Little Magician" for his uncanny ability to work behind the scenes to secure political advantage. He was a widower, which became a definite political advantage in the Jackson administration. With no spouse to hinder his efforts, the secretary of state wasted no time in extending every courtesy to John and Peggy Eaton. An appreciative president took note of who had supported him in the Petticoat Affair, and who had insulted his friend's new wife. Jackson was not a man to forgive his enemies.[27]

No matter how much he insisted that Peggy Eaton was a good woman, the affair would not die. For two years critics and reporters criticized Jackson's refusal to abandon the Eatons. The president became so intractable on the issue that he even sent his nephew and private secretary, Andrew Donelson, and Donelson's wife, Emily, away since they would not reconcile with the secretary of war and his wife. It was a difficult decision, but Jackson would not yield to his critics, even when they were family members.[28]

The always ingratiating Van Buren suggested a solution in April 1831. The president had contemplated removing cabinet members who would not embrace the Eatons, but this maneuver promised more heartache and negative press, especially if other cabinet secretaries resigned in protest. Van Buren's plan was simple. The secretary of state offered to resign, allowing the secretary of war to follow suit. The president could then request that his entire cabinet resign so that he could reorganize without identifying the Petticoat Affair as the cause. Loyal cabinet officers could be invited back into the government and opponents could be replaced with loyal men.[29]

Events unfolded as Van Buren had foreseen, but the public reaction was far more severe and hostile than he or Jackson had anticipated. No one was fooled. Peggy Eaton's ostracism obviously was the cause of the cabinet shakeup, and it suggested that Jackson could not govern effectively. One critic wryly compared the Jackson administration to "the reign of Louis XV when Ministers were appointed and dismissed at a woman's nod, and the interests of the nation were tied to her apron string." Still, perhaps the Eatons' departure would put the issue to rest, and Jackson could get on with the business of governing. The popular toast of the day reflected the desire to see the affair ended: "To the next cabinet—may they all be bachelors—or leave their wives at home."[30]

To ensure that the couple would not continue to wreak havoc in the capital, Jackson sent John Eaton to the Florida Territory to serve as governor. Two years later the president appointed Eaton minister to Spain. John and Peggy Eaton spent four years in Madrid, far away from the insular society of Washington, DC.[31]

For his loyalty to the cause, Jackson appointed Martin Van Buren to be minister to Great Britain, but an embittered John C. Calhoun, as vice president, cast a tie-breaking vote against the Little Magician's confirmation. Confident that the rejection "will kill him, sir, kill him dead," Calhoun was chagrined when Jackson tapped Van Buren to serve as vice president during Jackson's second term. Later, Van Buren won the presidency in the 1836 election, although he served only a single term.[32]

John Eaton remained out of sight but not out of mind. In 1840, after President Van Buren recalled him to the United States for failing to carry out his diplomatic duties, Eaton threw his support behind the president's rival in the 1840 election, William Henry Harrison. From retirement, Andrew Jackson learned of the betrayal, and he was enraged. "He comes out against all the political principles he ever professed and against those on which he was supported and elected senator," the former president groused. He did not speak to John Eaton again until the two men reconciled in 1844, a year before Jackson died.[33]

As for Peggy Eaton, she simply could not settle down to a comfortable middle-class life. After her husband died in 1856, she possessed the money to buy her way into high society. She created a new scandal at age 59 when she married her granddaughter Emily's 19-year-old dance tutor. Five years later the tutor ran off with Emily and his wife's fortune, leaving Peggy impoverished in her old age. She died in 1879 at a home for destitute women and was buried next to John Eaton in Oak Hill Cemetery. Surrounded as she was by many prominent Washingtonians, Peggy Eaton had finally joined the society figures she had sought to impress. One newspaper observed that as "cordially as they may have hated her, they are now her neighbors."[34]

The Rats leaving a Falling House

Figure 3.1. This drawing, *The Rats Leaving a Falling House*, reflects uncertainty about the Jackson administration following a cabinet shakeup related to the Petticoat Affair. Jackson is seated in a collapsing chair, with the "Altar of Reform" toppling next to him and rats scurrying at his feet. The rats are (left to right): Secretary of War John H. Eaton, Secretary of the Navy John Branch, Secretary of State Martin Van Buren, and Treasury Secretary Samuel D. Ingham. Jackson's spectacles are pushed up over his forehead, and his foot is planted firmly on the tail of the Van Buren rat. Courtesy of the Library of Congress.

NOTES

1. Jon Meacham, *American Lion: Andrew Jackson in the White House* (New York: Random House, 2008), 4, 5; Jeff Smith, "Lords (and Ladies) of Misrule: Carnival, Scandal, and Satire in the Age of Andrew Jackson," *Studies in American Humor* 3, no. 12 (2005): 53–54; Kirsten E. Wood, "'One Woman So Dangerous to Public Morals': Gender and Power in the Eaton Affair," *Journal of the Early Republic* 17, no. 2 (Summer 1997): 246.

2. H. W. Brands, *Andrew Jackson: His Life and Times* (New York: Doubleday, 2005), 63–65; John F. Marszalek, *The Petticoat Affair: Manners, Mutiny, and Sex in Andrew Jackson's White House* (New York: Free Press, 1997), 5–8; Meacham, *American Lion*, 33–34, 44–45.

3. Meacham, *American Lion*, 3–4.

4. The quote is found in J. Kingston Pierce, "Andrew Jackson and the Tavern-Keeper's Daughter," *American History* 34, no. 2 (June 1999): 23.

5. Jackson is quoted in Meacham, *American Lion*, 4.

6. Rachel Jackson is quoted in Meacham, *American Lion*, 5. See also Robert V. Remini, *The Life of Andrew Jackson* (New York: Harper, 2010 [1988]), 169–70.

7. Meacham, *American Lion*, 6–7. H. W. Brands indicates that they were sitting in the same room when the heart attack occurred. Brands, *Andrew Jackson*, 405.

8. Meacham, *American Lion*, 6–8.

9. Brands, *Andrew Jackson*, 423–24; Meacham, *American Lion*, 68–69; Smith, "Lords (and Ladies) of Misrule," 58.

10. Marszalek, *The Petticoat Affair*, 59; Wood, "'One Woman So Dangerous to Public Morals,'" 237–38.

11. Brands, *Andrew Jackson*, 422–23; Wood, "'One Woman So Dangerous to Public Morals,'" 238.

12. The information and the quote are found in Pierce, "Andrew Jackson and the Tavern-Keeper's Daughter," 22. See also Marszalek, *The Petticoat Affair*, 24–27.

13. The quotes are found in Wood, "'One Woman So Dangerous to Public Morals,'" 244. Meacham's description is found in Meacham, *American Lion*, 67. See also Peggy L. Coit, *John C. Calhoun: American Portrait* (Boston: The Riverside Press, Houghton Mifflin, 1950), 193; Marszalek, *The Petticoat Affair*, 30–33.

14. Marszalek, *The Petticoat Affair*, 33–37; Pierce, "Andrew Jackson and the Tavern-Keeper's Daughter," 22; Wood, "'One Woman So Dangerous to Public Morals,'" 245–46.

15. Marszalek, *The Petticoat Affair*, 38–42; Pierce, "Andrew Jackson and the Tavern-Keeper's Daughter," 22; Remini, *The Life of Andrew Jackson*, 173–74, 190; Wood, "'One Woman So Dangerous to Public Morals,'" 246–48.

16. The information and the quote are found in Pierce, "Andrew Jackson and the Tavern-Keeper's Daughter," 23. See also H. W. Brands, *Heirs of the Founders: The Epic Rivalry of Henry Clay, John Calhoun and Daniel Webster—The Second Generation of American Giants* (New York: Doubleday, 2018), 155–56; Marszalek, *The Petticoat Affair*, 42–43; Smith, "Lords (and Ladies) of Misrule," 56.

17. Smith, "Lords (and Ladies) of Misrule," 56–58; Wood, "'One Woman So Dangerous to Public Morals,'" 247–48.

18. Jackson is quoted in Pierce, "Andrew Jackson and the Tavern-Keeper's Daughter," 23.

19. McLane's quote is found in Pierce, "Andrew Jackson and the Tavern-Keeper's Daughter," 23. See also Brands, *Heirs of the Founders*, 156–57; Coit, *John C. Calhoun*, 193–94; David S. Heidler and Jeanne T. Heidler, *Henry Clay: The Essential American* (New York: Random House, 2010), 216; Marszalek, *The Petticoat Affair*, 47–50; Remini, *The Life of Andrew Jackson*, 190; Smith, "Lords (and Ladies) of Misrule," 56; Wood, "'One Woman So Dangerous to Public Morals,'" 253.

20. The quotes are found in Wood, "'One Woman So Dangerous to Public Morals,'" 248, 249. See also Marszalek, *The Petticoat Affair*, 86–88; Pierce, "Andrew Jackson and the Tavern-Keeper's Daughter," 24.

21. Brands, Andrew Jackson, 424–25; Coit, *John C. Calhoun*, 193–95; Heidler and Heidler, *Henry Clay*, 216; Marszalek, *The Petticoat Affair*, 53–54.

22. Jackson is quoted in Meacham, *American Lion*, 68. See also Pierce, "Andrew Jackson and the Tavern-Keeper's Daughter," 24–25.

23. Pierce, "Andrew Jackson and the Tavern-Keeper's Daughter," 24. See also Marszalek, *The Petticoat Affair*, 75–84, 101–3; Remini, *The Life of Andrew Jackson*, 191–92.

24. Pierce, "Andrew Jackson and the Tavern-Keeper's Daughter," 24; Wood, "'One Woman So Dangerous to Public Morals,'" 258–59.

25. Clay was not directly involved, but he chuckled at the contretemps, believing that the whole silly situation demonstrated Jackson's incompetence as an administrator and his unfitness for high office. Robert V. Remini, *Henry Clay: Statesman for the Union* (New York: Norton, 1991), 355. Demonstrating his wry sense of humor, Clay parodied a character's tribute to Cleopatra in Shakespeare's *Antony and Cleopatra* when he said of Margret Eaton that "age cannot wither nor time stale her infinite virginity." The quote can be found in several sources. See, for example, Coit, *John C. Calhoun*, 194; Heidler and Heidler, *Henry Clay*, 232; Marszalek, *The Petticoat Affair*, 84–86; Remini, *The Life of Andrew Jackson*, 194; Wood, "'One Woman So Dangerous to Public Morals,'" 267–68.

26. Coit, *John C. Calhoun*, 194; Pierce, "Andrew Jackson and the Tavern-Keeper's Daughter," 24; Wood, "'One Woman So Dangerous to Public Morals,'" 258–59.

27. Coit, *John C. Calhoun*, 194. See also Pierce, "Andrew Jackson and the Tavern-Keeper's Daughter," 24–25; Remini, *The Life of Andrew Jackson*, 194–95; Smith, "Lords (and Ladies) of Misrule," 57.

28. Brands, *Andrew Jackson*, 424–25; Brands, *Heirs of the Founders*, 157–58; Coit, *John C. Calhoun*, 200–2; Pierce, "Andrew Jackson and the Tavern-Keeper's Daughter," 25; Remini, *The Life of Andrew Jackson*, 192–93.

29. Brands, *Andrew Jackson*, 425–26; Brands, *Heirs of the Founders*, 157.

30. The quote can be found in Pierce, "Andrew Jackson and the Tavern-Keeper's Daughter," 26. See also Heidler and Heidler, *Henry Clay*, 231; Wood, "'One Woman So Dangerous to Public Morals,'" 263–64.

31. Marszalek, *The Petticoat Affair*, 158–66; Pierce, "Andrew Jackson and the Tavern-Keeper's Daughter," 26; Smith, "Lords (and Ladies) of Misrule," 60.

32. Calhoun is quoted in Pierce, "Andrew Jackson and the Tavern-Keeper's Daughter," 26. See also Brands, *Andrew Jackson*, 425–26; Brands, *Heirs of the Founders*, 157.

33. Jackson is quoted in Pierce, "Andrew Jackson and the Tavern-Keeper's Daughter," 26. See also Marszalek, *The Petticoat Affair*, 221–25.

34. The quote is found in Pierce, "Andrew Jackson and the Tavern-Keeper's Daughter," 26.

CHAPTER 4

"You Have Dishonored My House, and You Must Die!"

Daniel Sickles and Philip Barton Key II

The Sickles-Key scandal became one of the most salacious episodes of the nineteenth century, one of the few court cases of the era that could be characterized as a cause célèbre. Occurring as it did in 1859, on the eve of the Civil War, when passions were already inflamed, the case became a national obsession. An ambitious, up-and-coming US congressman from New York, Daniel Edgar Sickles, brutally shot and killed US district attorney Philip Barton Key II, the son of Francis Scott Key, author of the "Star Spangled Banner." Sickles had discovered that Key was having an affair with Sickles's beautiful, much younger wife. As if the facts were not sensational enough, at trial Sickles pleaded temporary insanity, the first use of the plea in American history. Although he was acquitted, Sickles became a pariah. A once-promising political career was derailed. He would go on to greater fame—or perhaps "infamy" would be a more apt description—but Sickles had already earned an indelible place in American history.[1]

Born on October 20, 1819, Sickles came of age during the 1830s and 1840s, a time of enormous growth and change in the United States. Although he was not to the manor born, he grew up in comfortable circumstances. His father, George Garrett Sickles, was a lawyer and politician. An only child, young Dan enjoyed opportunities unavailable to many young people of his era. He studied at the University of the City of New York (later known as New York University). Even during his school years, his bold personality and willingness to ignore social conventions were obvious. Charismatic, charming in a roguish way, and irrepressibly cocky, he was willing to ignore the advice and direction of his parents, teachers, and any adult who sought to instruct him on proper modes of behavior. Confident of his own superior abilities, he studied law under the tutelage of well-known lawyer-politician Benjamin Butler before winning election to the New York State Assembly in 1847.[2]

On September 27, 1852, when he was 32 years old, Dan Sickles married a beautiful young woman, Teresa Bagioli, who was half his age. Both families thought the union was a poor one, but the couple could not be dissuaded from defying their wishes. His burning desire to make a name for himself and earn a suitable income to support his vivacious young wife compelled Sickles to strive for bigger and better things in his career. He rose steadily through the ranks, first serving as corporation counsel for New York City before President Franklin Pierce appointed him as secretary to the US legation in London under James Buchanan.

Sickles returned to the United States in 1855 and threw himself again into elective politics. He won a seat in the New York Senate in 1856. After serving less than a year, he was elected to serve the third congressional district in the US House of Representatives. He was a Democrat.[3]

Even before his notorious encounter with Philip Barton Key, Sickles engaged in scandalous behavior. Flouting convention became his specialty. As a young man he frequented a high-priced bordello operated by an entrepreneurial businesswoman, Jane Augusta Funk, who also enjoyed ignoring social mores. Funk, who used the professional name Fanny White, met Sickles and, like so many others, was charmed by his reckless manner. She soon accompanied him on many a night on the town. She even visited him in Albany while he served as a state legislator. According to one apocryphal tale, his colleagues were so scandalized that the New York State Assembly censured him for his audacity in escorting a known prostitute into the legislative chamber. Another often repeated bit of salacious gossip had Sickles presenting Fanny White to Queen Victoria during a trip to England. The vignettes were entertaining and reflected popular opinion that Sickles was a scoundrel. No one much cared if they were true.[4]

Unbeknownst to the rakish congressman, even as he was out and about, his beautiful young wife was not content to sit at home alone. To all outward appearances, Teresa Sickles and her husband lived a charmed life. They had a 6-year-old daughter. They entertained politicians and celebrities in their impressive home near Lafayette Square, not far from the president's house. For all Sickles's indiscretions, real and imagined, it was not impossible to think that one day the New York politician, an undisputed up-and-comer, might move down the block to occupy that great house located at 1600 Pennsylvania Avenue.[5]

Yet Teresa Sickles would not wait for her real life to begin. She fancied a handsome, dashing young man who resembled her husband. As author Nat Brandt described Philip Barton Key II, a prominent US district attorney, comparing him to Daniel Sickles, "In some ways, the two men were alike—both debonair, ingratiating, wise to the ways of politics, egocentric and rebellious, arrogant and quick to take offense, yet sociable." They both shared an affinity for beautiful women. They also shared Teresa Sickles.[6]

The affair began innocently enough. Sickles had met the attractive young Key in March 1857 when the two men played an all-night whist game. Not long thereafter Key met Teresa Sickles. With the congressman frequently absent, Key frequently called upon the comely 23-year-old wife. Soon they appeared inseparable, attending balls and parties, receptions, and plays. It was only a matter of time before they became lovers in the spring of 1858.[7]

Daniel Sickles knew nothing of his wife's dalliance, but polite society could talk of little else. It was obvious to almost everyone in the insular world of Washington, DC, that Teresa Sickles and Philip Barton Key were lovers. Seeing them together, it was apparent that they shared sensibilities and secrets. They were casually playful and affectionate in public, seemingly with little worry about the possible consequences. How could they not be lovers? It later became clear that they met at an unoccupied house not far from the Sickles homestead. As Teresa Sickles eventually confessed to her husband, she and Key engaged in "intimacy of an improper kind." To put it bluntly, "I did what is usual for a wicked woman to do."[8]

The secret began to unravel on Thursday, February 24, 1859. Congressman Sickles and his wife had entertained dinner guests that evening. After dinner the guests headed for a dance at the Willard Hotel, a famous Washington landmark. Several guests departed in coaches, but Sickles stayed behind, offering to walk to the nearby hotel in a few minutes.

He was preparing to depart when a messenger arrived at his door. Handed a yellow envelope, Sickles tucked the message into his coat pocket and thought no more of it. Instead, he headed off to the hotel to join his guests.

The couple returned home in the wee morning hours of Friday, February 25. Teresa retired upstairs as the congressman slipped into his study to catch up on correspondence. He remembered the note that had been delivered earlier. Reaching into his pocket, he opened the envelope and unfolded the message. In less than a minute, his life changed forever. Sickles was stunned to read the explosive story of his wife's extracurricular activities:

> Dear sir with a deep regret I enclose to your address the few lines but an indispensable duty compels me so to do seeing that you are greatly imposed upon. There is a fellow I may say for he is not a gentleman by any means by the [name] of Phillip Barton Key and I believe the district attorney who rents a house of a negro man by the name of Jno. A Gray situated on 15th street between K & L streets for no other purpose than to meet your wife Mrs. Sickles. He hangs a string out of the window as a signal to her that he is in and leaves the door unfastened and she walks in and sir I do assure you with these few hints. I leave the rest for you to imagine. Most Respectfully Your friend R. P. G.[9]

Sickles did not know R.P.G.'s identity—it remains a mystery to this day—but the note was sickeningly persuasive. He might have thrown the page into the fireplace, dismissing it as unfounded rumor and nothing more, perhaps a political enemy's twisted effort to sow seeds of discord in his happy household. He certainly was tempted to ignore the allegation, but for one factor: The specificity was troubling. R.P.G. referred to a nearby house and seemed to know details about Key's (and Teresa's) comings and goings there. Sickles decided that he could not ignore the note. He had to know whether his wife had betrayed him with another man. It would be a simple matter to investigate.

Later that Friday he directed a friend, George Wooldridge, to search out the house and make inquiries at adjacent properties. It turned out that the neighbors who lived near the residence at 383 15th Street had seen a great deal, and they were willing to talk. They confirmed that a man and woman matching Philip Barton Key's and Teresa Sickles's descriptions had been spotted entering the premises on more than one occasion. The surreptitious comings and goings could mean only one thing. It was common knowledge among local inhabitants that something unseemly had occurred there.

Wooldridge reported back to Sickles that same Friday, but he had conflicting information about the day and time of the most recent rendezvous. It was possible that Teresa Sickles was not the mystery woman at 383 15th Street. Several neighbors thought the couple had entered the house on Thursday. Because Teresa was accounted for all day on Thursday, she could not have met Key. Perhaps the allegation was nothing but a horrible misunderstanding. Wooldridge promised to follow up. On Saturday he interviewed several eyewitnesses who confirmed that the assignation had occurred on Wednesday, *not* Thursday.

Dan Sickles was devastated. He had hoped that the mystery woman had met with Key on Thursday. The latest news led to only one reasonable conclusion: Teresa Sickles was having an affair with Philip Barton Key. Daniel Sickles was apoplectic. To be cuckolded by his wife was unforgivable, an affront to a man of his standing. Aside from that fact, he genuinely loved Teresa.[10]

That evening he marched home to confront his wife. Caught by surprise, Teresa Sickles vehemently denied the affair, but her protests were weak and lacked conviction. Sickles knew too much. He knew the address of the house where the assignations took place. He even knew the day and time of her most recent meeting with Key. Realizing that she could no longer deny the undeniable, she broke down. "I am betrayed and lost!" she exclaimed.[11]

She feared that Sickles, a man with a violent temper, would physically assault her, but he assured her that he would not. He believed her to be a victim of a scoundrel. Although he had not fully formulated a plan, Sickles knew he would exact revenge on Philip Barton Key. He insisted that Teresa write out a confession to assist his efforts. She had little choice but to comply with his instructions.

The woman spared no detail. "I have been in a house in Fifteenth Street, with Mr. Key. How many times I don't know; I believe the house belongs to a colored man. The house is unoccupied. Commenced going there the latter part of January; have been in alone and with Mr. Key. Usually stayed an hour or more; there was a bed in the second story. I did what is usual for a wicked woman to do . . . an intimacy of an improper kind . . . undressed myself and he also; went to bed together." She signed her maiden name: Teresa Bagioli.[12]

In the meantime Philip Barton Key knew nothing of the turmoil in the Sickles household. He knew only that he hoped to see Teresa again, and she had fallen inexplicably silent. He took a room in the Cosmos Club across Lafayette Park from her home. Using his opera glasses, he searched for a signal that she wanted to meet. He soon exhausted his patience.

On Sunday, February 27, 1859, Key could wait no longer. That morning he ambled out of the club and paced in front of the Sickles house, waving his handkerchief, a sign that he wished to arrange a rendezvous. Inside, a despondent Teresa Sickles did not see him. She lay on the floor, writhing in agony at her secret having been discovered. Her attendant, Bridget Duffy, attempted to console her, but Teresa would not respond.[13]

In another part of the house, Congressman Sickles was talking with a political supporter, Samuel F. Butterworth, a Tammany Hall operative visiting from New York. Butterworth had been visiting with a senator when Sickles summoned him to discuss options for handling the scoundrel Key. The man came to the Sickles house at once, finding his friend prostrate on a bed with a pillow over his head. Hysterical, the congressman poured out his thoughts and feelings to Butterworth. He also showed his friend Teresa's written confession. Stunned, the New Yorker offered what advice he could, but it did little to calm the wounded husband.

Butterworth excused himself and marched to a nearby bar to find a drink. Returning a few minutes later, he encountered George Wooldridge standing in the library of Sickles's house. The men discussed the sordid situation briefly, until Sickles abruptly entered the room.

"That villain is out there now making signs," Sickles exclaimed, or words to that effect. Butterworth and Wooldridge knew that Philip Barton Key was "the villain." Wooldridge had already seen Key walking in front of the house.

Butterworth understood that Sickles, in his volatile state, might erupt into violence. He initially sought to sooth the savage beast. "Mr. Sickles, you must be calm and look the matter square in the face," he said. "If there be a possibility of keeping the certain knowledge of this crime from the public, you must do nothing to destroy that possibility. You may be mistaken in your belief that it is known to the whole city."

"No, no, my friend, I am not," Sickles insisted. "It is already the town talk."

Realizing that the affair could not be hidden from public scrutiny, Butterworth changed his tune. He knew of nothing else he could say to stave off violence. "If that be so," he said, "there is but one course left for you, and as a man of honor you need no advice."

The three men considered the gravity of this remark. After a brief interlude Butterworth offered to venture outside and determine whether Key had rented a room at the Cosmos Club.

Oblivious to the drama playing out inside the Sickles residence, Key continued to signal his absent lover. He eventually saw Butterworth approaching. The two men knew each other. They stood at the southeast corner of Lafayette Square, on Madison Lane and Pennsylvania Avenue.

"Good morning, Mr. Butterworth. What a fine day we have," Key said.

Butterworth got to the point immediately. "Have you come from the Club?"

"I have."

Feigning nonchalance, Butterworth asked after a sick friend. Key acknowledged that the man was unwell. As Butterworth turned away, he saw Sickles bearing down on them.

Philip Barton Key saw Sickles, too. "How are you?" he said, offering his hand.

Daniel Sickles was furious. "Key, you scoundrel," he cried. "You have dishonored my house. You must die."

"What for?" he asked.

Without another word, Sickles pulled a pistol from his pocket and fired. The shot went wide. Realizing that he was in danger, Key pulled his opera glasses from his pocket and advanced on Sickles, grabbing the man's coat. He swung the glasses to hit Sickles and prevent him from firing again. Backing away, Sickles pulled free.

He fired again as Key threw the opera glasses. Sickles was not injured, but Key was. He staggered away, imploring his assailant not to shoot him again.

Sickles would not be dissuaded. He lunged at his wife's lover even as Key cried out, "Murder! Don't murder me! Murder!"

Sickles fired at close range, striking Key once more. Grabbing his groin, the man collapsed. "Don't kill me," he pleaded.

"You villain," Sickles repeated. "You have dishonored my house, and you must die!" He walked toward Key as he pointed his gun.

"I am murdered," Key shrieked as Sickles fired yet another shot and struck him.

Sickles stood over the bleeding man and fired at his head. Nothing happened. The gun misfired.

By this time several bystanders intervened. One fellow asked that Sickles relinquish the gun or, in any case, not fire again. Someone else checked on Key, who had fallen silent as he lay on the ground.

Hon. Daniel E. Sickles Shooting Philip Barton Key, in President's Square, Washington

Figure 4.1. This drawing, "Hon. Daniel E. Sickles Shooting Philip Barton Key, in President's Square, Washington," is reprinted from Felix G. Fontaine, *Trial of the Hon. Daniel E. Sickles for the Shooting of Philip Barton Key, Esq., U.S. District Attorney of Washington, D.C.,* February 27, 1859 (New York: R. M. De Witt, 1859), 24.

"He has violated my bed," Sickles told anyone who would listen. No longer enraged, he felt the need to justify his actions.

As a crowd gathered and several men lifted Key off the ground to carry him to a doctor, Sickles addressed the group. "Is the damned scoundrel dead?" No one answered, but it seemed clear to everyone that the "damned scoundrel" was dead, or soon would be.[14]

With the dead or dying paramour carted away, the congressman mulled over what he should do next. Having stepped from the line of fire, Butterworth now appeared at his friend's side. They discussed the options and agreed that Sickles must turn himself in to the authorities. The two men hopped into a carriage and headed over to the home of US Attorney General Jeremiah S. Black.

Sickles stayed at the attorney general's home until the police came to escort him to the station. On the way there he received permission to stop at his own home. He told Teresa what he had done before departing for the Washington, DC, jail.[15]

Word quickly spread about the deed as well as the reasons for Sickles's actions. Observers throughout the nation were riveted by the tale of two politically ambitious, high-profile, virile young men sharing the same impossibly beautiful woman. In a fit of pique, the jealous husband resolved to seek revenge against the hapless lover—in broad daylight with eyewitnesses, no less. The story was almost too good to be true.[16]

Faced with a plethora of criminal charges, Sickles assembled a crackerjack legal team to defend him. A prominent criminal lawyer from New York, James T. Brady, took the lead. Aside from Brady's professional competence, he and Sickles were longtime friends. Edwin M. Stanton, a renowned trial lawyer who later became secretary of war in the Lincoln administration, and John Graham, a lawyer known for his melodramatic appeals to jurors' emotions, also signed on to defend what seemed indefensible. Eight lawyers eventually joined the team.[17]

Robert Ould was the lead prosecutor. He had served as Philip Barton Key's principal assistant and was no stranger to the courtroom. He had a mind for detail and was known for his thorough preparation. Despite his familiarity with trials, he was soft-spoken, even meek. Fearful that Ould was outclassed by the flamboyant defense team, Key's relatives paid for an assistant, James Carlisle, to join the prosecution.[18]

Sickles had shot a man in cold blood in full view of witnesses. He had made no effort to conceal his crime, or his identity. The sole question should have been to decide whether the act amounted to murder or some lesser homicide crime, such as manslaughter. Yet Ould and Carlisle understood that they faced a daunting task. During jury selection on April 4, 1859, seventy-two of the seventy-five men initially called for in *voir dire* said they sympathized with the defendant. Two hundred potential jurors had to be excused before a group of twelve could be impaneled.[19]

In his opening statement Ould insisted that Sickles should be convicted of murder. His actions on February 27 showed a calculating murderer who had planned the crime for several days. He should not be acquitted, Ould told the jury, "no matter what may be the antecedent provocations in the case." Ould had gotten to the heart of the matter quickly. The outcome depended on whether the jury believed that the "antecedent provocations"—that is, the sexual affair—justified the homicide.[20]

John Graham delivered the opening statement for the defense. As expected, he painted a picture of a loving family man, a devoted husband and father, who confronted a "confirmed and habitual" adulterer. Citing the Bible, Graham argued that Sickles did what any self-respecting man would do under the same circumstances. His act was the fulfillment of "the will of Heaven."

Recognizing that some jurors might be unimpressed by this manifestation of divine intervention, Graham offered another possible explanation for Sickles's behavior. The poor man was out of his mind when he shot Philip Barton Key. "If he was in a state of white heat," Graham asked, "was that too great a state of passion for a man to be in who saw before him the hardened, the unrelenting seducer of his wife?"

Graham's opening statement lasted for three days. He continually argued that Philip Barton Key's character and his seduction of Teresa Sickles, not

Daniel Sickles's actions on February 27, 1859, were the appropriate focus. It was a criminal defense lawyer's tried-and-true strategy of putting the victim on trial rather than the defendant. Sickles appeared to be a sympathetic figure, a wronged husband and father who desired nothing so much as justice for his fractured family.[21]

The prosecution might have attacked Sickles's character to undercut the positive portrayal of the congressman as a wholesome family man. It would not have taken much effort to demonstrate that Sickles himself was a well-known womanizer. If Philip Barton Key was a philanderer of the first order, Daniel Sickles was his match. Instead of pursuing this course, however, Robert Ould presented witnesses to attest to the shooting without commenting on the defendant's possible motives. This trial strategy proved to be a costly mistake.[22]

Defense witnesses testified that Sickles was a desperate man, filled with anguish about his wife's affair. Ould repeatedly tried to exclude evidence of the affair, but too much information slipped out from witnesses. Teresa Sickles's written confession, which the trial judge excluded from the jurors' consideration, was printed in a story in the prominent magazine *Harper's Weekly*, which undoubtedly influenced the verdict.[23]

Edwin Stanton, always an eloquent advocate, was at his best as he delivered the defense summation. In soaring, vivid rhetoric, Stanton pontificated on the sanctity of the American family and the rights of an aggrieved husband. He spoke of a woman who has "surrendered to the adulterer," and described Daniel Sickles as a man driven temporarily insane when he shot his wife's paramour. This temporary insanity argument was a winning formula for the defense.[24]

The jury deliberated for a little longer than an hour before returning a "not guilty" verdict. The acquittal surprised no one. It was clear throughout the trial that the defense team had convincingly portrayed the despondent husband and father as temporarily insane. Courtroom spectators heartily cheered when the jury rendered its verdict. Stanton, not known for his gaiety, danced a jig when he heard the news. A jubilant Daniel Sickles hosted a party that evening for 1,500 well-wishers.[25]

Not everyone was thrilled with the outcome of the trial. The successful use of a temporary-insanity plea struck some legal commentators as an abuse of the legal system. That a man could shoot another man in cold blood in full view of eyewitnesses, whatever his motive, and essentially get away with murder seemed perverse, a travesty that opened the door for future acquittals.[26]

Daniel Sickles escaped formal justice, but he nonetheless paid a price for his violent act. His once promising political career was no longer limitless. Before the shooting, Sickles had been a slightly scandalous figure, but even his detractors had acknowledged his wit and charm. After the trial he remained a congressman, but he temporarily withdrew from public life. Public opinion turned against him when he reconciled with Teresa Sickles only a few months after his acquittal. If he were as despondent as he had claimed, how could he welcome this Jezebel back into his bed? The once lovable rogue with the gleam in his eye had been replaced by a dark, malevolent character who should be shunned at all costs.[27]

The trajectory of his career was momentarily halted, but history had not heard the last of Dan Sickles. He would make his mark again, albeit always with a whiff of scandal about him. Commissioned a major in the Union army during the Civil War, he lost a leg at the Battle of Gettysburg in 1863. Although he had disobeyed orders, Sickles had helped to save the day. He earned the Medal of Honor for his gallantry in battle, receiving the award thirty-four years after the fact. He retired from the army with the rank of major general.[28]

It was no small irony that Sickles was involved in another sexual scandal later in his career. While serving as the US Minister to Spain in the 1870s, he redefined the term "foreign affairs" when he seduced the deposed queen, Isabella II. It seems that Philip Barton Key was not alone in his propensity for sexual conquest.[29]

Sickles never escaped the taint of his actions in 1859. He still persevered in his career—even returning to the House of Representatives during the 1890s—but "Devil Dan" could not overcome the consensus that he was a scoundrel. He lived until 1914, when he died at the ripe old age of 94, outwardly unrepentant for having lived a life of debauchery. A *New York Times* article observed that "nobody with warm blood flowing through his veins can read the obituary notices of Gen. Sickles without a certain thrill of admiration. His was truly an adventurous spirit. Under the right inspiration, he might have been an intrepid explorer or a founder of thriving colonies." Despite the old man's long list of accomplishments as a lawyer, politician, and diplomat, there was always a roguishness about him. The *Times* concluded that Sickles "never quite lived down the effects of his mad action in 1859."[30]

Teresa Sickles was not as fortunate as her husband. She emerged from the scandal as a fallen woman. In an era of double standards, her actions were less forgivable than her husband's violent reaction. She and Daniel Sickles ostensibly reconciled, but behind closed doors they were estranged. No longer the young, attractive, desirable ingenue, Teresa suffered through her unhappy marriage until she died of tuberculosis in 1867. She was 31 years old.[31]

NOTES

1. "Dreadful Tragedy; Shocking Homicide at Washington; Philip Barton Key Shot Dead in Street by Daniel E. Sickles; Sad Story of Domestic Ruin and Bloody

Revenge," *New York Times*, February 28, 1859, 1; Edward W. Knappman, "Daniel Sickles Trial: 1859," in *Great American Trials: From Salem Witchcraft to Rodney King*, edited by Edward W. Knappman (Detroit, MI: Visible Ink Press, 2003), 27.

2. Chris DeRose, *Star-Spangled Scandal: Sex, Murder, and the Trial that Changed America* (Washington, DC: Regnery History, 2019), 9–15; Thomas Keneally, *American Scoundrel: The Life of the Notorious Civil War General Dan Sickles* (New York: Anchor Books, 2003), 6, 8, 9, 11. The *New York Times* article reporting his death listed Sickles's birth year as 1823. "Gen. Sickles Dies; His Wife at His Bedside; Long Estrangement Ended When Fatal Illness Attacked Veteran; Career a Stirring One; Soldier, Politician, and Diplomat, He Lost a Leg at Gettysburg, and Lived to Be Almost 91," *New York Times*, May 4, 1914, 1.

3. DeRose, *Star-Spangled Scandal*, 18–19, 21–22, 38–43; "Gen. Sickles Dies," 1, 3; Keneally, *American Scoundrel*, 1–2, 19–22, 30–32, 34, 35–46.

4. DeRose, *Star-Spangled Scandal*, 14–15, 122; Keneally, *American Scoundrel*, 16–17, 23, 26, 32, 33, 40, 47, 55, 83.

5. Keneally, *American Scoundrel*, 1–2, 4–5, 12, 17, 18, 20, 23–28.

6. Nat Brandt, *The Congressman Who Got Away with Murder* (Syracuse, NY: Syracuse University Press, 1991), 12. See also DeRose, *Star-Spangled Scandal*, 29–36, 55–56; Keneally, *American Scoundrel*, 66.

7. DeRose, *Star-Spangled Scandal*, 59–62, 69–73; Keneally, *American Scoundrel*, 66, 67–68, 82–102, 106–23.

8. Teresa Sickles is quoted in DeRose, *Star-Spangled Scandal*, 76. See also Knappman, "Daniel Sickles Trial," 128.

9. The letter is reprinted in many sources. See, for example, DeRose, *Star-Spangled Scandal*, 6. See also Brandt, *The Congressman Who Got Away with Murder*, 101, 103; "Dreadful Tragedy," 1; Keneally, *American Scoundrel*, 102, 107–8, 109–10, 113, 147–48, 157, 185, 188.

10. DeRose, *Star-Spangled Scandal*, 49–53; Keneally, *American Scoundrel*, 110–14, 120, 121, 123, 125, 127, 132–33.

11. Teresa Sickles is quoted in DeRose, *Star-Spangled Scandal*, 76. See also "Dreadful Tragedy," 1.

12. The confession is quoted in DeRose, *Star-Spangled Scandal*, 76–79. See also Brandt, *The Congressman Who Got Away with Murder*, 110.

13. Brandt, *The Congressman Who Got Away with Murder*, 117; DeRose, *Star-Spangled Scandal*, 81–84.

14. The incident, including the quotes, is recounted in DeRose, *Star-Spangled Scandal*, 82–86. See also Brandt, *The Congressman Who Got Away with Murder*, 117–22; "Dreadful Tragedy," 1; "Gen. Sickles Dies," 1, 3; Keneally, *American Scoundrel*, 123–32; Knappman, "Daniel Sickles Trial," 128.

15. Brandt, *The Congressman Who Got Away with Murder*, 132; DeRose, *Star-Spangled Scandal*, 86–87, 89–90; Keneally, *American Scoundrel*, 130, 231, 132, 140.

16. DeRose, *Star-Spangled Scandal*, 97–105; Keneally, *American Scoundrel*, 159–60.

17. Brandt, *The Congressman Who Got Away with Murder*, 153; DeRose, *Star-Spangled Scandal*, 111–14, 157–60; Keneally, *American Scoundrel*, 143, 144, 151–54; Knappman, "Daniel Sickles Trial," 129.

18. Brandt, *The Congressman Who Got Away with Murder*, 156; DeRose, *Star-Spangled Scandal*, 147–51; Knappman, "Daniel Sickles Trial," 129.

19. Keneally, *American Scoundrel*, 162–66; Knappman, "Daniel Sickles Trial," 129.

20. Ould is quoted in Knappman, "Daniel Sickles Trial," 129. See also DeRose, *Star-Spangled Scandal*, 177–85; Keneally, *American Scoundrel*, 166, 167–68.

21. DeRose, *Star-Spangled Scandal*, 193–98; Keneally, *American Scoundrel*, 173–80; Knappman, "Daniel Sickles Trial," 129–30.

22. Knappman, "Daniel Sickles Trial," 130.

23. DeRose, *Star-Spangled Scandal*, 219–24; Knappman, "Daniel Sickles Trial," 130.

24. Keneally, *American Scoundrel*, 190–96; Knappman, "Daniel Sickles Trial," 130–31; "The Sickles Trial; Arguments and Speeches on Both Sides; Verbatim Reports of the Addresses of Mr. Carlisle and the Prosecution and Mr. Stanton and Mr. Brady for the Defence; The Prayers for Instructions to the Jury; Verdict of the Jury—Mr. Sickles Acquitted; From the Special Reporter of the *N.Y. Times*," *New York Times*, April 27, 1859, 9.

25. DeRose, *Star-Spangled Scandal*, 288–92; "Gen. Sickles Dies," 3; Keneally, *American Scoundrel*, 197; Knappman, "Daniel Sickles Trial," 131; "The Sickles Tragedy; Trial of Daniel E. Sickles for the Murder of Philip Barton Key; Twentieth and Last Day's Proceedings; Verdict of Not Guilty; Extraordinary Scene of Excitement in the Court-room; How the Verdict was Received; Mr. Sickles Carried Off in Triumph by a Friend; Closing Scenes of the Trial," *New York Times*, April 27, 1859, 1; 8.

26. DeRose, *Star-Spangled Scandal*, 296–300; Knappman, "Daniel Sickles Trial," 131–32.

27. Keneally, *American Scoundrel*, 201–4, 205, 208, 209, 210, 215; Knappman, "Daniel Sickles Trial," 132.

28. "Gen. Sickles Dies," 3; John Keegan, *The American Civil War* (New York: Knopf, 2009), 195; Knappman, "Daniel Sickles Trial," 275–83, 287–90, 292–93, 295; Knappman, "Daniel Sickles Trial," 132.

29. Eric Foner, *Reconstruction: America's Unfinished Revolution: 1863–1877* (New York: Francis Parkman Prize Edition, History Book Club, 2005 [1988]), 575; Keneally, *American Scoundrel*, 334, 335, 338, 339, 353.

30. "Daniel K. Sickles," *New York Times*, May 5, 1914, 10. See also "Comrades in Arms Mourn Gen. Sickles; Men Who Fought with Him Hold Simple Memorial Service Over His Coffin; Place Flag and Flowers; To-day They Serve as Pallbearers at Service in Cathedral—Burial in Arlington," *New York Times*, May 8, 1914, 9; DeRose, *Star-Spangled Scandal*, 319–21; "Gen. Sickles Dies," 1, 3; Keneally, *American Scoundrel*, 353–54.

31. DeRose, *Star-Spangled Scandal*, 320; Keneally, *American Scoundrel*, 326–29.

CHAPTER 5

"I Never Kissed Miss Tilton, I Never Told a Lie!"

Reverend Henry Ward Beecher and Elizabeth Tilton

Henry Ward Beecher was a prominent nineteenth-century preacher and social activist, one of the most famous men in America, when the wife of his friend Theodore Tilton charged in 1870 that the famous man of God had seduced her. After he heard the charge, Theodore Tilton acted in a peculiar way. Rather than confront his wife's paramour privately or shout his outrage from the rooftops, he sat on the tale for years.[1]

Perhaps Tilton wished to preserve his friend's stellar reputation and prevent his wife's good name from being bandied about in the newspapers, to say nothing of protecting his own pride and avoiding the label of a cuckold. He had known Beecher for many years. As Beecher's protégé, Tilton had enjoyed more than his share of largess at the hands of the influential minister. When the reverend needed an editor for his newspaper the New York *Independent* on the eve of the Civil War, he installed Tilton. Beecher remained the titular editor, but Tilton ran the day-to-day operations. The young man also joined Beecher's church, Plymouth Congregational. He had much to lose and little to gain by making his charge public.

Beecher knew Tilton's wife, and the trio frequently socialized. To all outward appearances, it was a strong friendship. Tilton knew what his patron desired, and he strove to provide it. Yet, as the 1860s progressed, their relationship changed. For his part, Theodore Tilton became more radical in his moral and religious views. He championed the concept of "free love," a doctrine at odds with traditional views of marriage. Free-love supporters believed that standard mores were destructive because they confined men and especially women to loveless relationships that trapped them economically and harmed them emotionally. Most free-love supporters were not against monogamy, but they recoiled at prudish and silly Victorian values that deemed marriage the penultimate institution in human life. If a marriage was unhappy, free-love proponents urged couples to dissolve the union and seek companionship elsewhere. It was hardly the hippie "flower power" promiscuity of the 1960s, but free love was a radical concept at the time. Beecher did not support free love, and he said so from his pulpit.

According to the reverend, Theodore Tilton's evolving views on free love greatly upset Tilton's wife. By 1868 she was meeting regularly with Beecher, who provided solace by way of religious counseling and moral support. What happened during these long hours of comforting became a matter of no small controversy. Beecher might have been innocent of any untoward behavior—he was a charismatic man, and such figures attract all sorts of hangers-on—and Elizabeth Tilton changed her story repeatedly. Yet allegations of affairs and sexual escapades had dogged the minister for years.[2]

It was difficult, then and now, to assess the charge. After his wife told him her version of events in July 1870, Tilton hesitated to respond. He had worked for Beecher and, undoubtedly, he feared for future employment prospects if he passed along rumor and innuendo about one of the nation's most esteemed public figures. If true, the tale placed both men in an ironic position. Tilton, the avowed free-love supporter, was confronted with a wife who apparently had practiced what he preached. Beecher, the more traditional minister and an opponent of the free-love doctrine, had ignored the supposed sanctity of marriage. How much hypocrisy could each man afford to acknowledge?

Tilton was bothered privately by the allegations, despite his public silence. He made no public comments, but he did tell Elizabeth Cady Stanton, a famous women's rights advocate. Stanton had shared Reverend Beecher's abolitionist politics before the Civil War, but she also had spoken of the destructive male who sought to have his way with women privately while also dominating business, politics, and religion in public. The idea that such a powerful public figure could abuse his position of trust was sickening.[3]

After Stanton passed along the story to her fellow activists, including the notorious feminist Victoria Woodhull, it was only a matter of time before the incident became public. A proponent of free love, Woodhull was incensed that Reverend Beecher, a frequent opponent, was such a hypocrite. He denounced lax moral behavior from his pulpit, yet he had seduced his friend's wife. If true, the story highlighted exactly the sort of male domination and abuse of power that Woodhull, Stanton, and their fellow women's rights advocates had attacked for decades.

Woodhull was a public figure with both admirers and detractors in almost equal number. As a self-proclaimed spiritualist, she alarmed Americans suspicious of such quackery, and yet others found her oddly appealing. She and her younger sister, Tennessee (sometimes spelled Tennie C.) Claflin, who marketed herself as a "spiritual healer," had become financial advisers to Commodore Cornelius Vanderbilt, the renowned railroad-and-shipping magnate. The commodore insisted that he had earned vast amounts of money from the sisters' tips. The women became the first female stockbrokers and amassed an enviable fortune, which they parlayed into a newspaper enterprise, *Woodhull & Claflin's Weekly,* an outlet to promote their controversial views on feminism, free love, and various progressive causes.[4]

At first Woodhull remained silent after she learned of the Beecher-Tilton affair. The Reverend Beecher had been the subject of much speculation over the years. It was wise to proceed with caution. She met with Theodore Tilton to discuss the matter—they did more than discuss the matter, some wags suggested, implying that Woodhull and Tilton practiced their own form of free love—before offering Beecher an opportunity to admit the affair publicly.

The notion that Beecher would willingly call attention to his own misbehavior was absurd. He knew of Woodhull's reputation, and his inclination was to ignore her entreaties. His disagreements with Woodhull and her ilk were no secret. He did not see how he could declare himself a hypocrite without destroying his career.[5]

Woodhull never seriously expected the reverend to accede to her demands. Nothing short of Beecher's full public confession would have mollified the suffragette, in any case, and even that acknowledgment likely would have failed. As it was, when Beecher refused to bow to her demands, Woodhull dispatched a tantalizing letter to the *New York Times* and the New York *World* hinting at the secret she held, thus far, close to her vest. "Because I am a woman, and because I conscientiously hold opinions somewhat different from the self-elected orthodoxy which men find their profit in supporting, and because I think it my bounden duty and my absolute right to put forward my opinions and to advocate them with my whole strength, self-elected orthodoxy assails me, vilifies me, and endeavors to cover my life with ridicule and dishonor," she wrote, obviously delighting in the power that comes from possessing damaging information on a rival. "Let him that be without sin cast the stone. . . . My judges preach against 'free love' openly and practice it secretly; their outward seeming is fair [but] inwardly they are full of 'dead men's bones and all manner of uncleanness.'" It was a sanctimonious opening salvo.

Now came the promise of more news to follow: "For example, I know of one man, a public teacher of eminence, who lives in concubinage with the wife of another public teacher of almost equal eminence. . . . I shall make it my business to analyze some of these lives. . . . I have no faith in critics, but I believe in justice."[6]

Whether it was justice that fueled her demands or her anger at Beecher's failure to support women's rights—at least support them to the extent that Woodhull deemed appropriate—is a matter of debate. What is not disputed is Woodhull's propensity for releasing information in her own time, and on her own terms. She believed that Beecher's large family had attacked her in print, which caused her to leak bits and pieces of the story even as she corresponded with Reverend Beecher. To his dismay, he recognized that Victoria Woodhull was akin to a ticking bomb, but he did not know how to smother the fuse.[7]

Woodhull finally published the entire story in her magazine on November 2, 1872. "I am impelled by no hostility whatever to Mr. Beecher, nor by any personal pique toward him or any other person," she wrote. A skeptic could be forgiven for not taking this admission at face value. "Every great man of Mr. Beecher's type has had in the past, and will ever have, the need for, and the right to, the loving manifestations of many women," she continued, both implicitly attacking him and advancing her free love doctrine at the same time.

She recognized that she might be judged harshly for her revelation. "It is the paradox of my position that, believing in the right of privacy and in the perfect right of Mr. Beecher, socially, morally and divinely, to have sought the embraces of Mrs. Tilton . . . I still invade the most secret and sacred affairs of his life and drag them to the light and expose him." Lest anyone accuse her of hypocrisy, she offered a firm rationale. "But the case is exceptional and what I do I do for a great purpose." In short, the ends justify the means.[8]

If ever the term "bombshell" applied to news, it applied to Woodhull's article. She was eventually arrested for sending an obscene newspaper through the mails when she sent out copies of her article in *Woodhull & Claflin's Weekly*. In the meantime many Americans who knew nothing of Beecher's reputation for womanizing were stunned. His public persona had elevated him far above mere mortals with their petty, salacious problems. That this well-known man of God would so blatantly contradict the values he had espoused throughout a long career almost defied belief. He was a larger-than-life character. How could he have done such a thing?[9]

By the time the public learned of the Elizabeth Tilton scandal, Henry Ward Beecher had been an esteemed public figure for decades. He hailed from an amazingly accomplished family. His father, Lyman, was a well-known Presbyterian preacher from Boston. Lyman's thirteen children brought additional fame and glory to the Beecher name. Harriet Beecher Stowe, Henry's sister, was an author whose 1852 novel *Uncle Tom's Cabin* had publicized the horrors of slavery in ways that touched millions of antebellum Americans. Catharine Beecher was a groundbreaking educator who pushed for kindergarten training for children. Thomas K. Beecher was a Congregationalist minister and teacher. Charles Beecher was a prolific author, minister, and composer of hymns. Isabella Beecher Hooker became a social activist and suffragette.

The family was poor, but Lyman Beecher instilled the Protestant work ethic in his clan, as well as a deep appreciation of education. Although not viewed as one of the more promising children, Henry nonetheless enrolled in Amherst College and sought to make something of himself. He had suffered from a persistent stutter as a boy, but at Amherst he discovered a love of public speaking. As he excelled in oratory, he decided to enter the ministry. It was a daring choice given his father's prominence. Young Henry eventually attended Lane Theological Seminary near Cincinnati, Ohio, where his father was the headmaster.

For a decade after he left seminary, Beecher moved around from one church to another, a common practice among the clergy. He developed his distinctive style, rejecting the overly formal, florid rhetoric of his peers and speaking in a conversational tone, relying on humor, and preaching that the central message of the gospel was God's love. His father's style was to speak of fire-and-brimstone damnation and Calvinistic predestination, but the son was not a devotee of the old school. As his stature grew, he was an increasingly popular preacher. He made a name for himself throughout the 1840s. In 1847 he moved to the Plymouth Congregational Church in Brooklyn, New York, and his ascent continued.[10]

Beecher had not been much concerned about slavery as a young man, but his views evolved. In 1848 he helped raise $2,000 to purchase the freedom of two escaped female slaves after their father asked for his assistance. The Beecher family certainly harbored abolitionist tendencies—his sister, Harriet, had authored the most famous anti-slavery book ever written—but it had never been a driving force in Henry's life. Following his encounter with the girls, his views changed.[11]

Beecher was especially upset by the Compromise of 1850, a legislative package assembled by a legendary member of Congress, Henry Clay, to resolve an impasse over slavery. Among other things, the legislation allowed California to enter the Union as a free state while citizens in states where slavery had been abolished enforced the Fugitive Slave Act, which required them to return escaped slaves to their masters. This provision, Beecher argued in a widely reprinted essay called "Shall We Compromise," was odious because it placed Christians in an untenable position. Liberty and slavery were incompatible, and "one or the other must die." A genuine Christian must reject slavery and feed and clothe escaped slaves as an act of charity. No act of man should force a Christian to go against his conscience or his God.[12]

When violence erupted in the Kansas Territory a few years later, Beecher raised money to purchase rifles for abolitionists. In his view, supplying arms would be preferable to sending Bibles. Owing to this comment, the press labeled the weapons "Beecher's Bibles." Incensed southerners excoriated the minister, lodging countless death threats against the man who would denigrate their way of life.[13]

During the Civil War, President Lincoln recognized that Beecher's powerful oratorical skills could be put to good use. The president sent the minister on a European speaking tour. From one country to another, Beecher whipped up support for the Union and insisted that the Confederate States of America was an illegitimate government designed to perpetuate the sin of slavery. His fiery, unyielding language did much to dissuade Europeans from granting diplomatic recognition to the South.[14]

After the war his views sometimes appeared inconsistent. He had been an uncompromising abolitionist, expressing concern for the plight of slaves and freed blacks alike. After the war he sought a swift reconstruction plan to reunite the nation, apparently failing to understand how unreconstructed rebels might impose their will on former slaves. Beecher became an outspoken proponent of Darwinism, a perspective frequently attacked by conservative clergy who refused to embrace the concept of evolution. As a corollary to the theory in biology, Social Darwinism arose to say that just as the fittest survive in nature, so do they survive in society. Curiously, Beecher found the doctrine to be insightful and true. For a man who had displayed empathy for the less fortunate as part of the Christian faith, his postwar views were jarring.[15]

If the great man's intellectual positions sometimes struck observers as contradictory, his reputation as a lady's man also seemed out of character. A closer examination of his home life might have shed light on his predicament. He had married a woman, Eunice Bullard, who frequently nagged him. It didn't help that he was often away on speaking engagements or that the couple lost four of their eight children. Perhaps Beecher sought female companionship to compensate for the disappointments in his domestic life.[16]

Whatever the reasons, talk of his indiscretions followed him throughout his long career. In most cases the women chose not to speak or, if they did, they confined their remarks to a small circle of friends and acquaintances. It was an open secret among all who knew him that Beecher was a libertine, at least in private. The Tilton charge was different, though. Most of the women with whom he supposedly had affairs were acquaintances. Elizabeth was his good friend's wife. Moreover, with Elizabeth Cady Stanton and Victoria Woodhull involved in the affair, ongoing newspaper coverage was all but assured.[17]

With the charges now public, Beecher knew that he must clear his name. After Woodhull published her 1872 article, he demanded an investigation. As pastor of the Plymouth Congregational Church in Brooklyn, it was only natural that he turned to his congregants for assistance. Church members assembled an investigatory committee and launched an inquiry that lasted two months. To no one's surprise, the committee's report exonerated their preacher, finding that he had always lived "a life of great Christian usefulness and incessant work."[18]

The committee's findings, so blatantly sympathetic to Reverend Beecher and so insultingly dismissive of Elizabeth Tilton's allegation, infuriated Theodore Tilton. Anticipating the result, he had already filed a lawsuit against the minister, charging that Beecher had alienated his wife's affections. Tilton demanded $100,000 in damages, a princely sum. Given the shocking nature of the allegations during the repressive Victorian era, the legal proceedings promised to be explosive.[19]

The case came to trial in the Brooklyn City Court in January 1875. It lasted six months. Tilton presented a dozen witnesses, and Beecher offered ninety-five, most of whom were not fact witnesses. They vouched for his sterling character and Christian piety. To ensure his victory, Beecher retained six prominent lawyers, including William M. Evarts, a former US attorney general and future secretary of state and senator from New York. Evarts was widely heralded as the foremost trial lawyer of his time. Tilton's five lawyers included William Fullerton, known for his skillful cross examinations. With these lawyers attached to such a high-profile case, it was little wonder that the opening and closing statements lasted for two months.[20]

Both Henry Ward Beecher and Theodore Tilton testified, but Elizabeth Tilton did not. The interspousal immunity rule prevented one spouse from testifying in a case involving another spouse because the witness might be placed in an impossible position: forced to choose between committing perjury or providing information that harmed the marriage. The husband could testify with the stipulation that he not reveal "privileged communications" with his wife.

These limitations on the Tiltons' testimony meant that much of the firsthand information required to get at the facts was absent. Moreover, both Beecher and Tilton contradicted themselves repeatedly on the stand. Questions about Theodore Tilton's relationship with Victoria Woodhull—maybe they were lovers, and maybe they were not—also muddied the waters. By the end of the trial, everyone was exhausted. It was clear that someone, or everyone, was lying, but as to who the culprits were and what motivated them, no one could say with certainty.[21]

After all the press coverage and jockeying for position, the Beecher-Tilton trial reached an anticlimactic conclusion. The jury deliberated for a few days before deciding that no verdict could be reached. Nine jurors thought Beecher was innocent, and three were convinced that he had engaged in the affair. On July 1 the judge dismissed the case. Although a retrial might have been possible, Tilton did not pursue another round of proceedings.[22]

The minister told all who would listen that he was vindicated, but that conclusion was far from true. His parishioners cheered his return; teary-eyed, they watched, enthralled, as he read a hymn. The following Sunday they piled into the pews to hear a powerful, fiery sermon on the meaning of the New Testament. Yet the rest of the world viewed Beecher with suspicion. His public image was forever tarnished, and he even became a figure of ridicule in some quarters. One popular ditty, occasionally chanted by smirking children, included this refrain:

> Beecher, Beecher is my name,
> Beecher till I die!
> I never kissed Miss Tilton,
> I never told a lie![23]

Recognizing that he must rehabilitate his reputation, Beecher excommunicated critics from among his congregants. He also hit the speaking circuit, relying, as he often had, on the power of his oratory to raise him to a higher plane. He wanted for no audience, but the old luster was missing. Some of the flock turned out to see the fallen idol more out of curiosity than reverence, unafraid to hoot and call out insults when the mood struck

Figure 5.1. This drawing depicts scenes from testimony in the salacious Henry Ward Beecher–Elizabeth Tilton trial. The artist clearly believed that Beecher and Tilton had an illicit relationship. Courtesy of the Library of Congress.

them. Beecher commanded hefty speaking fees, but his name was greeted with amusement as much as anything. The legend had been reduced to a life, and a sorry one at that.[24]

None of the principals escaped damage. In 1878 Elizabeth Tilton published an open letter in the newspaper. It was notable primarily for its pitiful tone. She lamented her suffering as a fallen woman, reiterated the adultery charge, and confessed to "mental anguish" at the outcome of the trial. In her dotage she went blind and became a recluse, living with a daughter until Elizabeth died in 1897.

For his part, her husband remained a strange figure, an odd, ungrateful little hack who had attacked a beloved public man but could not bring him down. Beecher's adherents viewed the supposedly aggrieved husband as a crank who surrendered to his neuroses and discontents as he manufactured the entire affair for reasons that were never clear. Theodore Tilton would always be a pathetic footnote in history, they charged.[25]

Beecher went to his grave in 1887 having recovered some, but not all, of his former stature. When he learned of Beecher's passing, the mayor of Brooklyn declared a public holiday. The state legislature adjourned out of respect for the dead. Beecher's body lay in state in his church as fifty thousand people filed past to glimpse the old lion one final time. Despite the diminution in his reputation, he remained in death what he had been in life: a compelling, charismatic figure who commanded attention from all who knew of him.[26]

As for the 1875 trial, it demonstrated the sheer absurdity of the interspousal immunity rule. If a key participant in a trial—the woman at the heart of the adultery claim—could not be brought into court, the legal system contained a major flaw. In a later century, lawyers and judges assailed the rule, arguing that it was the useless relic of a bygone era—the Victorian period—where repressive preconceptions of sexual relations between men and women led to infuriatingly illogical outcomes. Perhaps the only positive legacy of *Tilton vs. Beecher* was its contribution to the modernization of an antiquated evidentiary rule.[27]

NOTES

1. Debby Applegate, *The Most Famous Man in America: The Biography of Henry Ward Beecher* (New York: Doubleday, 2006), 367–70, 382–83, 395–99; Eric Foner, *Reconstruction: America's Unfinished Revolution: 1863–1877*, Francis Parkman Edition (New York: History Books Club, 2005 [1988]), 520–21; Chuck Leddy, "Beecher: Abolitionist, Preacher, Lover; Henry Ward Beecher Was a Legend in His Time, for Both Theology and Scandal," *Christian Science Monitor*, July 11, 2006, 16.

2. Applegate, *The Most Famous Man in America*, 291, 292, 293, 308, 309, 333, 335–36; Stephen G. Christianson, "Tilton v. Beecher: 1875," in *Great American*

Trials: From Salem Witchcraft to Rodney King, edited by Edward W. Knappman (Detroit, MI: Visible Ink Press, 2003), 171–72; Richard Wightman Fox, *Trials of Intimacy: Love and Loss in the Beecher-Tilton Scandal* (Chicago: University of Chicago Press, 1999), 80, 82, 105, 112, 120–22.

3. Fox, *Trials of Intimacy*, 157, 159, 231–33, 303; Leddy, "Beecher," 16.

4. Amanda Frisken, "Sex in Politics: Victoria Woodhull as an American Public Woman, 1870–1876," *Journal of Women's History* 12, no. 1 (Spring 2000): 92; Helen Lefkowitz Horowitz, "Victoria Woodhull, Anthony Comstock, and Conflict over Sex in the United States in the 1870s," *The Journal of American History* 87, no. 2 (September 2000): 415.

5. Foner, *Reconstruction*, 520–21; Horowitz, "Victoria Woodhull," 415–16.

6. Woodhull is quoted in Mary Gabriel, *Notorious Victoria: The Life of Victoria Woodhull, Uncensored* (Chapel Hill, NC: Algonquin Books, 1998), 110–11.

7. Applegate, *The Most Famous Man in America*, 410–17.

8. Woodhull is quoted in J. E. P. Doyle, Compiler, *Plymouth Church and Its Pastor, or Henry Ward Beecher and His Accusers* (St. Louis: Bryan, Brand & Company, 1875), 23. See also Applegate, *The Most Famous Man in America*, 122.

9. Frisken, "Sex in Politics," 100.

10. Leddy, "Beecher," 16.

11. Applegate, *The Most Famous Man in America*, 106–7, 118, 129, 131, 186–89; "Henry Ward Beecher," *New York Times*, March 9, 1887, 4; Leddy, "Beecher," 16.

12. Applegate, *The Most Famous Man in America*, 242–43, 257–59.

13. Applegate, *The Most Famous Man in America*, 281; Bruce Catton, *The American Heritage New History of the Civil War*, Edited by James M. McPherson (New York: Viking, 1996 [1960]), 18, 20.

14. Applegate, *The Most Famous Man in America*, 327, 328–29, 338–57.

15. Leddy, "Beecher," 16.

16. Applegate, *The Most Famous Man in America*, 142–48, 151–53, 158–59, 166, 168, 219, 301–2, 336, 389.

17. Applegate, *The Most Famous Man in America*, 168, 190, 198, 304, 318, 319–20, 344, 346, 408–10, 417–18; Foner, *Reconstruction*, 520–21; Horowitz, "Victoria Woodhull," 415–16.

18. The report is quoted in Applegate, *The Most Famous Man in America*, 433–35. See also Fox, *Trials of Intimacy*, 54, 73, 80, 171–72, 247; "Rev. Henry Ward Beecher; Mr. Tilton's Accusation Against the Brooklyn Clergyman; An Extraordinary Story; The Evidence Against Mr. Beecher; Private Letters of the Parties Implicated; Mr. Tilton's Statement in Full," *New York Times*, July 22, 1874, 1.

19. Applegate, *The Most Famous Man in America*, 440, 442–53; Leddy, "Beecher," 16.

20. Applegate, *The Most Famous Man in America*, 283, 284, 443, 447–49, 450; Christianson, "Tilton v. Beecher: 1875," 173.

21. Applegate, *The Most Famous Man in America*, 414–16, 417, 420, 421, 423, 426, 436; "The Brooklyn Scandal; The Loader-Price Conspiracy; Examination Before Justice Riley; Mr. Beecher on the Stand; The Case Sent Before the Grand Jury; Price's Affidavit," *New York Times*, July 8, 1875, 2; Christianson, "Tilton v. Beecher: 1875," 173; "Rev. Henry Ward Beecher," 1.

22. Applegate, *The Most Famous Man in America*, 451–52; "The Brooklyn Scandal," 2; Christianson, "Tilton v. Beecher: 1875," 173–74.

23. The little ditty is quoted in Bruce J. Evensen, *God's Man for the Gilded Age: D. L. Moody and the Rise of Modern Evangelism* (New York and Oxford: Oxford University Press, 2003), 60.

24. Fox, *Trials of Intimacy*, 310.

25. Applegate, *The Most Famous Man in America*, 469; Christianson, "Tilton v. Beecher: 1875," 174.

26. Applegate, *The Most Famous Man in America*, 465–69; Fox, *Trials of Intimacy*, 18, 24, 315;"The Great Pastor Dead; Henry Ward Beecher's Peaceful End; Rest Coming to Him as He Had Wished; The Funeral Services on Friday Morning," *New York Times*, March 9, 1887, 1; "Henry Ward Beecher," 4.

27. Christianson, "Tilton v. Beecher: 1875," 174.

CHAPTER 6

"Ma, Ma, Where's My Pa? Gone to the White House, Ha, Ha, Ha!"

Grover Cleveland's Illegitimate Son

New York governor Stephen Grover Cleveland had just accepted the Democratic nomination for president in July 1884 when the Buffalo *Evening Telegraph*, a well-known tabloid of the day, reported that the candidate had fathered a child out of wedlock with a young woman who was soon confined to an insane asylum while another family adopted the child. Upstate New Yorkers had heard the whispered rumors for years, but to many other citizens the scandalous tale was riveting. Cleveland's Republican rival, James G. "Slippery Jim" Blaine—derided as "Blaine, Blaine, Continental Liar from the State of Maine"—had been tied to a scheme to trade congressional favors for cash payments, so he was grateful to share the negative press. Following the *Evening Telegraph* bombshell, the election became a contest between two deeply flawed men, with voters forced to choose the lesser of two evils.[1]

That Cleveland was the subject of a sex scandal appeared incongruous. He was a man of no small circumference, overly fond of food and drink—his various nicknames included "the Buxom Buffalonian" and "Uncle Jumbo"—and was known to be awkward around women. Unlike Blaine, who was a former speaker of the US House of Representatives, senator, and secretary of state, Cleveland's political résumé was short, but he had impressed voters with his strong work ethic and his rapid rise from obscurity. He was the son of a Presbyterian minister who died when Grover was 16 years old. As a young man he eked out a living working several jobs just to support his mother and eight siblings. He eventually became an attorney, a large step up in prestige and income for a self-made man.

During the Civil War Cleveland hired a substitute for $150 to take his place in the Union army, a routine practice during the time. He justified his action as necessary so that he could continue to support his large family. Having escaped military service, Cleveland used his time productively, hunkering down to establish his law practice and making connections among Buffalo's political and economic elite. He evinced an intense interest in politics, although he lost his first two forays in the arena. Rejected in his bid to capture a ward seat in 1864 as well as a subsequent effort to become district attorney, Cleveland relied on a friend, Oscar Folsom, to help him win a seat as the Democratic sheriff of Erie County, New York. The young lawyer was on his way.[2]

In his years as an elected official—first as mayor of Buffalo, New York, and eventually as governor of the Empire State—Cleveland developed a reputation for being scrupulously honest and fair-minded, a rare feat in an era rife with political corruption. With the 1884 revelation of a bastard child in his past, that reputation, so painstakingly developed over years of patient work, might disappear in an instant. He must respond, and quickly.

Despite his heretofore squeaky clean public image, Cleveland knew that to deny the allegations was to exacerbate his troubles. A bachelor at the time the incident occurred a decade earlier, he believed that it would be preferable to meet the charge head-on rather than dodge and obfuscate. To deny an incident with a paper trail and a list of witnesses would sink his political career at precisely the moment when he was poised to capture the highest office in the land.[3]

Cleveland had already faced many hurdles on his way to capturing the Democratic nomination. Tammany Hall political operatives were accustomed to controlling political leaders in New York State, and they were dismayed by Cleveland's momentum, to say nothing of his platform. The New York governor campaigned in favor of merit-based civil service reform, free public education, and lower tariffs. Such a man must be stopped at all costs. At the Democratic Convention in Chicago on July 8, 1884, Tammany men desperately sought to convince delegates to support someone other than Cleveland. They lost. The Democrats nominated Cleveland for president on the second ballot.[4]

If Grover Cleveland thought it was smooth sailing from the July convention to the November general election, he was sadly mistaken. In the explosive *Evening Telegraph* article, published on July 21, 1884, under the lurid headline "A Terrible Tale: A Dark Chapter in a Public Man's History," the Reverend George H. Ball laid out for readers the tale of a "beautiful, vivacious, and intelligent young lady," Maria Crofts Halpin. According to the good reverend, Grover Cleveland "won her confidence and finally seduced her." She became pregnant, but the prominent young lawyer, having promised to marry her, reneged. To add insult to injury, Cleveland employed two detectives and a "doctor of bad repute" to "spirit the woman away and dispose of the child."[5]

The charges electrified readers. A fierce debate ensued about whether a man of such low moral character was fit to serve as the nation's chief magistrate. The Reverend Ball, a minister at the Hudson Street Baptist Church who was known as a tireless public crusader for upholding morals and decency, claimed that he felt compelled to set forth the disturbing facts because he was upset that the Democrats had manufactured a fictional account of the candidate's fitness for high office. To prevent this morally suspect character from being forced upon "an unsuspecting electorate," he had leveled his charges in the public interest. "Since his candidacy is being pushed on the assumption of irreproachable morals, it would be criminal to allow the virtuous to vote for so vile a man as this under a false impression that he is pure and honorable." Ball's sanctimony was in full flower. "The American people have a right to know," he insisted.[6]

The news especially shocked Cleveland's supporters. He had always appeared to be an upstanding, clean-cut man. In fact, his straight-arrow image was a large part of his public appeal. No one could have guessed at his secret life.

The first question, of course, was whether the charge was true. It was possible that the incident, so apparently contrary to everything in the candidate's public record, had been manufactured from whole cloth. If so, it should be a relatively simple matter to track down the original source of the rumor and discredit the persons who had crafted such scurrilous lies.[7]

To conspiracy theorists, the timing was suspect. The article appeared fourteen weeks before the general election. Cleveland had been nominated earlier in the month, and the Democratic Party could not afford to reject him at this late date. After decades of humiliating defeats in presidential politics, the Democrats were favored to win. Cleveland was to be their knight in shining armor, but the stain on his character undoubtedly would harm his standing among voters. No one knew whether the story would be enough to sink his candidacy.

For many politicians, the natural reflex is to lie or attack the person who set forth the charge. Cleveland faced a special problem. His sincerity and willingness to reject the dissembling practiced by most politicians had been his most appealing trait. If he sought to cover up the scandal through traditional means, he would tarnish his reputation and diminish the appeal that had brought him so far.

He chose a direct approach, dashing off a telegram to his good friend and campaign surrogate from Buffalo, Charles Goodyear. "Whatever you do," he urged his friend, "tell the truth." Yes, Cleveland confessed, he had been "illicitly acquainted" with Maria Halpin, and she had become pregnant around that time. He was not sure that the child was his—Ms. Halpin was known to be promiscuous with several men, including married men in Mr. Cleveland's circle of acquaintances—but he had decided to acknowledge paternity and assist her in finding a suitable home for her baby. According to Cleveland's campaign staffers, the tale was not evidence of their man's depravity. On the contrary, the narrative demonstrated Grover Cleveland's sterling character. He might have disavowed any knowledge of the woman and her bastard child, preferring to leave her in the lurch lest the sordid episode tarnish his otherwise spotless record. Instead of pursuing this easy course, however, Cleveland had manfully stepped up to care for the widow and her son when lesser men might have headed for the hills. Surely his effort to help the poor widow did not disqualify him from serving as president, especially considering Blaine's far more recent transgressions involving misappropriation of funds, a matter pertinent to the gentleman's fitness to safeguard the public trust.[8]

At exactly the moment when the candidate was floundering, he received assistance from a group of Grand Old Party dissidents. A "committee of independent Republicans, dwelling in Buffalo," investigated the matter and exonerated the governor in uncompromising language. "The attack upon Gov. Cleveland's character is thoroughly discredited when we consider the sources from which it comes," the committee concluded in its report. Reverend Ball and other detractors did not possess firsthand knowledge of the facts. Moreover, when the committee requested notes and other details from the newspaper office, the editors were less than forthcoming. The committee insisted that its findings were "without partisan coloring." Indeed, the sixteen members who signed the report were Republicans, albeit their vested interest in having a man they knew from their hometown ascend into the presidency might have influenced their opinions.[9]

The 1884 election saw quite a few Republicans turn their backs on the Republican Party establishment owing to fears of corruption and untoward contributions from the conservative business community. They had acquired a nickname, the Mugwumps. The Mugwumps had supported Cleveland during his tenure as mayor of Buffalo as well as governor of New York. Eight hundred self-proclaimed Mugwumps from sixteen states were meeting in Cleveland when the story broke. Their reaction would determine the candidate's fate.

One delegate, a dedicated Cleveland man, spoke up against deserting their candidate. "I gather that Mr. Cleveland has shown high character and great capacity in public life but that in private life his conduct is open to question, while on the other hand, Mr. Blaine in public life has been weak and dishonest, while he seems to have been an admirable husband and father." When his fellow delegates nodded in agreement, he concluded with a flourish. "The conclusion I draw from these facts is that we should elect Mr. Cleveland to the public office for which he is admirably qualified to fill and remand Mr. Blaine to the private life which he is so eminently fitted to adorn."[10]

This was the essential narrative: a noble man had allowed a momentary private lapse in judgment to blemish his otherwise spotless record, but he was trying to do right by a fallen woman. It was a shrewd defense. He was a sinner, but he had made amends. Cleveland's supporters blithely accepted his story at face value and quickly moved to put the story behind them.

It helped that sympathetic outsiders rushed to the candidate's defense. Henry Ward Beecher, a prominent clergyman who had suffered through his own sex scandal a decade earlier, initially expressed doubts about Cleveland's character before accepting the official Democratic Party narrative and rallying to the candidate's cause. In contrast to Beecher, Joseph Pulitzer of the New York *World* never wavered in his support. He had been one of Cleveland's earliest and most vocal supporters. Pulitzer dismissed the charges with nary a second's hesitation. He was not a man to mince words: "If Grover Cleveland had a whole family of illegitimate children, he would be more worthy of office than Blaine, the beggar at the feet of railroad jobbers, the prostitute in the Speaker's chair, agent of the corruptionists, monopolists, and enemies of the Republic."[11]

Unfortunately for Cleveland, the story was not quite dead. Ms. Halpin had a different tale to tell. She had been absent from the scene, but news reporters soon tracked her down to ask about her recollection of events. Not surprisingly, her version cast the presidential aspirant in a negative light.

In a *Chicago Tribune* interview four days before the general election, Halpin presented voters with her own interpretation of the facts. Governor Cleveland was not the chivalrous gentleman he professed to be. "The circumstances under which my ruin was accomplished are too revolting on the part of Grover Cleveland to be made public," she told the reporter.[12]

In her version of events, she was not the fallen woman that Cleveland and his associates described. She was a 38-year-old widow employed as a clerk in a Buffalo department store when she encountered the hefty young lawyer on December 15, 1873. According to Halpin, Cleveland had been an ardent suitor, pursuing her for months with an off-putting zeal. She was on her way to a friend's birthday party when Cleveland ran into her on the street. He insisted that she join him for dinner, and he would not take no for an answer. Initially reluctant, she relented, accompanying him to the Ocean Dining Hall & Oyster House.

By her own account, Halpin enjoyed the dinner despite her initial reluctance to be there. After the meal ended Cleveland escorted her back to the boarding house where she resided. Events then took a turn for the worse. He all but forced himself into her room. Although she did not formally charge him with sexual assault or rape, she strongly intimated that the resultant encounter was not consensual.

Halpin did not report the incident to the police because Cleveland promised to destroy her career if she told anyone. It was not an idle threat. As the former sheriff of Erie County, Cleveland still had many friends in law enforcement. No doubt they would accept his word over hers if she filed charges. Fearful that she might be retaliated against, Halpin tried to put the episode behind her.[13]

The episode could not be so easily dismissed or forgotten. Her unexpected pregnancy meant that she could not escape the repercussions of that terrible night. She had never expected to see Grover Cleveland again after he had forced himself upon her, but the pregnancy changed everything. Five or six weeks later, she told him that she was pregnant. His reaction can be imagined.

The pregnancy advanced, as expected, and Maria Halpin bore a son in a hospital for unwed mothers on September 14, 1874. The boy was christened Oscar Folsom Cleveland, after Cleveland's best friend. (Grover Cleveland would later marry his friend's daughter.) Halpin was horrified when the child was "spirited away," and she was forced into the Providence Lunatic Asylum, a hospital for persons thought to be insane. The description is not quite apt, though; the asylum also treated patients who in a later era would be characterized as clinically depressed. Halpin insisted that she was not unbalanced and that her son had been snatched from her at Cleveland's direction. It was an insidious plot to undermine her credibility and punish her as a warning that she should be discreet.

She resided in the asylum for only a few days before the hospital's medical director recognized that she was not insane. Anxious to track down her boy after her release, she hired a well-known Buffalo attorney, Milo A. Whitney, to assist her in locating her son. Outraged at her treatment, Halpin said she would file charges for assault and abduction against Cleveland. Her brother-in-law arrived from New Jersey to join forces with Whitney.

Within days, according to Halpin, she received a proposed agreement that offered her $500 if she would relinquish custodial rights to the boy and drop the matter entirely. Without the means or wherewithal to battle Cleveland indefinitely, she abandoned her efforts to regain custody of the child. A doctor at the Providence Asylum later adopted Oscar.[14]

During the ensuing years, she watched as Cleveland's political career progressed. When reporters came calling in the summer of 1884 to investigate "Grover the Good's" unsavory past, Maria Halpin was upset by news reports portraying her as an irresponsible harlot prone to drinking, insanity, and neglecting her son. The campaign tale was more than the usual embroidery of the truth, she said. The official tale had Cleveland refusing to marry the young widow but fulfilling his responsibilities by establishing her in a business in Niagara Falls. He also provided child support. The campaign tale noted that Halpin was despondent because Cleveland would not marry her. In due course, according to Cleveland's staff, Maria Halpin returned to Buffalo and kidnapped the boy before he was adopted. Apprehended by the police, she lost custody permanently. Reviewing these supposed facts for reporters, she insisted that the campaign narrative was little more than fiction.[15]

The newspaper reporters did not know what to make of the competing narratives, but no matter. They gleefully reported on Maria Halpin's antics, delighting in vivid descriptions of her looks and demeanor. Her "wealth of dark hair and dark eyes of great depth and of strange, fascinating power" supposedly revealed something about her character, as did her "rotundity of figure."[16]

Cleveland wisely remained silent beyond his initial account. It was an era when presidential candidates were supposed to stay above the fray, leaving the electioneering to campaign staff and surrogates. Cleveland only made two speeches that summer and fall, never mentioning the scandal. He decided that all scandals were off-limits. Offered a packet of papers allegedly containing political dirt on James G. Blaine, he purchased the offending documents and burned them without examining the contents.[17]

Not surprisingly, public opinion followed predictable patterns. Democratic partisans expressed their support for their nominee, praising his heroic efforts to care for this unstable harlot and her little bastard of unknown origin. Even those Democrats who were disinclined to accept this whitewashed view of events chalked up the incident to youthful hijinks. Boys, after all, will be boys. (Cleveland was 36 years old at the time of the alleged rape, which made the characterization of his behavior as a young man's indiscretion highly unlikely, even if one were willing to give him the benefit of the doubt.)[18]

Republicans hooted and hollered that the Democratic nominee, always presented in the press as an unfailingly honest antidote to the corrupt James G. Blaine, was a libertine who did not deserve to be president. He possessed neither the character nor the ability to govern. One widely reprinted drawing, the creation of cartoonist Frank Beard, lampooned Cleveland by depicting a crying child reaching out to "Grover the Good," screaming, "I want my pa!" The cartoon famously appeared on the September 27, 1884, cover of *The Judge*, a satirical magazine modeled on *Puck*, a well-known American humor publication. A caption below the cartoon read, "another voice for Cleveland." Snickering Republicans invented a little ditty to accompany the image: "Ma, ma, where's my pa?"[19]

Despite Cleveland's efforts to eschew dirty politics, the election became a race between two campaigns to see how low they could go. Blaine's supporters could not and would not let go of the Halpin story. Cleveland's men retaliated by bringing up rumors about Blaine. Aside from his well-established penchant for financial corruption, rumors circulated that Blaine had engaged in premarital sex, marrying his wife in a shotgun wedding because he could not figure out a way to escape his predicament. Their child was born a mere three months after the wedding.[20]

Figure 6.1. This Frank Beard drawing, *Another Voice for Cleveland,* is from the September 27, 1884, cover of *The Judge.* Courtesy of the Library of Congress.

Cleveland eked out a victory over Blaine on November 4, 1884, winning just over 23,000 more popular votes than his rival out of almost ten million votes cast. In the Electoral College, Cleveland won 219 votes and twenty states to 182 votes and eighteen states for Blaine. He was the first Democrat to capture the White House since before the Civil War. Joyful Democrats chanted the little ditty about the president-elect's bastard son, but they added a twist: "Ma, ma, where's my pa? Gone to the White House, ha, ha, ha!" Another sarcastic refrain mentioned the illicit lover by name: "Hurrah for Maria! Hurrah for the kid! I voted for Cleveland and I'm damned glad I did!"[21]

Grover Cleveland went on to serve four years before losing his reelection bid in 1888. In 1892 Cleveland tried again, once more winning the presidency, becoming the first man, and so far, the only man, to serve two non-consecutive terms as president. While in the White House, he became the first president ever to be married in office when he wed 21-year-old Frances Folsom, the daughter of his good friend, Oscar Folsom, who had died in a carriage accident in 1875. Frances Cleveland became the youngest first lady in American history.[22]

Cleveland was grateful for the 1884 victory, but he remained bitter at the accusations lodged against his good character. Writing to a friend shortly after the contest ended, he said he would forgive some of his enemies, but some men were beyond redemption. His anger was evident. "I intend to cultivate the Christian virtue of charity toward all men except the dirty class that defiled themselves with filthy scandal and Ballism," he vowed, referring to the minister who ignited the firestorm in July. "I don't believe God will ever forgive them and I am determined not to do so."[23]

Observers wondered whether the lurid sex scandal of the 1884 election would become a routine feature in elections in years to come. Curiously, it did not, at least in presidential elections. Moral purity did not decline as a topic of conversation among the populace, but reporters and elites became less inclined to pursue wild stories of sexual impropriety among candidates for federal offices.[24]

In the #MeToo era of the twenty-first century, when sexual assault allegations against powerful men were taken more seriously than they were in the past, Cleveland no doubt would have been subjected to far more rigorous scrutiny. Blaming the victim for her promiscuity and characterizing the alleged assailant as a virtuous gentleman who sought only to aid a destitute, if deeply flawed, woman of low moral fiber would not be readily accepted. At least one historian has attempted to hold Cleveland accountable for his misconduct. In his 2011 book *A Secret Life: The Lies and Scandals of President Grover Cleveland*, Charles Lachman argued that Grover Cleveland raped Maria Halpin on that December evening in 1873. Cleveland's portrayal as the decent man who wanted to do the right thing by this young harlot was public relations spin at its most egregious.[25]

Cleveland survived a sex scandal that most likely would have wrecked his career because he seized upon a defense that served many a would-be scoundrel in years to come. He presented himself as an incredibly capable public figure who would carry out the people's business aside from his private failings. This was precisely the defense that candidates such as Bill Clinton and Donald Trump relied on to escape the consequences of their actions. In private life they fell short of the moral standards we would prefer in our elected officials, but their public policies were the paramount consideration for voters. Everyone is a sinner and let he who is without sin cast the first stone. This defense depends on the willingness of voters to place their own self-interests above concerns about the private moral character of the men and women they send to high office.[26]

NOTES

1. Ernest B. Furgurson, "Moment of Truth: Grover Cleveland's 1884 Presidential Campaign Was Rocked by a Sex Scandal. His Unconventional Response Saved His Political Career—and Offered a Case Study in Public Relations," *American History* 48, no. 4 (October 2013): 64; Charles Lachman, *A Secret Life: The Lies and Scandals of President Grover Cleveland* (New York: Skyhorse, 2012), 177, 204, 234; Patricia Miller, *Bringing Down the Colonel: A Sex Scandal of the Gilded Age, and the "Powerless" Woman Who Took On Washington* (New York: Sarah Crichton Books, Farrar, Straus and Giroux, 2018), 63; John H. Summers, "What Happened to Sex Scandals? Politics and Peccadilloes, Jefferson to Kennedy," *Journal of American History* 87, no. 3 (December 2000): 833–35; Mark Wahlgren Summers, *Rum, Romanism, and Rebellion: The Making of a President* (Chapel Hill: University of North Carolina Press, 2003), xi.

2. Furgurson, "Moment of Truth," 65–66; Miller, *Bringing Down the Colonel*, 62–63; Jules Witcover, *Party of the People: A History of the Democrats* (New York: Random House, 2003), 259.

3. Summers, "What Happened to Sex Scandals?" 833.

4. Furgurson, "Moment of Truth," 64.

5. The quotes are found in Summers, "What Happened to Sex Scandals?" 833. See also Susan Wise Bauer, *The Art of Public Grovel: Sexual Sin and Public Confession in America* (Princeton, NJ: Princeton University Press, 2008), 11; Lewis L. Gould, *Grand Old Party: A History of the Republicans* (New York: Random House, 2003), 100–1; H. P. Jeffers, *An Honest President: The Life and Presidencies of Grover Cleveland* (New York: HarperCollins, 2002), 106–8; Kerwin Swint, *Mudslingers: The Top 25 Negative Political Campaigns of All Time, Countdown from No. 25 to 1* (Westport, CT: Praeger, 2005), 206. Witcover, *Party of the People*, 261.

6. Ball is quoted in Summers, "What Happened to Sex Scandals?" 834. For more information on Ball's Republican Party affiliation, see, for example, Miller, *Bringing Down the Colonel*, 65.

7. Bauer, *The Art of Public Grovel*, 12; Lachman, *A Secret Life*, 219–24; Summers, *Rum, Romanism, and Rebellion*, 179.

8. Cleveland is quoted in Summers, "What Happened to Sex Scandals?" 834. See also Bauer, *The Art of Public Grovel*, 12, 16; Jeffers, *An Honest President*, 38, 108; Lachman, *A Secret Life*, 422; Miller, *Bringing Down the Colonel*, 65–66; Swint, *Mudslingers*, 207; Witcover, *Party of the People*, 261.

9. The committee report is printed in "The Charges Swept Away; A Political Scandal Speedily Settled; Report of a Committee of Independent Republicans, Dwelling in Buffalo, Concerning Accusations Against Gov. Cleveland," *New York Times*, August 12, 1884, 5.

10. The quote is found in Furgurson, "Moment of Truth," 67. See also Lachman, *A Secret Life*, 218–19; Summers, *Rum, Romanism, and Rebellion*, xi; Witcover, *Party of the People*, 261.

11. Pulitzer is quoted in Furgurson, "Moment of Truth," 66. See also Bauer, *The Art of Public Grovel*, 18–19; Jeffers, *An Honest President*, 108–9; Summers, *Rum, Romanism, and Rebellion*, 183. For more information on Beecher's and Pulitzer's defense of Cleveland, see also Miller, *Bringing Down the Colonel*, 64, 68–69.

12. Halpin is quoted in Lachman, *A Secret Life*, 287.

13. The incident is discussed in many sources. See, for example, Furgurson, "Moment of Truth," 66; Lachman, *A Secret Life*, 80–81.

14. Jeffers, *An Honest President*, 38–39; Lachman, *A Secret Life*, 82–83, 114, 115, 121–22; Miller, *Bringing Down the Colonel*, 58–64; Summers, *Rum, Romanism, and Rebellion*, 179–83; Swint, *Mudslingers*, 206.

15. Jeffers, *An Honest President*, 39; Lachman, *A Secret Life*, 106, 383; Miller, *Bringing Down the Colonel*, 63–66; Summers, *Rum, Romanism, and Rebellion*, 183–84.

16. The quotes are found in Lachman, *A Secret Life*, 242.

17. Bauer, *The Art of Public Grovel*, 12–13; Furgurson, "Moment of Truth," 67.

18. Lachman, *A Secret Life*, 222–24.

19. Bauer, *The Art of Public Grovel*, 19–20; Furgurson, "Moment of Truth," 64; Jeffers, *An Honest President*, 109–10; Lachman, *A Secret Life*, 278–79; Swint, *Mudslingers*, 206.

20. Jeffers, *An Honest President*, 111–12. Moreover, in a colossal blunder, Blaine inadvertently alienated the Irish Catholic vote when he spoke at a gathering of Protestant ministers in New York City on October 29, 1884. A Presbyterian clergyman, Samuel D. Burchard, said, "We are Republicans, and we don't propose to leave our party and identify ourselves with the party whose antecedents have been rum, Romanism and rebellion." Blaine was not responsible for the comment, but he failed to disavow the sentiment. After the comment, smacking of anti-immigrant feeling, was widely reported, Blaine struggled to distance himself from the remark. New York Catholics were outraged. Cleveland won the state by only 1,047 votes, and the comment probably helped secure the victory. Furgurson, "Moment of Truth," 67–68; Gould, *Grand Old Party*, 101–2; Jeffers, *An Honest President*, 113–14; Miller, *Bringing Down the Colonel*, 69–70; Swint, *Mudslingers*, 208–9, 210; Witcover, *Party of the People*, 261–63.

21. "Ma, ma" is quoted in Furgurson, "Moment of Truth," 68. See also Bauer, *The Art of Public Grovel*, 13; Summers, *Rum, Romanism, and Rebellion*, xi; Swint, *Mudslingers*, 207. "Hurrah for Maria!" is quoted in Witcover, *Party of the People*, 263. For the exact vote totals, see, for example, Joseph Nathan Kane, *Facts About the Presidents* (New York: Ace Books, 1976), 238.

22. Furgurson, "Moment of Truth," 68; Jeffers, *An Honest President*, 40.

23. Cleveland is quoted in Summers, "What Happened to Sex Scandals?" 835. See also Lachman, *A Secret Life*, 309.

24. Summers, "What Happened to Sex Scandals?" 835.

25. Lachman, *A Secret Life*, 82–85. If Lachman is the most critical of Cleveland's account, at the opposite end of the spectrum is Allan Nevins. The title of Nevins's 1932 book, *Grover Cleveland: A Study in Courage*, says it all. Nevins believes that Cleveland acted honorably, and that Maria Halpin was the promiscuous, damaged alcoholic that many Democrats believed her to be. Allan Nevins, *Grover Cleveland: A Study in Courage* (New York: Dodd, Mead, and Company, 1932).

26. Bauer, *The Art of Public Grovel*, 20–21; Furgurson, "Moment of Truth," 68; Witcover, *Party of the People*, 261–62.

CHAPTER 7

"It's a Good Thing I'm Not a Woman. I Would Always be Pregnant. I Can't Say No"

Warren G. Harding, Carrie Phillips, and Nan Britton

History has not been kind to Warren Gamaliel Harding, twenty-ninth president of the United States, but it did not start out that way. During his brief tenure as the nation's chief magistrate from March 4, 1921, until his sudden death on August 2, 1923, he was popular with the American people. He certainly looked the part of an American president. He was six feet tall with a full head of silver hair, a barrel chest, broad shoulders, a brooding countenance, and a booming, commanding voice. Aside from his physical attributes, many Americans admired his politics. He promised a "return to normalcy" following the horrors and bloodshed of the Great War in Europe. He championed policies to slash tax rates, and he appeared to be a model of stability in an unstable world where a global war, a Spanish flu pandemic, and the rise of Bolshevism and anarchism left citizens longing for quiet days ahead.

It was only after his death that Harding's reputation plummeted, although he knew that his secrets might soon be revealed. "It is my friends, my god-damned friends, who are keeping me awake nights," he once lamented. After he fell dead the public came to see the wisdom in the comment.

His administration was rife with political corruption, most notably the Teapot Dome scandal, where Secretary of the Interior Albert Fall accepted bribes to lease federal oil reserves at Teapot Dome, Wyoming, as well as two sites in California to private oil companies at low rates without the required competitive bidding. Harding's sexual affairs came to light much later, indicating that he was hardly the buttoned-down family man he was supposed to be. Harding once said, "I am not fit for this job and never should have been here," and subsequent historians and a skeptical public tended to agree.[1]

The Teapot Dome scandal is discussed in many sources. This chapter focuses on Harding's affairs with two women, Carrie Phillips and Nan Britton. Much of the historical ridicule heaped on Harding's legacy is the result of these two dalliances (among others) as well as his relationship with his ambitious, domineering wife.[2]

Harding met Florence Kling, the woman who became Mrs. Harding, in their hometown of Marion, Ohio, in 1886. She was five years his senior, and she had been married before. By all accounts Florence was a forceful personality. One writer described her as "a shrill, dowdy harridan who had relentlessly pursued him." She was the eldest child of Amos Kling, a prominent Marion businessman who had longed for a son. Although Kling eventually had a son, he raised Florence to be as assertive and outspoken as any man. Perhaps because of these expectations, Florence became strong-willed and pushy. She knew what she wanted, and she usually got it.

At age 19 Florence eloped with Henry "Pete" deWolfe, against her father's wishes. Amos Kling was upset because deWolfe's father was a rival and because Florence was too young to be married. In due course the couple produced a son. When the boy was six years old, deWolfe deserted his wife, and the couple divorced. If Amos Kling hoped that his daughter would settle down and attempt to please him, he soon learned otherwise.

Almost immediately following her divorce, Florence began dating a local journalist, Warren G. Harding, who had attacked her father in print. Perhaps the relationship was a defiant gesture toward her father. In any case, Amos Kling took it that way. Florence had been working as a piano teacher. Charity Harding, Warren's sister, became one of her students.

Aside from Harding's printed attacks, Amos Kling objected to Warren G. Harding because of a rumor circulating through Marion that the Harding family was contaminated with African blood. Amos Kling told his peers to boycott Harding's business interests. Angered by this threat, Harding erupted, threatening to "beat the tar out of the little man if he didn't cease."

Trading barbs with his future father-in-law was not the way to ensure domestic tranquility. After Florence married Warren G. Harding on July 8, 1891, at their new home, her father became completely estranged from the couple. He continued to spread rumors of black ancestry against his son-in-law, and he even financed a rival newspaper in hopes of driving Warren's newspaper out of business. Later in life Amos Kling reconciled with his daughter, but it was years before he begrudgingly accepted her husband into the family.

From Warren G. Harding's perspective, the marriage provided him with a strong partner. Florence Harding was far more than a partner, however. She had advised her father on business affairs beginning at a young age, and she set out to do the same with her new husband. She found a compliant and willing vehicle with which to realize her own thwarted ambitions. She could not compete as a man in a largely paternalistic world, but she could act through her husband. He was an empty shell, allowing her to control their joint finances and political designs.[3]

Harding recognized that he needed his wife to fulfill his ambitions, but his passions lay elsewhere. Of all the women with whom he was linked during his life, Carrie Fulton Phillips became the one most strongly associated with him. She was ten years younger but from the same small Ohio town as he. She was considered quite a beauty in Marion, typically described as statuesque, with red hair, the epitome of the Gibson Girl in vogue during that era. Virtually everyone was captivated with her vivaciousness, her quick wit, and her charming manner.

When they met, both Carrie Phillips and Warren G. Harding were already married to other people. He was 40 years old and well established in business and politics. She was a primary school teacher in a nearby town, married to Jim Phillips, a man who doted on her. The couples became best friends. They frequently dined together and even enjoyed joint vacations.[4]

Warren Harding and Carrie Phillips started an affair in 1905 during a time when their respective spouses were undergoing medical procedures. Florence Harding was in Chicago seeking treatment for a kidney ailment. Jim Phillips was grieving the death of his and Carrie's son. Warren suggested that the depressed man commit himself to a Michigan sanatorium, and Jim Phillips took his advice. In the absence of the spouses, Warren Harding visited Carrie Phillips and they found each other's arms as well as the bedroom. Their torrid affair continued for fifteen years. At Christmas 1907 they even acknowledged their love for each other, pledging to be together at some indeterminate future date.[5]

Much is known of the relationship because the lovers were prodigious letter writers. It is amazing that they continued the affair undetected for years. According to the letters, they met frequently, sometimes daily, and often in places where they might be compromised. The assignations ran the gamut, from the Phillips's home to out-of-town hotels, to automobiles, and even in the shrubbery in Carrie's garden.

Harding's letters were unambiguous professions of his love for Carrie and odes to his libido. He often penned them while his wife was in the house. One little ditty he wrote was a typical expression of soft-core pornography:

> I love your back, I love your breasts
> Darling to feel, where my face rests,
> I love your skin, so soft and white,
> So dear to feel and sweet to bite . . .
> I love your poise of perfect thighs,
> When they hold me in paradise.[6]

For her part, Carrie eagerly read the florid professions of love and devotion before tucking them away for safekeeping. She threw nothing away.

Thrilled with the illicit romance, she counted the days until she and her true love could be together.[7]

She eventually grew weary of waiting. Sometime in 1909 she expressed her frustration to Warren. He continually promised to leave Florence, but he never carried through with his promises. Harding was a public man, and he knew that if he divorced his wife to carry on with a younger woman, his political career would abruptly end.

By 1909 he had already served as a state senator and lieutenant governor of Ohio, with his eyes set on higher office. He had narrowly lost a gubernatorial bid, but he had emerged from the ranks as a man to watch. Against this back-drop, Carrie recognized that he was stuck. She repeatedly broke off the affair, only to return when he sent a fresh love letter vowing to change his ways.[8]

Incredibly, the two couples continued to travel together, even embarking on an extended tour of Europe and Egypt. Warren and Carrie found time to steal away for quick kisses and lovemaking on board the ship that snaked its way toward their destination. Jim Phillips and Florence Harding either remained blissfully ignorant of their spouses' activities or they deliberately turned a blind eye to the shenanigans.[9]

Warren Harding knew or should have known that his risky behavior could not be hidden forever. Marion was a small town, and it became an open secret that Warren and Carrie were lovers. On one memorable occasion, Inez McWhorter, Carrie Phillips's cook, entered the house to find Harding with his pants pulled down to his knees and Carried lying spread-eagled on the kitchen table. One telling detail lodged in McWhorter's memory. She had seen Carrie wearing a pair of brightly colored shoes earlier in the day. When she saw her employer lying on the kitchen table, Carrie still wore the novel footwear.[10]

The affair continued as the years passed, and Harding was satisfied with the status quo. His wife directed his budding political career while his mistress attended to his other needs. Despite the seemingly placid situation, all was not well. Carrie grew increasingly restless with Warren's vague, unfulfilled promises even as he was becoming nationally prominent in the Republican Party. In 1912 Harding nominated President William Howard Taft for a second term at the party's national convention, a high honor typically awarded to an up-and-comer. Two years later Harding won a seat in the US Senate representing Ohio.[11]

Carrie Phillips knew that her lover's ascent into national office would carry him away to Washington, DC. With his departure he would become less available to her, and he would be less likely to honor his numerous promises to leave his domineering wife. She opposed his decision to campaign for the Senate, and she mourned his victory.

A wiser man than Harding might have celebrated his Senate win and used his relocation to Washington, DC, to break off the affair. Warren Harding was not a wise man. As soon as he was established in the capital, he resumed his correspondence with his lover. Carrie had enjoyed spending time in Germany, and she set out for a lengthy visit. Harding's steamy letters followed her there. He would not marry her, but after she returned to Marion, he bought her a Cadillac to demonstrate his devotion.[12]

In 1915 Carrie Phillips resolved to end the stalemate. She sent back to him all the love letters that Warren Harding had written. Again, a wiser man with an eye on his political career would have burned the correspondence. Instead, he inexplicably returned the letters to her and asked that she destroy them. He came to regret his impetuosity.[13]

If Warren would not confront his wife about the affair, Carrie would do so. She wrote a love letter to Warren and sent it to his house. In the past she had been careful to avoid sending letters there. Florence Harding cared for the household, opening the mail and attending to personal affairs in her husband's absence. Not only would she probably open the letter, but, undoubtedly, she would recognize the scented stationery.

Florence opened the letter, precisely as Carrie had foreseen. Unfortunately for Carrie, the aggrieved wife did not immediately head to the courthouse to file for divorce. Florence Harding was not young, nor was she a beauty. She knew that her options for finding a replacement husband were limited. If she had not known of her husband's infidelity, she certainly knew that he was not passionately attached to her. Their relationship was first and foremost a business arrangement. Like so many women tied to philandering husbands before and since her time, she had made a clear-eyed assessment of her circumstances. Warren G. Harding was going places, and she would propel him there. Florence did not intend to give up without a fight.[14]

Carrie Phillips had been her friend and confidante throughout their long years of association. That friendship ended abruptly. Florence told Carrie that she must not pester the Harding family. In public, Florence denounced her husband's mistress as a *persona non grata*.

Carrie Phillips was not content to let bygones be bygones. She, too, had invested much time and energy into Warren G. Harding. Now, however, her relationship with the senator entered a new and dangerous phase.[15]

During her time in Germany, Carrie had become enamored of the country and its leadership. Her letters to Warren now contained "suggestions" about Senator Harding's position toward Kaiser Wilhelm. A new member of the Senate Foreign Relations Committee, Harding helped shape American foreign policy. Carrie's letters implied that she might reveal the details of their affair if he did not do her bidding.

In long, plaintive letters, the senator warned her that anti-German feeling was growing across the country. She must temper her public sentiments or risk triggering heightened scrutiny from government agents. The appeal did little to mute her pro-German public remarks. Harding even reached out to

Jim Phillips for assistance. If anything, Carrie Phillips became more outrageous after the men in her life urged restraint, staging a one-woman protest while her patriotic neighbors marveled at her audacity.

Just as Carrie had constantly nagged her paramour to leave his wife and make a life with her, she nagged him to embrace her politics. As always, he mostly ignored her. Harding voted in favor of the United States entering the Great War despite her veiled threat that he must oppose the war or face the consequences. Following the November 1918 armistice, she bitterly complained to anyone who would listen, and more than a few who would not, that Germany had been treated unfairly.[16]

He must have known that his position was precarious, but somehow Harding persevered in the face of his damaging secret. Luck had been with him so far, and his luck continued into the 1920 election season. That year Republicans were confident of victory in the presidential election. Woodrow Wilson, a Democrat, had served for eight turbulent years. Americans had suffered through a bloody European war as well as a Spanish flu epidemic that proved to be even more deadly than the war had been. Most citizens longed for a quiet time, and the Republicans promised to deliver.

Three strong presidential candidates emerged from the Republican ranks. General Leonard Wood was an especially appealing public figure. He possessed all the right credentials. He was a major general in the US Army as well as a physician. He had earned the Medal of Honor. He also had commanded the legendary Rough Riders, with Theodore Roosevelt as his second, during the Spanish American War. He had served as military governor of Cuba and governor general of the Philippines. To anyone who paid attention to Republican politics, Wood was a formidable public figure.

Illinois governor Frank Lowden, a former congressman, also proved to be a strong candidate. He was a conservative Chicago lawyer who appealed to Americans concerned about profligate spending, although he was later embarrassed when reports revealing his reckless campaign expenditures surfaced in the battle for the 1920 Republican nomination.

Hiram Johnson, a colorful California senator, was another possibility, although he was not as strong a candidate as Wood and Lowden. Johnson represented the progressive wing of the Republican Party. He had been Theodore Roosevelt's running mate during TR's maverick presidential bid as the head of the Bull Moose Progressive Party in 1912.

Warren G. Harding initially was no one's choice for president of the United States in 1920. He had been a mediocre senator at best. He missed two-thirds of the floor votes, and he could always be counted on to be among the least well-informed legislators on any issue. Every Congress is populated by a handful of so-called backbenchers, nonentities who are satisfied to sit in the back, enjoy the perquisites of high office, and try to avoid ruffling the feathers of the more talented and hardworking members.

Harding was just such a man. He poured his energies, such as they were, into writing love letters and reveling in his position as a man of influence.[17]

Harding had three things in his favor that ultimately propelled him into the White House. First, because he was an inoffensive nonentity, Harding had amassed few political enemies. He was a pleasant enough fellow who simply glided through a room without leaving angry political opponents in his wake. Second, he looked the part of a president. His impressive physique, silver hair, and booming voice reminded more than a few people of Hollywood's idea of how a president should appear. It was one of the first times that media stereotypes helped to elect a candidate to high office.

The third and arguably most important factor in his favor was Harry Micajah Daugherty. A politically well-connected Ohio Republican, Daugherty was a shrewd behind-the-scenes operator who understood the emerging brand of politics as few others of his generation did. Wood, Lowden, and Johnson were ferocious competitors who could be counted on to battle one another to a draw at the Republican National Convention. Daugherty proposed Harding as a compromise candidate. If no one else could secure enough ballots to capture the prize, perhaps Senator Harding would emerge as a suitable dark horse.[18]

Harding was as astonished as anyone at this strategy. He had never harbored serious presidential ambitions. "You know I am unsuited for this high office even if it were possible for me to attain it," he told Daugherty. For all his many faults, a lack of self-awareness when it came to his statesmanship was not one of Harding's failings. Despite this blunt self-appraisal, Harding could not dissuade his would-be manager. Daugherty was determined to serve as a kingmaker whether the object of his labors desired it or not.[19]

Daugherty had one other person to persuade, and she was not as pliable as her husband. Florence Harding had hoped that Warren would continue serving in the US Senate. If he remained in Washington away from Marion, he would not be around that horrid floozy who had stolen away his affections and, more importantly, his attention. Florence Harding was as astonished as her husband that he might be a suitable presidential candidate—she knew he was little else than a walking haircut with an overactive sex drive—but she eventually allowed him to be nominated.[20]

Before Harding won the nomination, Republican Party operatives sought assurances that the candidate would not embarrass the party. George Harvey, a former Democratic Party supporter of Woodrow Wilson who had become a political conservative after falling out with Wilson, was an aficionado of backroom politics. He met with Harding privately on the eve of the convention to gauge the Ohio senator's malleability. Harvey was a proponent of big business who rejected the progressive ideals championed by the Wilson administration. In considering Harding, he needed a man who was not going to work on behalf of the poor, downtrodden, or sickly.

He needed a man who was every bit as interested in protecting large corporations as he was.[21]

Harding held few, if any, ideological principles, but he styled himself a Republican, and he could be manipulated. Harvey had not been a Harding man, but he liked what he saw. This was a fellow he could work with.

"We think you may be nominated tomorrow," Harvey told Harding. "Before acting finally, we think you should tell us . . . whether there is anything that might be brought against you or make you inexpedient."

Harding reflected on the question for a few minutes. No, he told Harvey. He could not think of anything that would disqualify him from accepting his party's nomination for president.

Exactly as Harry Daugherty had foreseen, the Republican National Convention in Chicago was deadlocked. With few options, the delegates turned to Harding on the tenth ballot. One disappointed Republican acquiesced to the choice, referring to the Ohio senator as the "best of the second raters."[22]

It was far from a ringing endorsement, but the assessment mattered little. Warren G. Harding, the weak, compliant, philandering Senate backbencher became the Republican nominee for president of the United States in 1920. It was almost too shocking to believe. "Now what do you think of that," he mused. "I have been nominated for president! I can't believe it!"[23]

Carrie Phillips was not pleased. In one angry letter she mocked Warren's presidential ambition. In another letter, written shortly before he accepted the nomination, she presented an ultimatum. If he withdrew from politics, divorced Florence, and married her, she would remain silent. For the first time, however, she presented another option. Harding could buy her silence for $25,000.[24]

It was an extraordinary sum, especially for a man engaged in public service. In his reply, Harding told her so. He counteroffered. He could pay her $5,000 a year. It was the last letter he wrote to her. Carrie never replied.[25]

In the absence of an exchange of letters, Harding turned his attention elsewhere. He had numerous demands on his time. If he hoped to become president, he and his advisers must develop a strategy. Florence was in the thick of things, meeting with party officials and negotiating in a ruthless manner that her husband could never have mastered. For his part, he followed the conventions of the day, conducting a "front porch campaign." He delivered his acceptance speech from his Marion home and remained mostly ensconced there during the fall campaign season.

Recognizing that he could not cover up the affair indefinitely, Harding eventually confessed to the party elders. By that time the Republicans could not reject Harding and hope to capture the White House in 1920. For good or bad, they were stuck with him as the party's standard-bearer.[26]

With few available options, Republicans realized they would have to neutralize the threat as soon as possible. Albert Lasker, a Republican "fixer"

Figure 7.1. Warren and Florence Harding are pictured on June 16, 1920, four days after the end of the Republican National Convention, when the Republican Party nominated Warren G. Harding for president. Courtesy of the Library of Congress.

serving as the party treasurer, met with Carrie Phillips and offered her a deal. The party would meet her demand for $25,000, and she would receive $2,000 a month for as long as Harding served as president. She and her husband would be dispatched on a yearlong trip around the world, ostensibly for Jim Phillips, a merchant, to purchase silk in China and Japan. In return she must remain silent about the affair.[27]

Carrie knew a good deal when she saw it. She immediately accepted the offer. Harding went on to win the 1920 general election by a landslide, capturing more than sixteen million popular votes (as well as 404 electoral votes and thirty-seven states) compared to nine million popular votes (along with 127 electoral votes and eleven states) for his opponent, Ohio governor James M. Cox. The party's hush money was well spent. The public would not learn of Harding's relationship with Carrie Phillips until many decades after his death. In fact, they would learn of his affair with another young woman, Nan Britton, long before they learned the details of the Carrie Phillips liaison.[28]

Nanna "Nan" Popham Britton was thirty-one years younger than Harding. She was born in Marion, Ohio, in 1896. Marion was a small town where everyone invariably knew everyone else. Nan's father, Dr. Samuel H. Britton, was Harding's friend. Harding's sister taught school, and Nan was her student.[29]

As a young girl Nan became obsessed with Harding. He was married, as everyone knew, but he had no children. He cut a dashing figure about town as he walked to and from work, conversing with his neighbors and enjoying the conviviality of the town's movers and shakers.

At the age of 15, Nan did not hide her obsession. She hung photographs of the man on her bedroom walls. She lingered around the offices of the *Marion Daily Star*, which Harding owned and edited at the time, so she could glimpse him walking home from work. She found excuses to talk with him whenever she could.

Dr. Britton was concerned enough about his daughter's infatuation that he spoke to Harding about it. At the doctor's request, Harding met with the young woman and told her that she would find a man closer to her age someday. The meeting did not have the desired effect. She continued to "bump into" him around town. The term "stalker" was not common parlance at the time, but it certainly is the term that would be used to describe Nan Britton today.[30]

She graduated from high school in 1914, just as Harding was campaigning for a seat in the Senate. After she moved to New York, she continued reaching out to him. According to Nan, she was 20 years old in July 1917 when the senator finally reciprocated her attention and, in her words, she "became Mr. Harding's bride."[31]

They began a secret affair that lasted for six and a half years. As he had with Carrie Phillips, Harding would find time to slip away from his duties for a short tryst. Sometimes the assignations occurred in his Senate office and, later, in the White House. According to Nan, one notorious episode happened in a White House coat closet that measured no more than "five feet square." The Secret Service detail, as helpful as always, knocked on the door when Florence Harding approached, a signal that the president had best finish up so he could elude detection.[32]

As the result of one encounter, apparently on the couch in the senator's office, Nan Britton became pregnant. Her daughter, Elizabeth Ann, was born on October 22, 1919. Although Harding never met his daughter, he provided financial support. The affair and coverup continued until his unexpected death on August 2, 1923.[33]

Harding was only 57 years old when he died. He had been experiencing heart problems, but he appeared to be on the mend. (Some conspiracy theorists thought that his wife had poisoned him—she refused to allow an autopsy, after all—but the rumors were never confirmed.) The American public did not know of his sexual affairs or the many scandals that were about to erupt within his administration. Consequently, his death triggered widespread mourning across the nation. Times were good—the Roaring Twenties and their attendant economic prosperity were well underway—and Harding was a symbol of happy days following the instability and misery of a world war. Little did the public know of his extracurricular activities. Just as the 1920s appeared to be a rollicking period of plenty and prosperity while masking deeper structural problems on the economic and political fronts, Harding's public image was a facade that disguised the incompetence and corruption rampant within his administration.[34]

Nan Britton took the news of his death especially hard. Not only was the man of her dreams unexpectedly gone, but he had not left a will or other instructions for the care and upkeep of his daughter. Nan approached his family for assistance but, predictably, Florence Harding refused to entertain a financial arrangement. Having lost the source of her power, the former first lady was fighting a losing rear-guard action to preserve her late husband's legacy. She would never agree to care for the illegitimate offspring of his supposed young lover.[35]

With no sure means of support, Britton worked as a secretary, barely eking out a living. In 1927 she produced a tell-all book, *The President's Daughter*, about her relationship with the twenty-ninth president. By this time Harding's reputation had suffered immeasurably as news of the numerous financial improprieties in his administration became well known. The book was the latest revelation that this man who looked the part of a president had not been as well suited for the post as the public had believed. Harding's friends and family worried that this new development, coupled with the barrage of negative stories since the president's death, would only serve to further blacken his name in the pages of history.[36]

Britton experienced enormous difficulty finding a publisher. By the standards of the day, the material was considered prurient and unworthy of distribution. Britton founded an organization, the Elizabeth Ann Guild, that eventually printed and distributed the book.

Everything about *The President's Daughter* came under attack. Arkansas congressman John N. Tillman introduced a bill into the House of Representatives to ban the sale of the book, which he called "a blast from hell." Aside from attacks on the veracity of the substance, critics posed questions about the style. The text may have been written by Richard Wightman, head of the Bible Corporation of America. Nan Britton worked for him at the time the book appeared in print, and much of the prose matched prose he had written in other works.[37]

Long after the book appeared, Harding's supporters vilified Nan Britton as a publicity-seeking gold digger who had fabricated the affair so that she could force a payoff from his family. It was "slut-shaming" long before the term existed. Many decades later a DNA test conclusively demonstrated that Elizabeth Ann was, in fact, Harding's biological daughter. In the meantime Nan received death threats and was denounced as "a degenerate pervert" for daring to accuse a great man of infidelity after he was dead and could not defend himself.[38]

One man was not satisfied to sit by idly and watch Harding's reputation suffer. Charles Augustus Klunk, a Marion hotel owner and Harding friend, professed his outrage and disgust. In his view *The President's Daughter* must be answered in detail. He penned a blistering book as a rebuttal, labeling Britton a "degenerate" for publishing lies about a great man after his death. Fearful that she must take a stand or lose what little credibility she possessed, Britton sued him for libel. Not surprisingly, she lost *Britton vs. Klunk* when the jury returned a verdict of "no cause for action," largely because the jurors considered her a person of low moral character for self-publishing her exposé.[39]

It did not help that Britton could offer no physical evidence apart from her daughter. Harding had asked her to destroy the love letters he had written to her. Unlike Carrie Phillips, who had parlayed her love letters into a large financial windfall, Britton, to her everlasting regret, had complied with his request. Without tangible evidence, her story was difficult for some observers to believe. Having written an unseemly tell-all book, Nan impressed skeptics as but another ambitious tramp out to profit from a real or imagined relationship with an important public figure.[40]

Throughout the rest of her life, Britton never retreated from her claim that Warren G. Harding had fathered her daughter. She did retreat from public view, however, afraid that Harding supporters and cranks would continue harassing her if she reiterated her story. She died in Sandy, Oregon, on March 21, 1991, at age 94.[41]

Her daughter, whose married name was Elizabeth Ann Blaesing, lived briefly in Ohio with her aunt and uncle before rejoining her mother after *The President's Daughter* appeared. She lived a long life, seldom referring to her supposed relationship to Harding. After she died at age 86 on November 17, 2005, DNA testing confirmed what her mother had said all along.[42]

As other chapters in this book attest, sexual scandals, especially involving powerful men, are nothing new. They are as old as human nature. Henry Kissinger famously noted that power is the ultimate aphrodisiac. Movie actors, rock stars, and elected officials often are surrounded by groupies and so-called "star fuckers" who are desperate to enjoy the reflected glory of celebrity. Even by the lax moral standards of many public figures, Warren G. Harding stands in a class by himself.

Although some scholars contend that Harding's political accomplishments have not received the credit they deserve, the consensus is that he was a terrible president. He possessed few of the qualities desired in a great, or even merely adequate, leader: wisdom, judgment, steadfastness, and dedication to a noble cause. He was a terribly inattentive president, and no wonder. He spent much of his time thinking about his affairs, writing love letters, or arranging his latest rendezvous. Owing to his surviving correspondence, we know far more about his love life than we should. Harding nicknamed his penis "Jerry," and he wrote about the appendage in the third person in letters that he sent to Carrie Phillips. Jerry took on a life of its own, becoming an alter ego with hopes, dreams, and desires that Harding expressed in numerous letters.[43]

We know, courtesy of Nan Britton, that the New York Police Vice Squad once burst into a hotel room as Senator Harding and his young lover completed their lovemaking. The officers would have hauled the couple to jail but for the realization that this fellow was a powerful lawmaker. After they verified the man's identity, the police departed, spewing apologies and showing the proper deference that a US senator would expect from mere mortals.[44]

The Phillips and Britton affairs are well documented and not easily discounted. Harding's other alleged affairs are open to debate. He was thought to have had an affair with Grace Cross, his staff secretary. In one account a young Warren Harding had an affair with Susie Hodder, Florence Harding's best friend since childhood. Hodder gave birth to Harding's daughter, Marion Louise. He reportedly had a son with Rosa Cecilia Hoyle, a maid from California. Harding's affair with a woman named Augusta Cole resulted in an abortion as well as Ms. Cole's confinement to a sanatorium. He also enjoyed the company of chorus girls, although not all their identities are known. Some chorus girls, such as Maizie Haywood and Blossom Jones, can be identified, as can a "Miss Allicott," but the others are lost to history. A New York woman reputedly committed suicide after Harding bought her a house as a consolation prize when he seduced her but refused to marry her.[45]

"It's a good thing I'm not a woman," he told reporters. "I would always be pregnant. I can't say no." As presidential epitaphs go, the statement does not rank with George Washington's farewell address or Abraham Lincoln's Second Inaugural, but it is a fitting summary of the legacy of the twenty-ninth president of the United States. Harding's escapades remind discerning students of history that sometimes the sex scandal is not a one-time aberration, a serious misstep in an otherwise wholesome, productive life. Sometimes the sex scandal *is* the life, and everything else is the aberration.[46]

NOTES

1. Harding's quote "It is my friends . . ." is found in Ed Wright, *History's Greatest Scandals: Shocking Stories of Powerful People* (San Diego, CA: Thunder Bay Press, 2013 [2006]), 34. Harding's quote "I am not fit for this job and never should have been here" is found in Michael Farquhar, *A Treasury of Great American Scandals: Tantalizing True Tales of Historic Misbehavior by the Founding Fathers and Others Who Let Freedom Swing* (New York: Penguin Books, 2003), 204. See also Jared Cohen, *Accidental Presidents: Eight Men Who Changed America* (New York and London: Simon & Schuster, 2019), 233–55; Nancy E. Marion, *The Politics of Disgrace: The Role of Political Scandal in American Politics* (Durham, NC: Carolina Academic Press, 2010), 65; Phillip G. Payne, *Dead Last: The Public Memory of Warren G. Harding* (Athens: Ohio University Press, 2009), 192–220; Wright, *History's Greatest Scandals*, 28–29.

2. John H. Summers, "What Happened to Sex Scandals? Politics and Peccadilloes, Jefferson to Kennedy," *Journal of American History* 87, no. 3 (December 2000): 836.

3. The phrase "a shrill, dowdy harridan who had relentlessly pursued him" is from Farquhar, *A Treasury of Great American Scandals*, 21. On the rumor about African blood, see, for example, John W. Dean, *Warren G. Harding* (New York: Times Books, 2004), 19. See also Carl Sferrazza Anthony, "The Duchess: First Lady Florence Harding and the Tragedy of Being Ahead of Her Time," *Social Science Journal* 34, no. 4 (October 2000): 504; Carl Sferrazza Anthony, *Florence Harding: The First Lady, the Jazz Age, and the Death of America's Most Scandalous President* (New York: William Morrow & Company, 1998), 6, 23–24, 61, 167, 186, 198; Marion, *The Politics of Disgrace*, 65; Charles L. Mee Jr., *The Ohio Gang: The World of Warren G. Harding* (Lanham, MD: M. Evans, an Imprint of Rowman & Littlefield, 1981), 54–55, 57; James David Robenalt, *The Harding Affair: Love and Espionage During the Great War* (New York: Palgrave MacMillan, 2009), 25–26.

4. Farquhar, *A Treasury of Great American Scandals*, 22; Robert H. Ferrell, *The Strange Deaths of President Warren G. Harding* (Columbia and London: University of Missouri Press, 1996), 157; Payne, *Dead Last*, 99, 171–75; Robenalt, *The Harding Affair*, 28–29; Wright, *History's Greatest Scandals*, 29.

5. Dean, *Warren G. Harding*, 26; Ferrell, *The Strange Deaths of President Harding*, 157; Robenalt, *The Harding Affair*, 16–17; Wright, *History's Greatest Scandals*, 30.

6. The poem is quoted in Anthony, *Florence Harding*, 89.

7. Mee, *The Ohio Gang*, 43, 63–65.

8. Wright, *History's Greatest Scandals*, 30.

9. Mee, *The Ohio Gang*, 64.

10. Wright, *History's Greatest Scandals*, 31.

11. Mee, *The Ohio Gang*, 45–47.

12. Wright, *History's Greatest Scandals*, 32.

13. Dean, *Warren G. Harding*, 26–27; Wright, *History's Greatest Scandals*, 31.

14. Some commentators have compared Florence Harding to Hillary Clinton as they tried to understand why a strong, capable woman would remain married to a serial cheater. In Harding's era a woman certainly had fewer available options than in the Clinton era seventy years later. See, for example, Payne, *Dead Last*, 206–9.

15. Wright, *History's Greatest Scandals*, 31–32.

16. Dean, *Warren G. Harding*, 35; Robenalt, *The Harding Affair*, 255–57; Wright, *History's Greatest Scandals*, 31–33

17. Wright, *History's Greatest Scandals*, 32–34.

18. Farquhar, *A Treasury of Great American Scandals*, 205; Louis L. Gould, *Grand Old Party: A History of the Republicans* (New York: Random House, 2003), 220–21; Michael Kerrigan, *Dark History of the American Presidents: Power, Corruption, and Scandal at the Heart of the White House* (London: Amber Books, Ltd., 2011), 142; Wright, *History's Greatest Scandals*, 32–33.

19. Harding is quoted in Wright, *History's Greatest Scandals*, 32. See also Kerrigan, *Dark History of the American Presidents*, 142.

20. Dean, *Warren G. Harding*, 51–52; Wright, *History's Greatest Scandals*, 33.

21. Dean, *Warren G. Harding*, 63–64.

22. The quote is found in Russell, *The Shadow of Blooming Grove*, 383. See also Kerrigan, *Dark History of the American Presidents*, 142.

23. Harding is quoted in Wright, *History's Greatest Scandals*, 33.

24. Dean, *Warren G. Harding*, 35; Wright, *History's Greatest Scandals*, 33.

25. Wright, *History's Greatest Scandals*, 33.

26. Harvey is quoted in Summers, "What Happened to Sex Scandals?" 836.

27. The amount differs. Some sources list $25,000, while others say it was $20,000. See, for example, Farquhar, *A Treasury of Great American Scandals*, 22; Gould, *Grand Old Party*, 221; Marion, *The Politics of Disgrace*, 65; Wright, *History's Greatest Scandals*, 34.

28. Gould, *Grand Old Party*, 222–27. Joseph Nathan Kane, *Facts About the Presidents* (New York: Ace Books, 1976), 311–12.

29. Ferrell, *The Strange Deaths of President Harding*, 50.

30. Farquhar, *A Treasury of Great American Scandals*, 22; Ferrell, *The Strange Deaths of President Harding*, 50–51; Mee, *The Ohio Gang*, 64.

31. Britton was quoted in Ferrell, *The Strange Deaths of President Harding*, 72. See also Mee, *The Ohio Gang*, 75.

32. Cohen, *Accidental Presidents*, 234–35; Farquhar, *A Treasury of Great American Scandals*, 22–23; Marion, *The Politics of Disgrace*, 65–66.

33. Cohen, *Accidental Presidents*, 236–43; Kerrigan, *Dark History of the American Presidents*, 143; Marion, *The Politics of Disgrace*, 65–66; Robenalt, *The Harding Affair*, 247, 347.

34. Cohen, *Accidental Presidents*, 243–55; Farquhar, *A Treasury of Great American Scandals*, 23; Robenalt, *The Harding Affair*, 348.

35. Peter Baker, "Test Results Are In: At Last, Secret About Harding Is Out," *New York Times*, August 13, 2015, A12.

36. Cohen, *Accidental Presidents*, 258; Dean, *Warren G. Harding*, 162–63; Kerrigan, *Dark History of the American Presidents*, 143; Marion, *The Politics of Disgrace*, 65–66; Payne, *Dead Last*, 126–27; Summers, "What Happened to Sex Scandals?" 836.

37. Baker, "Test Results Are In," A12; Payne, *Dead Last*, 127–44.

38. Baker, "Test Results Are In," A12; "DNA Tests of the Relevant Descendants Show That Warren Harding Had a Love Child by Nan Britton, a Woman 31 Years His Junior," *National Review* 67, no. 16 (September 7, 2015): 13; Robenalt, *The Harding Affair*, 350–51.

39. Anthony, *Florence Harding*, 530; Ferrell, *The Strange Deaths of President Harding*, 68–76.

40. Dean, *Warren G. Harding*, 163. Dean's book was published in 2004, before DNA evidence revealed that Harding fathered Nan Britton's daughter. See, for example, Baker, "Test Results Are In," A12.

41. Anthony, *Florence Harding*, 532.

42. Baker, "Test Results Are In," A12.

43. Ferrell, *The Strange Deaths of President Harding*, 46; Robenalt, *The Harding Affair*, 168, 275, 332.

44. Robenalt, *The Harding Affair*, 270.

45. Anthony, *Florence Harding*, xiii, 61–62, 149–50, 194, 262, 302, 310, 354, 356, 393; Kerrigan, *Dark History of the American Presidents*, 140.

46. The quote is from Kerrigan, *Dark History of the American Presidents*, 140.

CHAPTER 8

"She Had the WAYS; He Had the MEANS"

Wilbur Mills and Fanne Foxe

"They used to say that not even God could defeat Wilbur D. Mills in an Arkansas election," an October 1974 *New York Times* article observed. "That has changed. The Lord is now given a slight edge."[1]

At the time the article appeared, Mills was a 65-year-old United States Democratic congressman from Arkansas and chairman of the powerful Ways and Means Committee, which developed tax policy for the nation. A longtime legislator who ruled his committee with an iron fist, Mills was among the most powerful and influential figures in the nation's capital. A colleague once remarked as a testament to the chairman's power, only half in jest, "I never vote against God, motherhood or Wilbur Mills." To all outward appearances, the Arkansas legislator was a respectable, conservative, and even staid figure. What few people outside the beltway knew in October 1974 was that Wilbur Mills was out of control, and he had been that way for some time.[2]

Matters came to a head in the wee morning hours of Monday, October 7, 1974. Around two o'clock that morning, a black 1973 Lincoln Continental automobile barreled down a street near the Washington Monument in Washington, DC. As they conducted a routine patrol, two US Park Service policemen, Privates Larry Brent and Thomas Johann, noticed that the car's headlights were off, and the vehicle was traveling at a "high rate of speed." The officers jumped into their cruiser and pursued the Lincoln, stopping it near the Tidal Basin, a partially man-made reservoir between the Potomac River and the Washington Channel that dates from the 1880s. Directly across the basin sat the Jefferson Memorial, brightly illuminated with powerful floodlights.

Stepping from their cruiser, Officers Brent and Johann approached the car. The driver rolled down the window, apparently to greet the officers. Judging by the odor, one or more of the vehicle's occupants—three men

and two women—had been drinking alcohol. Following standard proce-
dure, the officers asked to see identification for each person.

One occupant in the back seat was a balding, elderly man with dark-
framed glasses and a bulbous nose. The man's face was badly scratched,
and his nose was bloody. An attractive curly-haired woman wearing a long
evening dress sat next to the man inside the car. She was obviously much
younger than he was.

When she realized that she would have to identify herself, the curly-
haired woman became hysterical. To the officers' surprise, the woman
pushed the door open, climbed out of the car, and ran for the nearby Tidal
Basin. She screamed as she ran, alternating between English and Spanish
words. Still hysterical and out of control, she landed in the Tidal Basin. Accounts differ as to whether she hurled herself into the water or tripped and
fell. Most witnesses believed it was the former.

Officers Brent and Johann were not sure why she had reacted so dramat-
ically. It may have been a suicide attempt, but most likely she was fleeing
the scene. If she hoped to skedaddle before the officers discovered her identity, however, she chose her escape route poorly. The woman might have
run along the tree-lined boulevard and eluded capture by flagging down a
passing motorist or disappearing into an adjacent copse. Of all her options,
jumping into the Tidal Basin was the worst choice. The basin spans 107
acres and is approximately ten feet deep in some places. Even an expert
swimmer would have a difficult time fleeing in the water.

Whatever her motive, the officers were worried for her safety. The woman
was obviously intoxicated and might drown, although the water where she
was wading was not deep. After a few seconds, Officer Brent fished her out
of the basin. He handcuffed her when she tried to break away and jump
back into the water.

The strange night grew even stranger. No sooner had the woman entered
the water than the bleeding man stumbled from the car and tried to follow
her in. Lawrence Krebs, a television cameraman who had arrived on the
scene as soon as he heard that a woman was in the Tidal Basin, witnessed
most of the event. He recalled one of the officers speaking to the man.
"Come on, Congressman," the officer admonished him, "you don't need
this kind of publicity." Krebs immediately recognized the influential Ways
and Means committee chairman. In his opinion, "unless he's got a dupli-
cate in life, it was Wilbur Mills." A spokesman for the congressman later
denied that Mills had been on the scene, but there was little doubt of his
presence.[3]

According to a police spokesperson, at some point after the woman
jumped into the Tidal Basin, "one of the people who was on the scene"
identified the man with the bulbous nose and bleeding face as Wilbur Mills.
Accounts vary as to who disclosed his identity. Mills may have identified

himself or someone else may have said it. As a high-profile member of Congress, Mills was a prominent figure on television and in the newspapers. The officers almost certainly knew who he was. Even if they did not recognize his face, they knew his name.

Early eyewitness accounts had Mills throwing his weight around after he stepped from the car. "I'm a congressman," he supposedly cried out to the officers, "and I'll have you demoted." Officer Brent's official report did not mention the remark. In fact, the police report did not mention Wilbur Mills being present at the scene.[4]

As the officers learned later, the woman inflicted the scratches on Mills's face and bloodied his nose as soon as the police pulled the car over. She was desperate not to be apprehended. It was little wonder that she sought to avoid the harsh spotlight. The woman, whose real name was Annabella Battistella, was a 38-year-old stripper who used the stage name Fanne Foxe, aka the "Argentine firecracker."[5]

Because they could not be certain of her mental condition, the police escorted Ms. Battistella to St. Elizabeth's Hospital for observation. She was treated and released. One officer drove the Lincoln Continental, which bore Arkansas license plates and was registered in Wilbur Mills's name, transporting the other occupants to the congressman's apartment building in Arlington, Virginia. No one was cited for drunk driving or public intoxication. Observers later questioned whether the report that failed to mention Mills might have been an attempted cover-up, but the park police denied such an intent.

If the police sought to hush up the incident, they failed. When the story appeared in the newspapers, it attracted enormous attention. Readers gleefully soaked up details of the dowdy congressman and the slinky stripper cavorting together in a late-night romp along the Potomac. Fanne Foxe quickly earned the nickname the "Tidal Basin Bombshell."[6]

Wilbur Mills, a titan of the United States Congress, had humiliated himself. Occasionally a sex scandal, while squalid, suggests that the man involved possesses virility galore. He emerges, ironically, as a more sympathetic figure because he is desirable to the opposite sex and he is a flesh-and-blood human being. The short, homely Arkansas congressman, however, appeared as the punchline to a national joke. As they learned of the episode, Americans chortled at the diminutive, intoxicated, bespectacled congressman with the big glasses, even bigger nose, and a scratched, bloody face who had been beaten up by his much younger stripper girlfriend. He was not a dashing man about town with a certain roguish charm. He was a pathetic old man who had fallen prey to a hardened, conniving temptress. In one evening Congressman Mills all but destroyed the career he had painstakingly built over many decades of unrelenting labor.[7]

The climb had been painstaking, indeed. Pundits sometimes describe a public figure's rise as "meteoric," noting how quickly the person has ascended into the spotlight. Mills's success was anything but meteoric. He slowly made his way up the proverbial career ladder, one rung at a time.

Wilbur Daigh Mills was born on May 24, 1909, in the little town of Kensett, Arkansas, population 905, about sixty miles north of Little Rock. He attended public schools and performed well. He was the valedictorian of his high school class and salutatorian of his class at Hendrix College in Conway, Arkansas. During his childhood his father was the town grocer and bank president. The elder Mills later served as superintendent of schools before becoming school board chairman and the district's banker.

Reflecting on his life, Wilbur Mills recalled the moment when he resolved to pursue a political career. He was 10 years old when Congressman William A. Oldfield visited the town. Impressed with the reception afforded this public man, the boy saw that he, too, could earn respect if he served in high office. For almost two decades afterward, he thought about how to position himself to maximize his voter appeal. Thinking back on his decision years later, he admitted that "I've never regretted the decision."

Budding politicians often practice law before running for office, so Mills chose to enter the legal profession. He wanted a head start on his contemporaries; consequently, he enrolled in Harvard Law School after graduating from college in 1930. For a small-town Arkansas boy to earn a seat at one of the most prestigious law schools in the country was no mean achievement.

He subsequently returned to Arkansas but found it difficult to open a law practice at the height of the Great Depression in 1933. After he was admitted to the Arkansas bar, he became a cashier in his father's bank. It was not the exalted position he had hoped to find, but it introduced him to prominent people in the town. Those associations would serve him well.

After only a year Mills felt he could compete in local politics. In 1934 the citizens of White County elected him to serve as a county judge. Four years later he campaigned for a seat in the United States House of Representatives for the second district of Arkansas. Amazingly, he won. He served in the seat for thirty-eight years.

Wilbur Mills was 29 years old and the second-youngest House member when he set off for Washington, DC. At five feet eight inches tall with undistinguished features, he was not a handsome man, nor was he especially flamboyant. He soon distinguished himself, however, by his keen intellect and diligent attention to detail. Impressed with the hardworking Arkansas legislator, Speaker Sam Rayburn appointed Mills to the House Banking and Currency Committee in 1939, and to the Ways and Means Committee in 1943.

Mills dutifully labored long hours as a pedestrian House member. According to all accounts, he bided his time without complaint. Because Congress operated on a seniority system, by 1957 he had served long enough to become the Ways and Means Committee chairman. In that capacity he and his staff authored much of the federal tax code and oversaw Social Security and military spending as well as tariff legislation.

He reflected the standard states' rights positions of most southern politicians of the time. Although he was not a race-baiting demagogue, Mills voted with the southern bloc, which favored segregation and resisted any federal efforts to assist people of color. "I couldn't stay in Congress unless I voted the way I do on these highly emotional issues," he explained late in his career.[8]

Although his self-destruction appeared to occur during an isolated moment of absurd weakness in 1974, Mills had spent decades building up (or, rather, breaking down) to that incident. By his own admission, he started drinking in the evenings after work to relax before dinner. Gradually, he drank more alcohol and ate less dinner. "During some 54 years from when I took my first drink to when I took my last, I was not aware of any progression of my drinking at all," he wrote in a 1979 article published in the *Saturday Evening Post*. "The last two years of my drinking, as I look back on them, were living hell."[9]

If Wilbur Mills's background was blandly conventional for a member of Congress, his girlfriend's origins were far more exotic. She was born on February 14, 1936—St. Valentine's Day—in Nueve de Julio, a town 175 miles southwest of Buenos Aires, Argentina. Her father, Oswaldo Villagra, was of Indian-Spanish heritage. He worked as a male nurse and local politician.

At the age of 20, Annabella Villagra married Eduardo Battistella, a nightclub pianist. She followed him around the club circuit as he eked out a meager living. When they depleted their funds, she turned to dancing and eventually to stripping. With her curvaceous figure and increasingly uninhibited performances, she enjoyed a modicum of success.

The couple moved to the United States in the early 1970s in search of greater economic opportunities. They had four children, but their marriage was strained by their dual careers. Predictably, they divorced. Along the way, though, they befriended their neighbors, an older couple named Wilbur and Polly Mills.[10]

It was easy to see what attracted Mills to the much younger stripper. She was physically attractive and, with her soft Latin accent and bronze skin, exotic. She also listened to him talk about the things he had missed in his life. She encouraged him to be free and easy, tossing away his cares and inhibitions. He found the attentions of the younger woman almost as intoxicating as the alcohol he guzzled each night.

For her part, Battistella thought that Wilbur Mills was the stable father figure she had never had. "I guess it is not ridiculous that any woman would like to be married to Wilbur Mills," she told an interviewer in December

1974. "I think he could be a perfect husband. I would like to marry somebody older than my former husband."[11]

After they finished chuckling at the famous man's shenanigans, pundits wondered aloud what had made Mills behave in such a reckless fashion, despite the stripper's obvious charms. He was well respected and powerful, a man who had clawed his way up to the top of the heap in Washington, DC. Now that he apparently had everything that a member of Congress could desire, he seemed to throw it all away. For his part, Mills explained that he was an alcoholic, and he had been taking prescription medication for back pain following surgery a year earlier. For observers who cared to psychoanalyze the man, he might have been so afraid of success—feeling that he was an imposter who did not deserve to succeed—that he had deliberately sabotaged his career as a perverse means of ensuring that he would not enjoy the fruits of his labors.

This last explanation seems to be borne out by Mills's behavior after the Tidal Basin incident hit the newspapers. He managed to eke out a victory in the November 1974 election—his constituents had returned him to Washington for so many years that they may have forgotten how to vote against him—but he should have learned his lesson and stayed away from the glamorous Fanne Foxe. He did not.[12]

On December 1, 1974, as the Argentine Firecracker performed a burlesque show at the run-down Pilgrim Theater in Boston, in the heart of the "Combat Zone," an area infamously littered with strip clubs and sex film theaters, Mills turned up backstage. Fanny saw him lurking in the wings and called him onstage. "I'd like you to meet somebody," she told the audience. Waving him in, she called, "Mr. Mills, Mr. Mills! Where are you?"

Incredibly, Mills wandered out in front of the audience and exchanged a few words with the stripper. She kissed him on the cheek, and he headed backstage. Later, he hung around long enough to be photographed with his Tidal Basin buddy.[13]

Democrats, especially junior members of Congress, had been critical of Mills's ham-fisted control of the Ways and Means Committee for years. In the Watergate era, when crooked politicians who had grown too autocratic and intoxicated by their own power were ignominiously booted out of office, few elected officials were sympathetic to colleagues who failed to fulfill the public trust. No one thought that Wilbur Mills was corrupt in the same way that Richard Nixon, the disgraced and recently resigned president of the United States, was corrupt, but they acknowledged that it was time to surrender his committee chairmanship. He lost the coveted leadership post but remained in the House of Representatives until his term ended in 1977. Mills occasionally had been mentioned as a possible presidential candidate, but those dreams died the moment his stripper girlfriend entered the Tidal Basin.[14]

Figure 8.1. On December 1, 1974, Congressman Wilbur Mills was photographed with Argentine stripper Fanne Foxe (née Annabelle Battistella) outside a burlesque theater in Boston, Massachusetts, where she was starring in a production that promoted her as "The Washington Tidal Basin Girl." Courtesy of Granger Historical Picture Archive.

Mills was humiliated, but he had brought it on himself. In the days, weeks, and months that followed, his wife, Clarine "Polly" Mills, suffered through everything expected of a political wife. She stoically appeared at public events and acted as though the sordid tales of her husband's ribald antics bothered her not at all. Somehow, she smiled sweetly, swallowed her pain, and got through it. Whatever her private thoughts, she never voiced anything other than total commitment to her husband. The couple remained together until his death at age 82 on May 2, 1992.[15]

If Mills's fortunes declined after the Argentine Firecracker blew up in his face, Fanne Foxe's career thrived. She immediately increased her appearance fees. Before the Tidal Basin episode, she commanded approximately $3,500 for a two-week engagement. Afterward, she commanded as much as $15,000 as curious tourists arrived to see what all the fuss was about. Fame had a downside as well. In December 1974 she was arrested for indecent exposure during a show in Sanford, Florida—the gig that paid $15,000—but authorities later dropped the charges. Ironically, the arrest kept her in the spotlight and increased public interest in her celebrity.

Trading on her fifteen minutes of fame, she was not satisfied to confine her appearances to strip clubs. She appeared on a popular television program, *The Mike Douglas Show.* Later, she also snagged a role playing herself in a low-budget western film called *Posse from Heaven,* released in October 1975. The plot of the film, to the extent that it had a plot, was easily summarized: "Heavenly forces send a guardian angel to assist an ex-cavalryman named Appletime [to] find love and meaning in life." Foxe appeared as an angel's apprentice, trying her hand at slapstick comedy along with a bit of singing and a bump-and-grind display of her other talents. Her character offered pearls of wisdom to an ex-cavalryman in need of advice from an aging stripper. Lest anyone miss Fanne's claim to fame, film posters advertised the feature with a not-so-subtle reference to her ex-boyfriend's former career: "She had the WAYS; he had the MEANS."[16]

She continued cashing in on her infamy in 1975. She published a tell-all book, the appropriately titled *The Stripper and the Congressman,* detailing her seventeen-month affair with Wilbur Mills. The 180-page ghostwritten memoir regaled readers with stories, some known, others only hinted at, about her relationship with the Arkansas congressman. Yes, it was sexual. In fact, Fanne Foxe was pregnant with his child until she had an abortion. She also discussed her visits about town with Mills and how his wife sometimes joined them. Musing about the incident that ensured her notoriety, she insisted that if "it hadn't happened, I think me and Congressman Mills would have married."[17]

Criticized for her rank opportunism, Foxe was unrepentant. She said in a subsequent interview that "Congressman Mills knew that I was writing the book. What may shock him is the fact that I put almost everything into it." The book was not a flattering portrait of herself or anyone else. She twice attempted suicide. During her tumultuous marriage to Eduardo Battistella, she tried to run him over with her car. The couple engaged in wife swapping, and Foxe had two abortions in addition to the one she underwent while carrying Wilbur Mills's child. As an aging stripper, she frequently underwent cosmetic surgery to turn up her nose, flatten her stomach, and firm up her sagging breasts.[18]

Whatever else could be said about her, Fanne Foxe was a realist. She understood that fame was fleeting, especially for someone as modestly talented as she. She had to parlay her reputation into paying engagements quickly. She was pushing 40, and the public would not remember her forever. "I have three children and I am not being supported by a man," she explained. "It is hard to earn a living, and I have financial obligations to meet."[19]

Foxe appeared in *Playboy* magazine in 1976 and 1977. She also granted a lengthy interview to another men's magazine, *Cheri*, in 1977. She eventually returned to Argentina, where she faded into obscurity. After a lengthy absence from the headlines, Fanne Foxe briefly reappeared when she died at age 84 on February 10, 2021. Today she is remembered as the floozy who brought down a sad, silly congressman in a crazy incident that still elicits guffaws and wonder at the absurdity of it all.[20]

NOTES

1. Roy Reed, "Mills Forced to Campaign Hard Following Tidal Basin Incident," *New York Times*, October 19, 1974, 65.

2. The quote is found in "The Rise and Decline of Mr. Mills," *New York Times*, December 8, 1974, 252. See also Nancy E. Marion, *The Politics of Disgrace: The Role of Political Scandal in American Politics* (Durham, NC: Carolina Academic Press, 2010), 209.

3. The quotes and details are found in John M. Crewdson, "Mills in Seclusion After Report He Was Intoxicated in Car Stopped by Police: Mills Not at Session," *New York Times*, October 10, 1974, 23.

4. Mills was quoted in "Wilbur's Argentine Firecracker," *Time* 104, no. 17 (October 21, 1974): 21; The incident was reported in many sources. See, for example, Crewdson, "Mills in Seclusion After Report He Was Intoxicated in Car Stopped by Police," 23; Kim Long, *The Almanac of Political Corruption, Scandals & Dirty Politics* (New York: Delta Paperbacks, 2007), 230–31; Marion, *The Politics of Disgrace*, 209; "Mills Derided in Congress Over Link to Stripper," *New York Times*, December 3, 1974, 32, 85.

5. Long, *The Almanac of Political Corruption, Scandals & Dirty Politics*, 230; Marion, *The Politics of Disgrace*, 208–9.

6. Crewdson, "Mills in Seclusion After Report He Was Intoxicated in Car Stopped by Police," 23; "Mills Aide Reports Representative Ill," *New York Times*, October 12, 1974, 62; "Mills Says He's 'Still Embarrassed,'" *New York Times*, October 17, 1974, 28.

7. Dennis Hevesi, "Wilbur Mills, Long a Power in Congress, Is Dead at 82," *New York Times*, May 3, 1992, 54.

8. Mills is quoted in Hevesi, "Wilbur Mills," 54. See also Marion, *The Politics of Disgrace*, 208–9.

9. Wilbur Mills, "My Life on the Rocks; The Tragic Fall of Wilbur Mills, Once a Candidate for the Presidency, and How He Fought Back to Respectability Is Told to His Friend and Professional Colleague Roger Zion," *Saturday Evening Post* 251, no. 4 (May/June 1979): 32.

10. Michael Farquhar, *A Treasury of Great American Scandals: Tantalizing True Tales of Historic Misbehavior by the Founding Fathers and Others Who Let Freedom Swing* (New York: Penguin Books, 2003), 149; "Wilbur's Argentine Firecracker," 21–22.

11. The information and the quote are found in "Fanne: Acting 18 and Feeling 50," *Time* 104, no. 25 (December 16, 1974): 23.

12. Marjorie Hunter, "Mills Reveals Alcoholism; Plans to Stay in Congress," *New York Times*, December 31, 1974, 45.

13. The incident and quotes are found in "Mills Derided in Congress Over Link to Stripper," 32. See also Farquhar, *A Treasury of Great American Scandals*, 149–50.

14. Hevesi, "Wilbur Mills," 54; Richard D. Lyons, "Mills Quits as Chairman; Young Democrats Advance," *New York Times*, December 11, 1974, 1, 27; Marion, *The Politics of Disgrace*, 209.

15. Hevesi, "Wilbur Mills," 54; Marion, *The Politics of Disgrace*, 209.

16. Farquhar, *A Treasury of Great American Scandals*, 150; Mary Vespa, "Fanne Foxe, Tidal Basin Bombshell, Writes a Sizzler to Pay the Bills," *People* 4, no. 12 (September 22, 1975): 12.

17. Foxe is quoted in Vespa, "Fanne Foxe," 12.

18. Foxe is quoted in Vespa, "Fanne Foxe," 12. See also "Fanne: Acting 18 and Feeling 50," 23.

19. Foxe is quoted in Vespa, "Fanne Foxe," 12.

20. "And Now . . . DC's Dynamic Duo," *Playboy* 23, no. 9 (September 1976): 132; Farquhar, *A Treasury of Great American Scandals*, 150; Peter Wolff, "Fanne Foxe Finally Tells All! Meet the newest member of the 'Cheri' family!" *Cheri* 1, no. 9 (April 1977): 14–15, 91, 96–98; Robert D. McFadden, "Fanne Foxe, Who Plunged into a Reservoir and Emerged Famous, Dies at 84," *New York Times*, February 25, 2021, A21.

CHAPTER 9

"If Anybody Wants to Put a Tail on Me, Go Ahead. They'll be Very Bored"

Gary Hart and Donna Rice

It was yet another scandalous story, almost a cliché, of a powerful man who throws away his political career in pursuit of sex with a younger woman. In 1987 Gary Hart was an up-and-coming US senator from Colorado, a two-time presidential candidate whose good looks, formidable intellect, and widespread name recognition temporarily assured him front-runner status in a crowded field of lackluster Democratic hopefuls for the 1988 season. As a candidate he seemed too good to be true—and, as it turned out, he was.

Tales of Hart's relentless womanizing circulated regularly, tarnishing his otherwise impeccable credentials. He was a serious, articulate man with serious, well-expressed ideas, exactly the sober-minded, pragmatic, thoughtful candidate the Democratic Party needed as an antidote to the Reagan era. Yet no matter what he said or did, Hart could not escape his reputation as a 50-something lothario. Apparently, the senator, frustrated at the media's continued interest in his private life, thought he could put the rumors to bed, pun intended, by challenging the press corps to dig up evidence on his alleged sexual escapades. Unbeknownst to the candidate when he uttered the remark, intrepid reporters had already done that, hoisting him on his own petard and, in the process, transforming Gary Hart into a symbol of hubris, hypocrisy, and horniness. As a general rule, a public man who pledges to be squeaky clean should refrain from posing for a photograph with a physically attractive former cheerleader, who is not his wife, sitting on his lap while they each hold a drink and he wears a T-shirt adorned with the words "Monkey Business Crew," the name of a luxury yacht.[1]

Despite his later reputation as a high-flying playboy, Hart was a product of a midwestern, conservative household. As a young man he entertained thoughts of a career in the ministry. His early life was prosaic and unremarkable. He was born Gary Warren Hartpense in Ottawa, Kansas, on

November 28, 1936. His father was a farm equipment salesman. No stranger to hard work, young Gary labored on the railroad.

Raised as an evangelical Christian in the Church of the Nazarene, Hartpence won a scholarship to attend a church-affiliated college, Bethany Nazarene College (later renamed Southern Nazarene University) in Bethany, Oklahoma. He graduated with a philosophy degree in 1958. While in college he met Oletha "Lee" Ludwig, the woman who would become his wife. The couple married after he graduated from college. Afterward, they headed off to Connecticut so that Gary could attend divinity school at Yale University. He earned his bachelor of divinity degree in 1961, the same year that he shortened his name to "Hart" because it was easier for others to remember than "Hartpence."

Even as he completed his divinity degree, the young man decided that he would not become a minister. Perhaps he decided that "Hartpence" was a suitable name for a minister, but he needed something snappier and more memorable if he pursued a career in public service. Gary Hart moved over to Yale's law school in 1961, and he earned his bachelor of law three years later.

After graduation he moved to Washington, DC. It was an exciting time to be a young Washington-based lawyer. Hart joined the Department of Justice in 1964 just as the DOJ was aggressively enforcing civil rights laws enacted by Congress. After a year he moved over to the Department of the Interior, where he served as a special assistant to the Interior solicitor. These formative experiences did much to shape the young man's devotion to progressive Democratic politics.

Having served his time in government, in 1967 Hart accepted a position with the law firm of Davis Graham & Stubbs in Denver, Colorado. The Centennial State would become his home and political base in the decades that followed. In his newly adopted state, he searched for a new way to use his talents. Practicing law was financially lucrative, but Hart was attracted to politics.

He first came to national prominence when South Dakota senator George McGovern, running for president in the 1972 Democratic primaries, hired Hart to serve as his national campaign director. New rules for selecting the party's presidential nominee allowed for greater emphasis on primary elections, which benefited an outsider like McGovern. In previous presidential contests, party bosses were far more influential in selecting delegates than they were in 1972. Hart and another staffer, Rick Stearns, realized they could use the rule change to McGovern's advantage. They focused their efforts on winning twenty-eight states with caucuses, where a candidate could meet potential delegates and make a direct case for his candidacy without filtering his message through party leaders. The strategy paid handsome dividends for McGovern, helping him to secure the nomination. He went on to lose the general election to the incumbent president, Richard M. Nixon, in a landslide.

Although McGovern suffered a devastating loss, Hart emerged as a national figure as the Democratic Party sought to rebuild its brand. After the American people learned details about Nixon's involvement in the Watergate break-in, Democrats were poised to capture numerous local, state, and federal elective offices around the country in 1974. Recognizing an opportunity to change Colorado politics and advance his career, Hart challenged two-term Republican senator Peter Dominick for his seat. Hart had several factors in his favor. Colorado was leaning Democratic, Dominick had been an ardent Nixon supporter, and the 37-year-old Democrat was an able and attractive candidate. In November 1974 Hart won 52.7 percent of the vote to Dominick's 39.5 percent.[2]

When he swore his oath of office in Washington, DC, in January 1975, Hart's reputation preceded him. Many Democratic leaders viewed him as a rising star. Comparisons to John F. Kennedy—in positive ways as well as negative—would be a hallmark of the senator's later career, but even in the early days he was cast as the new JFK. He won a plum assignment on the Senate Armed Services Committee as well as positions on the Environment and Public Works Committee and the Intelligence Committee.[3]

Hart participated in some of the most high-profile Senate activities of the 1970s. Idaho Senator Frank Church chaired a subcommittee investigating abuses by the Central Intelligence Agency, the Federal Bureau of Investigation, and the Internal Revenue Service. Commonly known as the Church Committee, named after its chairman, the group spent much of 1975 and 1976 exposing decades-long malfeasances. Although he was only a freshman senator, Hart became a high-profile committee member. Later, Hart served as chairman of the Senate Subcommittee on Nuclear Regulation. Following the well-publicized accident at the Three-Mile Island nuclear reactor near Harrisburg, Pennsylvania, Hart assumed a prominent role in the subsequent investigation.[4]

During two terms in the Senate, Hart distinguished himself as a neoliberal young Turk who challenged his party's progressive orthodoxy. Hart believed that government could be an instrument of change, but he rejected the traditional liberal view that the federal government could cure all manner of social ills through expensive, often poorly run programs. Dubbing himself a pragmatist, Hart questioned the way government funds were spent, especially on social programs such as Medicare and Medicaid. He also counseled caution in foreign affairs, not only as a means of reducing expenditures but also to prevent American forces from becoming embroiled in endless overseas conflicts.[5]

Hart's reputation proved that a politician's strengths simultaneously can be his weaknesses. He was obviously whip smart, intellectually curious, and hardworking. Aside from those impressive qualities, his admirers frequently mentioned his cool demeanor, a calmness under pressure that suggested he would be a steady leader if he ran for the White House and won. He seldom displayed emotion in public. Hart was a policy wonk who was comfortable discussing data and the intricacies of policy formulation and implementation but seemed disinterested in courting voters.

His cerebral approach to policy and his lack of passion in his speeches and public appearances caused his critics to complain that he was aloof, condescending, and narcissistic. Hart seldom disguised his antipathy for the campaign trail. He seemed to think that retail politics was dirty, somehow beneath him, and he could not be bothered to communicate with ordinary citizens who did not share his intellectual prowess. He also expressed frustration with the media because he believed that reporters focused on the wrong things, such as scandals and "gotcha" moments, when they should highlight policy issues that affected people's lives directly.[6]

In 1980 he stood for reelection. Considering his high-profile successes in crafting public policy, the senator was surprised when he faced more than token opposition. His Republican opponent, Colorado secretary of state Mary Estill Buchanan, was a moderate, but she fiercely attacked Hart for supporting President Jimmy Carter's administration on several controversial issues, notably the treaties relinquishing American control of the Panama Canal. Buchanan repeatedly linked Hart to the unpopular Carter, noting that he voted with the president 80 percent of the time. It was a clever strategy, and it almost worked. Hart won the election, but it was a close-fought contest. He barely eked out 50.2 percent of the vote.[7]

Hart returned to Washington, DC, in January 1981, but Jimmy Carter did not. Former California governor Ronald Reagan had handily defeated Carter. Senator Hart soon found himself confronting a presidential administration that was diametrically opposed to his understanding of proper governance. Although Hart had always prided himself on his willingness to cut wasteful government spending, which often put him out of step with liberals in his party, he nonetheless believed that government could and should exercise a positive effect on citizens' lives. Reagan, by contrast, viewed government—especially the big, fat, bloated federal government—as the problem, not the solution to people's problems. Where the Carter administration tried to reform government to improve its performance, the new administration pushed for cuts to government programs, except for defense, merely for the sake of trimming government. The Reagan administration championed increases in defense expenditures while reducing or eliminating social welfare programs.[8]

The Colorado senator was increasingly outraged by Reagan's agenda. As the 1984 election season approached, Hart contemplated running for president to counteract what he saw as the willingness of most Republicans to cut government programs that helped America's less fortunate citizens. He had not distinguished himself in the Senate as a legislator of the first rank, but neither had he disgraced himself. His good looks and fondness for expressing bold ideas impressed enough Democratic voters that Hart was convinced he might win. He threw his hat into the ring. Jimmy Carter's former vice president, Walter F. Mondale, eventually won the nomination, but Hart, with lower name recognition and far fewer financial resources, came in a close second. It was a promising beginning for a novice presidential candidate.

As he grew in stature and threatened Mondale's candidacy during the 1984 primary elections, his adversaries attacked him in a series of negative advertisements. He was too liberal, too erudite, too pie-in-the-sky and academic for the presidency. During a televised debate on the road to the nomination, Mondale ridiculed Hart's penchant for proposing new government programs and coined a slogan that came to define the 1984 election season. Echoing a television commercial for the Wendy's hamburger chain, Mondale suggested that Hart's proposals were flashy but contained little substance. "Where's the beef?" Mondale sarcastically asked.

When the party faithful convened in San Francisco in July 1984 for the Democratic National Convention, Mondale enjoyed a commanding lead in the delegate count, although he was forty short of securing the nomination. It was clear that he would win in the end, but the question was whether the party would be unified heading into the fall. Everyone understood that taking on a genial incumbent president would be tough, and party leaders needed to be united in their quest to take on Reagan. As the second-place finisher, Hart angled for a spot on the ticket as vice president, a reasonable possibility. Mondale eventually chose the first female major party vice presidential candidate, New York congresswoman Geraldine Ferraro, but Hart had become a party favorite. In an address to the delegates, the Colorado senator pledged his fidelity to the Democrats despite his defeat. "Our party and our country will continue to hear from us," he said. "This is one Hart you will not leave in San Francisco."[9]

Mondale was probably the strongest nominee the Democrats could field that year, but Reagan nonetheless defeated him in the general election by a landslide. In retrospect, it was unlikely that any Democrat would have defeated Reagan in 1984. Hart's loss to Mondale in the Democratic primary was a mixed blessing. With his newfound name recognition, Hart could look forward to 1988, when Reagan would retire from the presidency, leaving an open seat and no other Democrat who could match the Colorado senator's standing in the party. He represented a new generation of leaders—younger, more energetic, and brimming with new ideas and optimism.[10]

Because he thought 1988 would be his year, Hart declined to campaign for a third term in the Senate in 1986. Freed from the day-to-day responsibilities of legislating, he had two years to travel the country, meeting key Democrats and shoring up his base in the expectation that he would run for president. During this time, as he received heightened scrutiny, rumors circulated that Hart had cheated on his wife. Frustrated that the stories would not die, he ignored the topic, dismissing such talk as absurd and unworthy of comment.

New York governor Mario Cuomo, widely regarded as a formidable candidate, announced in February 1987 that he would not run for president in 1988. With Cuomo's decision to opt out of the race, Gary Hart was the front-runner for the Democratic nomination. He formally announced his candidacy on April 13, 1987. On that same day *Newsweek* magazine printed a story about the candidate's two trial separations from his wife. It was an ominous sign of things to come.[11]

In an earlier era, candidates and presidents could count on the media to ignore stories of serial infidelity. Reports of sexual escapades involving Warren G. Harding and John F. Kennedy were well known among the press corps, but they did not make their way into print until long after the men were dead. The press corps's willingness to look the other way had eroded by the 1980s. A public figure could expect his or her private life to no longer be private.

Gary Hart's prickly personality did not help matters. Some candidates become friendly with reporters, cultivating them and providing media scoops upon occasion. Even elected officials who do not feel a natural affinity for the press will often feign friendship to ensure more favorable news coverage. Hart would have none of it. He viewed the media with disdain, and he made no secret of his opinion. With the continued interest in his sex life, he became even more distant and aloof than he had been in the past.

Hart's haughtiness would come to haunt him. On April 22, 1987, an anonymous telephone caller told the *Miami Herald*'s political editor, Tom Fiedler, that the rumors about Hart's adultery were true, at least in one instance. Fiedler had written a front-page story in the *Herald* scolding reporters as "irresponsible" for publishing stories about Hart's private life without corroborating evidence. The caller, later identified as Dana Weems, a model, said she knew for a fact that Hart had engaged in sexual relations with her friend. According to the caller, the friend was planning to meet with Hart at the candidate's Washington, DC, townhouse on May 1.[12]

In an earlier era the *Miami Herald* might have dismissed a salacious tip offered by an anonymous source, but the times they were a-changin.' Fiedler dispatched a team of reporters to stake out the candidate's townhouse. They observed Hart entering the premises with a young blonde woman who was not his wife. She apparently stayed the night and spent much of the next

day with him. The *Herald* ran a story on May 3 detailing the team's observations.[13]

That same day, in what turned out to be exquisitely bad timing for the
Hart campaign, the *New York Times Magazine* printed an interview that columnist E. J. Dionne Jr. had conducted with Hart. Responding to a question
about his alleged sexual affairs, an exasperated Hart told Dionne, "Follow
me around. I don't care. I'm serious. If anybody wants to put a tail on me,
go ahead. They'll be very bored." A myth grew up around this comment.
For many years, political commentators assumed that the *Miami Herald*
reporters took him up on the offer and followed him around. In fact, they
had already observed the mystery woman with the candidate by the time
that Dionne's column appeared.[14]

The appearance of two stories on the same day about the leading Democratic contender's marital infidelity attracted enormous press attention.
Hart knew that he had to act immediately. Had he appeared before the
press as soon as the story broke, oozing sincerity, contrite, and seeking
forgiveness for his sins, he might have survived the media onslaught. He
chose another tack.

On Monday, May 4, Hart appeared at a press conference, but he was unrepentant. He complained about the unfair press coverage and castigated
reporters who had nothing better to do than follow him around. He refused
to apologize and insisted that the young woman, who by this time had
been identified as Donna Rice, was a campaign aide and nothing more.[15]

In the meantime Donna Rice held her own press conference. She supported Hart's story that they had not engaged in a sexual liaison. Had this
been the only incident on an otherwise spotless record of a squeaky clean
candidate, the public might have been willing to accept the story at face
value. As it was, "the facts floated on a sea of innuendo."[16]

Reporters scrambled around to find out as much as they could about
Donna Rice. They learned that she was a 29-year-old former cheerleader at
the University of South Carolina as well as a former Miss South Carolina
in the Miss World Pageant. She had worked as a pharmaceutical company
representative and a part-time actress, appearing on the soap opera *One Life
to Live* as well as on an episode of the popular television police show *Miami
Vice*. Fairly or unfairly, the press repeatedly described her as a "party girl,"
presumably implying that she was sexually promiscuous.[17]

She met Gary Hart at a New Year's Eve party in Aspen, Colorado, hosted
by rock singer Don Henley. "I knew who he was, but almost everyone at
the party was a celebrity, so I didn't take much notice of Hart," she later
recalled. They did not talk again until she saw the senator at a yacht party
in Miami on March 1, 1987. She was with friends and they stumbled into
the party by happenstance. Suddenly, there was the senator she had met
a few months earlier. She did not spend time alone with the senator, but

she gave him her phone number. She was "very interested in getting into fundraising," she told him.[18]

Two days later, Billy Broadhurst, a friend of Louisiana governor Edwin Edwards—the governor was a notorious womanizer himself—scheduled a boat trip to cruise Florida's Intracoastal Waterway. Broadhurst knew Hart and invited him along. Donna Rice's friend Lynn Armandt came with Rice, making the group a foursome. "It was Hart who called and asked me to go," Rice remembered. The boat was named the *Monkey Business*.[19]

Rice always insisted that the plan was to enjoy a short boat trip, but eventually the group wound up in Bimini. The customs office was closed when they arrived, and so they had to spend the night. According to Rice, the boat did not live up to its name. The women slept on the *Monkey Business*, but the men spent the night on another vessel that Broadhurst had moored on the island.

At no time did Gary Hart try to seduce her, Rice reported. He was a perfect gentleman. If she had felt there was something more to his intentions, she would have been upset. In her view they were not sexually attracted to each other.

For someone who was not attracted to the senator, Donna Rice's decision to visit Hart at his Washington townhouse seemed curious. Once again she offered an innocent explanation. The same four people were present on Friday evening, May 1. They stayed at Hart's townhouse briefly before heading to Broadhurst's house to eat steaks. Afterward, they returned to Hart's townhouse so that Rice could retrieve an address book she had inadvertently left behind. Broadhurst, Armandt, and Rice left at some point. (The *Miami Herald* article insisted that Rice did not leave with the others.) In the morning Rice returned with a manila envelope that Armandt asked her to deliver. Broadhurst and Armandt arrived shortly thereafter. The group went for a drive to Mount Vernon, George Washington's home in nearby Virginia.

According to Rice, the remainder of the day was essentially the same sort of G-rated entertainment that had preceded it. At no time did she and the front-runner for the American presidency engage in intimate physical touching, much less sexual intercourse. The explanation, of course, satisfied no one. The list of Hart's sexual dalliances was simply too long for a skeptical public and press corps to accept an innocent story of friends enjoying each other's company.[20]

Hart withstood the relentless media attention as best he could, but the stories would not stop. Every deficiency, every failure, every grievance that had ever been aired about Gary Hart came to light. Reporters seized on a story about incensed creditors who still had not been paid for debts the senator had incurred during his 1984 presidential bid. The names of women who had engaged in affairs with him were bandied about. No longer could he hide from the so-called "character issue."

Public opinion polls suggested that the public was not as fixated on Hart's private life as the media appeared to be. A May 1987 *Newsweek* poll found that 64 percent of respondents believed that media coverage of the alleged affair was "unfair," and 70 percent thought that media surveillance of a candidate was inappropriate. Most surprisingly, 53 percent of respondents said that marital infidelity did not affect a president's ability to

Figure 9.1. Gary Hart, a senator from Colorado from 1975 to 1987, ran for the 1988 Democratic presidential nomination, but his campaign imploded when Hart was caught in a sex scandal in 1987. Courtesy of Keystone Pictures USA/Alamy Stock Photo.

govern. Even other political figures were somewhat sympathetic. When asked about the issue, Governor Cuomo shrugged it off. In his view there were "skeletons in everybody's closet."[21]

Despite public support, Hart could not recast the debate. The scandal drowned out his campaign messaging. Realizing that he could no longer run for the presidency and address crucial public policy problems in the face of the ongoing scandal, Senator Hart suspended his campaign on May 8, 1987.[22]

At a feisty press conference, he again refused to accept responsibility for the brouhaha. "I said that I bend, but I don't break, and believe me, I'm not broken," he defiantly told the media. "If someone's able to throw up a smokescreen and keep it up there long enough, you can't get your message across. You can't raise the money to finance a campaign; there's too much static, and you can't communicate. Clearly, under the present circumstances, this campaign cannot go on. I refuse to submit my family and my friends and innocent people and myself to further rumors and gossip. It's simply an intolerable situation." Paraphrasing Thomas Jefferson, he growled, "I tremble for my country when I think we may, in fact, get the kind of leaders we deserve."[23]

It was a remarkable performance. Unsympathetic political commentators likened Hart's speech to Richard Nixon's infamous farewell address on November 7, 1962, after Nixon had lost his quest for the California governorship. Both Nixon and Hart adopted a belligerent stance, blaming others, especially the media, for their failures.[24]

Not long after Hart folded his campaign, a photograph surfaced of the senator wearing a T-shirt with the words "Monkey Business Crew" printed on the front and Donna Rice seated on his lap. They are pictured on a dock. The smiles on their faces suggest they have indeed been up to monkey business. Perhaps they were just friends, as they both insisted, but the photograph suggests otherwise. The *National Enquirer* tabloid plastered the evocative shot on its June 2, 1987, cover beside the words "Gary Hart Asked Me to Marry Him." Hart had already suspended his campaign, but the photograph caused a new round of snickering and eye-rolling. He may have been a serious man with serious ideas, but the photograph intimated that he occasionally entertained other ideas as well.[25]

Amidst all the brouhaha, Hart retreated to Ireland to avoid the glare of unwanted publicity. He remained in seclusion, but he also stayed in touch with his campaign staff and left open the possibility that he would return. To everyone who spoke with him during that time, he appeared strangely ambivalent about the race. Sometimes he talked about returning, and on other occasions he emphatically denied such intentions. When he left Ireland at the end of August, he was still uncertain.

On December 15, 1987, Hart announced that he had changed his mind. He was returning to the campaign trail. He had been the front-runner in May, but seven months later much of his support had eroded. He was yesterday's news. It was a longshot, and he knew it. "This will not be like any campaign you have ever seen because I am going directly to the people," Hart said in announcing his return. "I don't have a national headquarters or staff. I don't have any money. I don't have pollsters or consultants or media advisers or political endorsements. But I have something even better. I have the power of ideas, and I can govern this country."[26]

Incredibly, against the odds, Hart's popularity rose. Soon, he was second only to Massachusetts governor Michael Dukakis in the polls. It seemed to be a remarkable comeback story. Unfortunately for Hart, it did not last. The same old negative stories circulated again. He had changed his name from "Hartpence." He had lied about which year he was born, changing it from 1936 to 1937 for reasons that were unclear. (Hart said that it was a simple error in his campaign materials.) He had not paid his campaign debts from 1984. He was a serial womanizer. The stories that had driven him from the race in May remained as topical as ever for some people in December. Gary Hart, in short, was inauthentic, a poseur, a phony.

Skipping the Iowa caucuses, Hart campaigned vigorously in the New Hampshire primary in February 1988, an early test of a candidate's viability. He received 4,888 votes, or about 4 percent of the total. Less than a month later, during the Super Tuesday contests in March, Hart captured approximately 5 percent of the vote. It was clear that he would not be the Democratic Party nominee. He withdrew from the race a second time, never to return. Governor Dukakis eventually won the Democratic nomination before losing to Republican George H. W. Bush in the November 1988 general election.[27]

No longer a member of the United States Senate, and with his presidential aspirations dashed, Hart returned to the private practice of law. Still vitally interested in public policy, he remained a man of strong convictions and progressive ideals, always on the periphery of politics even as he refused to run for elective office. In the ensuing years, he focused on America's standing in the world as well as new developments, such as terrorism. In 1998 President Bill Clinton asked Hart to serve on the United States Commission on National Security/21st Century (USCNS/21), a blue-ribbon panel created by Defense Secretary William Cohen to provide a comprehensive review of American national security requirements in the coming century. Hart co-chaired the bipartisan commission with former New Hampshire senator Warren Rudman, a Republican. The commission expressed concerns about the state of homeland security and offered a series of recommendations to prepare for potential terrorist attacks. In fact, Hart became a shrill critic of American national security policy, urging officials to devote more resources and attention to terrorism. The September 11, 2001, terrorist attacks underscored the importance of his message, and they made him appear prescient.[28]

Always interested in education, Hart completed a doctorate in politics at Oxford University in 2001. His dissertation was titled "The Restoration of the Republic: The Jeffersonian Ideal in 21st Century America." Oxford University Press published a book based on the dissertation the following year.[29]

His Oxford classmates recognized that Hart remained interested in the presidency, and they encouraged his interest. In 2002 he began thinking about another campaign. It had been long enough since his earlier problems that perhaps a new generation of voters would look beyond the sins of the past. He launched a blog during the spring of 2003, the first potential candidate to test the waters for 2004. When his plans generated a lukewarm response, he declined to run.[30]

Instead, Hart threw his support behind Massachusetts senator John Kerry. Observers speculated that Kerry might appoint Hart to a cabinet post if he won the presidency. Hart's stature was large enough that he might have served as secretary of defense or perhaps homeland security. He might have served on the National Security Council. After winning the Democratic nomination, however, Kerry lost to incumbent Republican president George W. Bush in the general election.[31]

Gary Hart will always be remembered for his womanizing and the high-profile implosion of his 1988 presidential campaign. When he dies and his obituary is written, the scandal will be featured prominently. Despite the embarrassment he suffered, however, he went on to enjoy a reasonably important career in public service, becoming a member of the Council on Foreign Relations, serving on the advisory board for Operation USA, an international relief agency, and serving as the US Special Envoy for Northern Ireland during the Obama administration. None of these positions compares to the power and prestige of serving as president of the United States, of course, but they are the positions that a serious man holds during a long and rewarding career.[32]

Donna Rice initially did not fare well from the scandal fallout. Recalling the intense media scrutiny of 1988, she said, "I was blindsided and thrown into a media feeding frenzy. I kept saying, 'I just wanna go home.'" Stories about her life denigrated her as a ditzy "party girl" and emphasized her looks, portraying her as promiscuous and opportunistic. For months after the story broke, everywhere she went she encountered rapacious reporters anxious to expand on the story. "I felt I was put on trial," Rice lamented. "The media fixated on me for the next 18 months. My reputation was destroyed worldwide."[33]

She eventually moved on with her career. In 1994 she married business-man Jack Hughes. That same year she began working at Enough Is Enough, a nonprofit organization devoted to fighting against online pornography to make the Internet safer for families and children. In 2002 she became president and chair of the organization. As the years progressed and she disappeared from the headlines, Donna Rice Hughes settled into a satisfy-ing life.[34]

She briefly returned to public attention in 2018 when director Jason Reit-man's film *The Front Runner* appeared in theaters. Based on the 2014 book *All the Truth Is Out: The Week Politics Went Tabloid* by journalist Matt Bai, the film recounted the 1987 scandal for a new generation of Americans. Starring Hugh Jackman as Gary Hart and a relative unknown, Sara Paxton, as Donna Rice, *The Front Runner* received mixed reviews and suffered poor box office results.[35]

By the twenty-first century, the Gary Hart–Donna Rice scandal paled in comparison to subsequent scandals. In an era when one president of the United States engaged in sexual acts with a White House intern and another president paid a pornographic film actress to remain silent about their affair, a photograph of a woman sitting on a presidential candidate's lap hardly excites the prurient interest of many Americans. Yet the Hart-Rice episode represented a turning point in American political history. The days when a candidate could engage in extramarital affairs—or, if the two partic-ipants are to be believed, *appeared* to engage in such acts—while the press corps turned a blind eye were over. After 1987 there were no private lives for elected officials, especially those running for the presidency. Intense media scrutiny of a candidate's life from cradle to grave, public and private, was fair game. As illustrated in later chapters of this book, the consequences were historic and severe.

NOTES

1. Nancy E. Marion, *The Politics of Disgrace: The Role of Political Scandal in Ameri-can Politics* (Durham, NC: Carolina Academic Press, 2010), 212; Jules Witcover, *Party of the People: A History of the Democrats* (New York: Random House, 2003), 635.

2. For more information on Hart's background, see, for example, Diana Kle-banow, "'Pressed' to Destruction: The Saga of Gary Hart," *USA Today* 143, no. 2838 (March 2015): 56–57; Marion, *The Politics of Disgrace*, 212; John Pearson, "Gary Hart," in *Our States: Colorado* (Toledo, OH: Great Neck Publishing, August 31, 2020): 1–4; "Shocking, Lurid, and True! A Hart-Stopping Campaign," *Biography Magazine* 3, no. 9 (September 1999): 18.

3. Pearson, "Gary Hart," 1–4.

4. Klebanow, "'Pressed' to Destruction," 56–57; Pearson, "Gary Hart," 1–2.

5. Sandra Sobieraj Westfall, "Donna Rice 30 Years After Political Scandal: How the Woman at the Center of Gary Hart's Presidential Campaign Monkey Business Went from 'Rock Bottom' to Healing," *People* 90, no. 21 (November 12, 2018): 78.

6. John J. Miller, "He, Gary Hart," *National Review* 55, no. 9 (May 19, 2003): 34.

7. Pearson, "Gary Hart," 1–2.

8. See, for example, Rick Perlstein, *Reaganland: America's Right Turn, 1976–1980* (New York: Simon & Schuster, 2020), 391–92, 914; Richard Reeves, *President Reagan: The Triumph of Imagination* (New York: Simon & Schuster, 2005), 6–7, 209.

9. Hart is quoted in "Excerpts from Hart Speech to Convention Exhorting Party for Campaign," *New York Times*, July 19, 1984, A18. See also Klebanow, "'Pressed' to Destruction," 56; Pearson, "Gary Hart," 2–3; Witcover, *Party of the People*, 622–25.

10. Witcover, *Party of the People*, 635.

11. Pearson, "Gary Hart," 2–3.

12. Westfall, "Donna Rice 30 Years After Political Scandal," 79.

13. Witcover, *Party of the People*, 635.

14. Hart is quoted in E. J. Dionne Jr., "Gary Hart: The Elusive Front-Runner," *New York Times*, May 3, 1987, SM 28. The myth is repeated in many sources. See, for example, Klebanow, "'Pressed' to Destruction," 57; Kim Long, *The Almanac of Political Corruption, Scandals & Dirty Politics* (New York: Delta Paperbacks, 2007), 261; Marion, *The Politics of Disgrace*, 212.

15. Klebanow, "'Pressed' to Destruction," 57; Pearson, "Gary Hart," 3–4.

16. The quote can be found in E. J. Dionne Jr., "Courting Danger: The Fall of Gary Hart," *New York Times*, May 9, 1987, 1.

17. "Shocking, Lurid, and True!" 18; Westfall, "Donna Rice 30 Years After Political Scandal," 78.

18. The incidents and the quotes are found in Matt Bai, *All the Truth Is Out: The Week Politics Went Tabloid* (New York: Vintage, 2015), 76–78; Marion, *The Politics of Disgrace*, 212; Westfall, "Donna Rice 30 Years After Political Scandal," 79.

19. Rice is quoted in Bai, *All the Truth Is Out*, 77. See also Marion, *The Politics of Disgrace*, 212.

20. The story is set out in several sources. The most detailed account is found in Bai, *All the Truth Is Out*, 77–78.

21. Cuomo is quoted in John Dillin, "Press Unfair to Hart? Polls Show Public Concern; Experts Back Tough Scrutiny," *Christian Science Monitor*, May 12, 1987, n.p.

22. Long, *The Almanac of Political Corruption, Scandals & Dirty Politics*, 261; Marion, *The Politics of Disgrace*, 212.

23. Hart is quoted in Bai, *All the Truth Is Out*, 21. See also "New Morality, New Journalism," *National Review* 39, no. 10 (June 5, 1987): 15.

24. Angry, hurt, and humiliated, Nixon unloaded his wrath on the media. "I leave you gentlemen now," Nixon said. "And you will now write it. You will interpret it. That's your right. But as I leave you, I want you to know—just think how much you're going to be missing. You won't have Nixon to kick around anymore, because, gentlemen, this is my last press conference and it will be one in which I have welcomed the opportunity to test wits with you." Nixon is quoted in Stephen E. Ambrose, *Nixon: Volume I—The Education of a Politician, 1913–1962* (Touchstone, a Simon & Schuster Book, 1987), 671. See also Conrad Black, *Richard M. Nixon: A Life in Full* (New York: Public Affairs, 2007), 442.

25. Bai, *All the Truth Is Out*, 77; James Fallows, "Was Gary Hart Set Up?" *The Atlantic* 322, no. 4 (November 2018): 27; Klebanow, "'Pressed' to Destruction," 57; Long, *The Almanac of Political Corruption, Scandals & Dirty Politics*, 261; Witcover, *Party of the People*, 635.

26. Hart is quoted in Matthew L. Wald, "Hart, in Surprise, Resumes Campaign for White House; Democrats in Disarray; Coloradan Cites Dismay That Others Have Not Pressed for Some of His Ideas," *New York Times*, December 16, 1987, A1. See also E. J. Dionne Jr., "Hart Unsettles Democrats, Which Pleases Republicans," *New York Times*, December 16, 1987, B7.

27. E. J. Dionne Jr., "Gephardt Is Second; Vice President Jubilant as His Troubled Week Ends in Triumph," *New York Times*, February 17, 1988, A1; Klebanow, "'Pressed' to Destruction," 57; Witcover, *Party of the People*, 640.

28. Miller, "He, Gary Hart," 36.

29. Gary Hart, *The Restoration of the Republic: The Jeffersonian Ideal in 21st Century America* (Oxford and New York: Oxford University Press, 2002). See also Fallows, "Was Gary Hart Set Up?" 28; Miller, "He, Gary Hart," 34.

30. Miller, "He, Gary Hart," 34–36.

31. Bai, *All the Truth Is Out*, 224–25.

32. Simon Carswell, "US Appoints Gary Hart as Envoy to Northern Ireland," *Irish Times*, October 22, 2014, 7; Jim Dee, "Pushing Our Politicians," *Belfast Telegraph*, November 1, 2014, 7.

33. Rice is quoted in Westfall, "Donna Rice 30 Years After Political Scandal," 79. See also Jon Nordheimer, "Donna Rice Aims to Resume Life After Hart," *New York Times*, June 20, 1987, 34.

34. "Shocking, Lurid, and True!" 18; Westfall, "Donna Rice 30 Years After Political Scandal," 80.

35. Fallows, "Was Gary Hart Set Up?" 27; Westfall, "Donna Rice 30 Years After Political Scandal," 77–78.

CHAPTER 10

"This Shadow Life Made a Mockery of My Marriage"

Bob Packwood

Robert William "Bob" Packwood was a longtime Republican senator from Oregon when multiple women alleged that he had sexually assaulted them. As a progressive Republican and chairman of the powerful Senate Finance Committee, Packwood had done much to aid women's rights. He supported causes near and dear to their hearts: abortion rights, equal opportunity in the workplace, and family leave. Yet it became clear in 1992 that the senator had two faces: a public one and a private one. In private he had compiled a long, dismal record of unwanted kissing, touching, and groping women, many of whom worked for him. He was a Dorian Gray–like character: handsome and engaging on the outside while corrupt and rotten within.

Before the charges emerged, Packwood was widely respected as a hard-working centrist Republican, a vanishing breed of pragmatic lawmaker able to bridge the chasm between Democrats and Republicans. He parlayed his ability to reach across the aisle and get things done into a twenty-six-year career in the United States Senate. He had become an elder statesman of his party before the allegations surfaced.[1]

Packwood was born on September 11, 1932, in Portland, Oregon. His great-grandfather, William Henderson Packwood, was the youngest member of the Oregon Constitutional Convention of 1857. With this pedigree, it was little wonder that Packwood developed an early interest in politics.

In 1954 he graduated from Willamette University in Salem, Oregon, before going on to New York University Law School on the Root-Tilden-Kern Scholarship, arguably the most prestigious public service scholarship in the country. Packwood excelled in law school, earning national awards in the moot court competition. He also served as the student body president.

Admitted to the Oregon bar in 1957, he practiced law to earn a living. It was clear, however, that Packwood was interested in pursuing a political career. He was a young man in a hurry. In 1960 he was elected chair of the

Multnomah County Republican Central Committee. Two years later he won a seat in the Oregon House of Representatives. At 29 he was the youngest member of the state legislature.

His first campaign demonstrated Packwood's willingness to work long hours and his intuitive understanding of the election process. He assembled a crackerjack team of volunteers who canvassed door to door, distributing leaflets and yard signs. They blanketed neighborhoods to elect their man. The operation was so effective that the Republican Party recruited the freshman legislator to create a political action committee to fund up-and-coming Republican candidates for local and state offices across the state of Oregon. It became known as Packwood-style campaigning. Many state Republicans attributed their success in state politics in 1964—a banner year for Democrats throughout the country—to Packwood's influence. He was obviously a guy to watch in the future.

From 1963 until 1969, Packwood mastered the intricacies of the legislative process and nurtured relationships with state Republican Party leaders, especially among a new generation of elected officials. By the end of the decade, when Republicans needed a candidate to run against the Democratic incumbent, Senator Wayne Morse, Packwood was a natural choice.[2]

Packwood was taking a major chance in challenging the incumbent. Morse was a legend in Oregon politics. He had served in the Senate since 1945, and he had developed a reputation as a maverick, bucking his party when it suited his purposes. He had been a Republican early in his career before declaring himself an independent and finally becoming a Democrat. One issue especially caused a rift between Morse and his fellow Democrats: the Vietnam War. President Lyndon B. Johnson insisted that Democrats support the war, but Morse was bitterly opposed, becoming a strong voice against the administration.

For all the advantages of incumbency, Morse was a surprisingly vulnerable candidate in the 1968 election. As a *Washington Post* editorial noted, the "Senator's sharp tongue, his skill in debate, his astonishing ability to filibuster all by himself, and his disposition to speak his mind regardless of what the consequences might be tended to make him something of a lone figure." Packwood shrewdly recognized the political advantage in attacking Morse where he was weak, namely on his party loyalty. The young upstart argued that Morse, a Democrat, was reckless because he would not vote to fund the war effort of a Democratic president. Packwood pointed out that the attention Morse devoted to the war was attention that he did not devote to the needs of Oregon's citizens. According to Packwood, the usual reason that voters supported long-serving incumbents was because the legislator could bring federal largesse into the state, but Morse was estranged from his party and therefore ought to be retired.[3]

It turned out to be an effective strategy. Despite his aggressive campaigning style, no one expected Packwood to pull off a victory. He had little name recognition and he could not match Morse's contacts, despite the senator's mercurial nature. On election day, November 5, 1968, the margin of victory was razor thin. Packwood initially appeared to have won by 3,445 votes. Morse demanded a recount of about 100,000 ballots, as did Packwood.

The recount spilled into December. Morse narrowed the gap, but the final tally showed that Packwood had won by 3,263 votes, which meant that he had captured 50.2 percent of the vote to Morse's 49.8 percent. Morse's advisers informed him that he would have won "if several thousand illegal ballots had not been counted." Yet he had run out of options to contest the results. Wayne Morse officially conceded the election on December 30, 1968.[4]

Thirty-six-year-old Bob Packwood arrived in Washington in January 1969 as the youngest member of the United States Senate, displacing Edward M. Kennedy, who had been the youngest senator until that time. Packwood was determined to be a good Republican, but he never aligned himself with the conservative wing of the party. As a moderate, he supported commonsense gun restrictions and favored civil rights legislation. When Republican president Richard M. Nixon nominated two southern Supreme Court nominees, Clement Haynsworth and G. Harrold Carswell, Packwood voted against confirmation in both cases because the men favored racial segregation. More importantly, Packwood also became the first Republican to break with his party on impeaching President Nixon.[5]

His pro-choice position impressed many women's organizations. Here was a Republican member of Congress who could be counted on to treat women as persons, not infantilizing them with paternalistic legislation telling them what they could and could not do with their bodies. Throughout his career, he received awards from groups such as Planned Parenthood and the National Women's Political Caucus for his progressive agenda.[6]

Packwood was in the thick of many Senate battles as he was reelected in 1974, 1980, and 1986. He often went his own way, defying easy categorization. He was an ardent environmentalist, which was unusual for a Republican. As chair of the Senate Finance Committee, he helped rescue President Reagan's 1986 tax-cut legislation, which appeared to be headed for defeat. In 1993 he threw his weight against President Clinton's health-care reform bill, assuring that the measure would not pass. His admirers saw him as that rare breed of politician who makes decisions based on his reading of the bill, not on party affiliation. Detractors viewed him as a prickly iconoclast who was difficult to deal with owing to arrogance and inconsistency in his positions.[7]

In his personal life, Packwood was married from 1964 until 1990. Later, his ex-wife, Georgie Oberteuffer Packwood, remarked that she never knew

Figure 10.1. Senator Bob Packwood is pictured in 1977. Courtesy of the Library of Congress.

the dark side of his personality. Even as he sponsored legislation benefiting women and families, the senator lived a "shadow life." He became a shameless sexual predator. "This shadow life made a mockery of my marriage, 25 of the prime years of my life," his ex-wife bitterly reflected.[8]

Packwood kept his secret for two decades. He was likely aided by the culture of that era. When he entered the US Senate, some powerful men assumed that sexual conquests were a perquisite of the position. Multiple volumes could be written on the history of influential members of Congress engaging in affairs with staffers, lobbyists, and hangers-on. In some cases the women were willing participants, even initiators, but all too often they were victims of predators who leveraged their positions to prey on people weaker than they were. Sometimes the question of consent was unclear as less powerful men and women felt compelled to give in to the more powerful figure out of fear of losing a job or social position.

Bob Packwood's long pattern of sexual harassment and assault was well known among congressional staffers and interns, who were warned to avoid being alone with him. To the public, however, his facade was secure. Yet the secret, so carefully concealed for so many years, could not remain hidden from the public forever.

His transgressions came to light beginning in October 1992. Packwood was running for reelection against a popular Democratic congressman, Les AuCoin, in what promised to be a close race. In the meantime reporters from the *Washington Post* were investigating allegations from ten women that Senator Packwood had forcibly kissed and groped them in a series of incidents stretching back twenty years. The *Post* contacted Packwood's office in October about the incidents. Chief of Staff Elaine Franklin, fearing an "October Surprise" with information about sexual abuse charges appearing in newspapers a month before Election Day, dismissed the allegations as part of a politically motivated "witch hunt."[9]

Packwood knew that a brief statement from his chief of staff was insufficient to satisfy reporters. Accordingly, he agreed to sit down to an interview with the *Washington Post* investigative journalists on October 29, 1992. When asked about the charges during the interview, he emphatically and unequivocally denied them. "I am so hesitant of anything at all that I just, I don't make any approaches," he said. "It's simply not my nature, with men or women, to be forward." He pointed out that he had hired many women to serve on his Senate staff throughout his twenty-three-year career. If his behavior was as egregious as the complainants alleged, "why do they come to work here?" The senator promised to review his staff records to determine if he could find additional information on the women who had complained.[10]

Much to the senator's relief, the *Post* reporters told him on October 31 that they would not finish their investigation before Election Day. Therefore, any news stories on the allegations would wait until later in November. It was a welcome development because the election was too close to call on election night. When the ballots were all counted, Packwood had won with 52 percent of the vote. Had the allegations surfaced before Election Day, he knew that the vote might have gone against him.[11]

The story was not dead, however, and Packwood needed to supply a statement beyond his initial denials. Over the course of nine days, he submitted materials on the backgrounds of the accusers, indicating that some of the women were attracted to him and some women had been sexually promiscuous. This "blame-the-victim" defense divided the senator's staff. Some staffers wanted to fight aggressively against all the allegations, but others believed that smearing the accusers' reputations would backfire. Often in cases where a man has been accused of sexual misconduct, he tries to turn the focus off his own behavior and onto the character of the persons accusing him of wrongdoing. Some staffers argued that attacking the women would only reinforce his propensity for predatory behavior. Moreover, for a public figure who prided himself on his record of promoting women's rights, viciously assailing their credibility would be the worst sort of hypocrisy imaginable.

Packwood reluctantly agreed that he should not besmirch the good names of his accusers. It soon became clear that the tactic would not work in any case. The list of women who reported that Packwood had harassed and assaulted them grew. Some victims were hesitant to speak out initially, but as they read accounts of the senator's victims, they began to emerge. As it turned out, Packwood had been a sexual predator for his entire Senate career.[12]

Their stories were disturbingly consistent. In 1969 Julie Williamson, a 29-year-old legal secretary, came to work in Packwood's Senate office in Portland. She had worked for his 1968 campaign and she looked forward to continuing her association with the progressive young senator. Little did she know how different he was behind closed doors than he appeared in public. The articulate and charismatic champion of idealistic causes became a creepy sexual assailant.

One afternoon not long after she joined his staff, Williamson was on the telephone when Packwood slipped behind her and kissed her on the back of the neck. Stunned, she wheeled around. "Don't you ever do that again," she admonished him.

The senator would not be denied. He followed her into another room, grabbed at her clothes, pulled her ponytail, and stood on her toes. "I was really frightened," she recalled. Realizing he could not remove her clothes, the senator eventually wandered away as though nothing had happened. She quit her job shortly thereafter.

Confronted with this account more than twenty years later, Packwood denied that the incidents had occurred. He said that he and Williamson had discussed a "continued warm relationship," but their association "passed like a summer storm." The senator produced a written statement from his friend Anne Elias, who knew Williamson. The statement indicated that Elias believed that Williamson had desired a romantic relationship with Packwood. The statement neglected to mention that Williamson, extremely upset and agitated, arrived at Elias's apartment immediately following the episodes and told Elias that Packwood had made improper advances.[13]

Had Julie Williamson been the only woman to describe a close encounter with Bob Packwood, her statement might have been dismissed as a misunderstanding or a personal vendetta, as the senator alleged. Yet she was hardly alone in lodging accusations against him. In the mid-1970s, 30-year-old Jean McMahon, then an employee of the Oregon Department of Education, applied for a job in Packwood's Portland office. They initially met in his hotel room to talk about having McMahon draft a speech for the senator. A few weeks later Packwood was in town, and he asked her to meet him again in his hotel room so they could discuss her work on the speech.

McMahon later admitted that she was naïve to meet the senator in his hotel room. During the first visit, however, Packwood had been a perfect gentleman. The second visit was far different. As she recalled years later, the visit "ended up in one of those classic unpleasant situations where it was obvious he had other ideas on his mind and didn't want to talk about the speech," she said. Packwood was out of control. "I can remember being chased around the table and being grabbed and kissed once."

She tried to leave, but the senator blocked her exit. "There didn't seem to be any way to calm him down and get him back to what I thought we were going to do," she said. "The feeling I remember is of him trying to get power over me both physically and psychologically." When McMahon later contacted Packwood's staff to discuss the speech, no one was aware that she had been assigned to complete that task. Packwood said he did not remember McMahon or the incident she described. He also said he never used outside speechwriters, strongly suggesting that he had invented the speechwriting assignment as a pretext to entice McMahon to enter his hotel room.[14]

The stories continued. Paige Wagers was a 21-year-old college graduate who snagged a job as a mail clerk in the senator's Washington, DC, office. Working in the least prestigious position in the Senate office, she was surprised when Packwood noticed her and invited her to play bridge with several aides. Later, he buzzed her on the intercom and asked her to enter his office. He was her boss, of course, and so she complied with the request.

As soon as she came into the office, Packwood locked the door and embraced her, running his fingers through her hair, and kissing her on the lips.

He said he liked her wholesome good looks. "It was very clear that it was a sexual thing," Wagers remarked during an interview years later. "It was very hard to get him to let go of me."

She eventually talked her way out of the office. Shaken, she described the encounter to other staffers. Their nonchalant attitude surprised her. It was common knowledge among the staff that Packwood was a sexual predator. They recommended that she simply refuse any requests from the senator to enter his office alone. Wagers followed their advice when Packwood twice summoned her into his office following the initial incident.

Wagers moved on to a job at the US Department of Labor, but that did not end the harassment. Years later, in 1981, she ran into Packwood in a subterranean hallway inside the capitol. He maneuvered her into a private office by saying he wanted to discuss her work at the Labor Department. Wagers naively assumed that he was serious about his intentions until she saw a couch inside the office. He was steering her to the couch, but she refused. "I made it clear in the nicest way possible that I wasn't interested." She was embarrassed, she said, for allowing herself to be caught alone again with Packwood after she knew he was a sexual predator.

Wagers told friends about the second encounter, but they advised her not to report him to anyone in the Senate. Packwood was a powerful senator, and he probably would not be punished. Wagers, however, was a relatively low-level government employee who would acquire a reputation as a troublemaker. "That's the way Washington is," she observed during a subsequent interview. "You have to build. You can't have enemies. You can't be discredited from the time you come in." The problem with these one-on-one encounters, Wagers reflected, is that they quickly degenerate into a "he said–she said" exchange. "But because only the two of you were in the room, there is no way you can prove it. You're vulnerable. You're totally out on a limb." That is precisely why predators maneuver their would-be victims into quiet, out-of-the-way alcoves and offices. The power differential—who believes the lowly worker over the powerful, influential public figure?—ensures that the assailant lives to strike another day.[15]

Like many successful elected officials, Bob Packwood was consumed by his job. He was "always on," always working on the next bill or project. He worked long hours, often arriving at his desk before sunrise and laboring into the night. To ease the pressure he faced, Packwood consumed alcohol, usually in the evenings after a long day working on legislation. During the early years, he drank beer and wine in moderation. By the late 1970s he drank liquor as well, and his consumption gradually increased as he drank steadily throughout the day. "I don't think my basic nature changes" because of alcohol, he told interviewers in 1992.[16]

His staff and others who encountered him after he had been drinking all day, however, begged to differ. They saw a man who easily lost his temper when he had consumed a few too many drinks. His sexual assaults often occurred when he was intoxicated. He had always been predatory, but his attacks increased during the late 1970s and early 1980s as his alcohol consumption increased.

One woman who asked that her name not be used told the *Washington Post* reporters that she was a 21-year-old clerk on Packwood's staff when she stopped by his office to deliver some papers one evening in 1982. To her surprise and initial delight, the senator invited her to sit and chat. He knew her name and asked about her plans to return to college. He was drinking wine and offered her a glass, but she declined. At that moment the meeting took a turn for the worse.

Packwood rose from his chair and lunged at her. He grabbed the young woman and forced his tongue into her mouth. Panicked, the young woman "squirmed" out of his embrace and fled from the office, leaving behind her purse and winter coat despite the cold outside. "I was embarrassed, insulted and feeling like an idiot," she said. The woman left his employ shortly after the encounter. She told friends about the attack, but she never filed a formal complaint. "I wasn't important enough for anybody to believe," she explained. "I didn't know where to turn. I didn't know who to complain to, and he would probably just deny it, have me fired, and that's all that I needed at the time."[17]

On and on it went as ten women laid out their experiences with Packwood over the years. Even when they weren't recipients of his sexual advances, other women recalled instances when the senator repeated sexually explicit jokes in their presence. Maura C. Roche was a 22-year-old college intern in 1989 when Packwood pulled a binder from an office drawer and read off-color jokes to her. She sat, stunned, wondering how to respond. "I didn't know what I should do," she remembered. "I just sat there and took it." When asked about the incident, Packwood said he did not remember it.[18]

Packwood spent decades championing women's issues, and yet he remained a sexual predator. Many of the men and women on his staff defended him as a hardworking legislator who cared deeply about progressive issues. His personal failings were substantial, but they rationalized their work for the senator as noble and worthwhile even as they reluctantly turned a blind eye to his alcoholism and sexual advances.

A former Packwood aide, a woman who asked to remain anonymous, said that she repeatedly rebuffed his attacks. "He couldn't seem to help himself," she said. "I cannot tell you how many people sat down with him and said, 'You are going to come to a bad end. All your career's work on women's issues and on progressive issues is going to turn to dust.'"[19]

Following the November 22, 1992, publication of a *Washington Post* article detailing Packwood's twenty-year pattern of behavior, the senator was under enormous pressure to issue a statement explaining his behavior. "If any of my comments or actions have indeed been unwelcome or if I have conducted myself in any way that has caused any individual . . . embarrassment, for that I am sincerely sorry," the initial statement read. Critics immediately pounced on the statement, which they argued was too little, too late. A *New York Times* editorial opined that the statement "betrays a basic misunderstanding about the charge against him. It's not just about embarrassment. It's that he used the power of his position for sexual purposes." The editorial noted that Packwood's behavior did not exist in a vacuum. Many powerful men in the US Senate, and in a variety of elected positions, used their power to coerce unfortunate subordinates to endure all manner of sexual harassment and assaults.[20]

On December 10, 1992, in his first public appearance since the *Washington Post* article appeared, the senator went further than he did in the original statement. Saying that he accepted "full responsibility" for his actions, Packwood acknowledged that his conduct went far beyond inappropriate or offensive behavior. It was, he admitted, "just plain wrong." Earlier in the month, he had entered a clinic for alcohol treatment and evaluation, although Packwood said that his drinking problem was not an excuse for his behavior.

"I am here to take full responsibility for my actions," he told a crowd of reporters. "I will not debate the recent accounts of my actions toward my staff and those who worked with my office. The important point is that my actions were unwelcome and insensitive. The women were offended, appropriately so, and I am truly sorry."[21]

Critics noted how convenient it was that Packwood accepted responsibility *after* the November 1992 election. They urged him to "clear the air" and resign, but the senator would have none of that talk. He said that he understood that the "bond of trust" with voters had been broken, but he asked for "the chance to earn back your respect." In acknowledging his horrible behavior, Packwood said that he hoped his constituents would look at his conduct and judge him on the weight of his entire record. He also promised to cooperate with an investigation that the US Senate's ethics committee had recently launched.[22]

Comprised of three Democrats and three Republicans, the committee formally launched its investigation following the *Washington Post* story. Packwood dragged his feet, insisting that he would cooperate but also repeatedly insisting that he needed to get back to his important Senate duties. Committee members heard testimony from many more women who outlined a series of sexual abuses across the spectrum of the senator's career.[23]

During an appearance before the committee in October 1993, Packwood did himself no favors when he mentioned that he had kept a diary for years. Investigators seized on this admission, arguing that they needed to see the diaries to determine the nature and extent of his contact with women during his time in the Senate. Packwood resisted, contending that the diary contained private information that should not be open to public scrutiny. Constitutional advocates questioned whether requiring Packwood to divulge the content of his diaries constituted a violation of his Fifth Amendment privilege against self-incrimination. Despite these concerns, the Senate voted 94 to 6 to require him to turn over the more than 8,200 pages of the document to the ethics committee.[24]

On December 16, 1993, US District Court Judge Thomas Penfield Jackson ordered the senator to turn over the diary because the material was, in the words of the ethics committee, "unquestionably relevant" to the investigation. Concerned that the diaries contained all manner of personal material, including the senator's sexual fantasies and his unvarnished opinion of his colleagues, Packwood appealed Judge Jackson's decision. He lost on appeal. A court-appointed special master, Kenneth Starr, was directed to sift through the diary pages and determine whether any entries contained material that was purely personal, involved medical records, or disclosed confidential information between Packwood and his attorneys. The ethics committee eventually received over 5,000 pages of material.[25]

After reading through the submission, the committee realized that Packwood had edited the diary, removing passages and omitting some pages. Committee members insisted that the senator turn over an additional 3,200 pages—essentially, everything from the diary—but Packwood resisted. He knew that the entries included not only incriminating statements about his sexual assaults, but potential criminal violations such as Packwood's decision to skirt campaign finance laws. If he edited the entries to alter or interfere with the congressional investigation, he also might face obstruction of justice charges. Moreover, if Packwood's testimony under oath before the committee contradicted information contained in the diary, he might be guilty of perjury.[26]

Some senators, most notably California's Barbara Boxer, urged the committee to hold public hearings as they explored Packwood's transgressions. After much wrangling, committee members declined. It was one thing to air dirty laundry behind closed doors, but senators were reluctant to shine a public spotlight on misconduct by one of their own. For some senators, Packwood's actions hit uncomfortably close to home. For others, they feared opening a Pandora's box if they held public hearings on what they viewed as an internal Senate matter. While public hearings would have increased transparency, the hearings probably would not have altered the outcome. In May 1995 the ethics committee concluded that "substantial credible evidence" existed that Senator Packwood had engaged in sexual misconduct, tampered with evidence, and solicited favors from business-people on several occasions, such as when he attempted to secure a job for his ex-wife to reduce his alimony payments.[27]

Packwood had spent his Senate career as a self-professed independent, and he again wrapped himself in that mantle. In the past he had bucked his party on substantive issues in service of some higher purpose, such as effecting progressive policies that arguably advanced the public interest. Faced with allegations of misconduct, he portrayed himself as a maverick who refused to surrender to the liberal press, dogmatic women's groups, and rampant political correctness. It was not a good look for the senator. He could not make a case that his defense served any purpose other than protecting himself from his own inexcusable behavior.

The ethics committee eventually published its findings in a comprehensive ten-volume report numbering 10,145 pages. In public remarks delivered shortly after publication, ethics committee chairman Mitch McConnell said that Packwood's "habitual pattern of aggressive, blatantly sexual advances, mostly directed at members of his own staff or others whose livelihoods were connected in some way to his power and authority as a Senator" were unacceptable. In addition, Senator Packwood exacerbated his offenses by "deliberately altering and destroying relevant portions of his diary."[28]

Much of the material in the committee's report consisted of excerpts from Packwood's diaries. It was damning stuff. The senator reported a pattern of seedy conduct that reinforced the public image of senators as out of touch with their constituents, existing in a world of high-priced lobbyists, enjoying fancy meals and outings, and preying on a multitude of young, vulnerable female staffers ripe for exploitation. Senators reviewing the information were right to be concerned about how the public would perceive the Packwood diaries. No one who read the material came away with good feelings about Packwood in particular, or Washington lawmakers in general.[29]

Between the time that the sexual abuse charges first surfaced late in 1992 until publication of the ethics committee's report almost three years later, Senator Packwood deliberately kept a low profile. One news report labeled him "a spectral figure in Oregon." He refused to grant interviews to the state's leading newspaper, and he did not hold town hall meetings to greet voters, a tradition among many members of Congress. In fact, Packwood did not even own a home in the state. He lived in a trailer for a time.[30]

A sampling of public attitudes revealed that the junior senator from Oregon was a pariah. "The maverick stud didn't work for him in the end because he forgot his roots," said Lee Bergstein, a political consultant. "He had stopped practicing the kind of retail politics that people in this state like." James Moore, a political science professor at the University of Portland, commented on Packwood's tone-deaf defense of his actions. "He was a procedural master, brilliant in many ways, but what did him in with the Senate was the same thing that got him in trouble with the women—he couldn't read human nature. It wasn't that he doesn't get it on women's issues. He doesn't get it on people." Outside of the political class, citizens abandoned the lawmaker who once had been a champion of the disenfranchised. "Sympathy? For Bob Packwood?" asked Ana Thompson, a flower shop owner. "No way."[31]

The ethics committee had several options for punishing Packwood's misconduct. The committee might have recommended that he be stripped of his Senate Finance Committee chairmanship permanently, or that the Senate censure him. The committee chose the harshest recommendation possible. On September 7, 1995, the ethics committee unanimously recommended that Bob Packwood be expelled from the Senate.[32]

The full US Senate still had to vote on the expulsion, but it was likely that most members would accept the committee's recommendation. Realizing that his expulsion probably was inevitable, Packwood approached Senate Majority Leader Bob Dole and offered to resign if he could have ninety days before it went into effect. The majority leader did not immediately reject the proposal, and he promised to consider it. He was sympathetic to Packwood's situation. Following the exchange with Packwood, Dole met with the Democratic majority leader, Tom Daschle of South Dakota, to negotiate the terms of Packwood's departure.

Before Dole and Daschle reached a decision, Packwood granted an interview to explain his reasoning. "I would hope as a matter of comity that I could have a decent grace period," he said. "I need enough time here with the staff that knows me to get things in order." It was a necessary interval, he argued, because many outstanding issues had to be addressed. "This is not like throwing things in boxes. I have things to go to the archives. Do I take them to the archives myself? I have scores of things to do that are very time-consuming. This isn't like, 'You're fired, clean out your desk.'"[33]

Once again, Packwood had misjudged the level of disdain that his colleagues and the public felt toward him. When word of the proposed delay circulated, outrage from Republicans as well as Democrats forced Dole to change his plans. He initially scaled back the time from ninety days to sixty days before agreeing to thirty days. Finally, everyone agreed that Packwood would depart on October 1, which was three weeks away. Packwood could vote during that time, but he could not manage any bills or speak on legislation. He was removed as chairman of the Senate Finance Committee.[34]

As planned, Packwood left the Senate in disgrace on October 1, 1995. A Democrat, Ron Wyden, won a special election to replace him. Although Packwood went on to enjoy a successful career as a lobbyist, he had lost the power and prestige that came with a seat in the world's most influential legislature. His name was forever blackened by his decades of misconduct.[35]

A *New York Times* editorial concluded that "the Ethics Committee reached a proper judgment, and Mr. Packwood departs, too late, but with the burden of shame he has earned." Perhaps Maura C. Roche, one of the nineteen women who eventually came forward to charge the senator with sexual abuse, expressed it best when she reflected on Bob Packwood's fall from grace. "What I learned from all this," she said, "is that it is possible to go up against someone that's far more powerful than you and prevail."[36]

NOTES

1. Florence Graves and Charles E. Shepard, "Packwood Accused of Sexual Advances; Alleged Behavior Pattern Counters Image," *Washington Post*, November 22, 1992, A1.

2. "Sen. Morse Concedes Election to Packwood," *Washington Post*, December 31, 1968, A4. For more information on Packwood's background, see, for example, Timothy Egan, "Packwood Is Leaving as a Pariah in His State," *New York Times*, September 9, 1995, 8; Mark Kirchmeier, *Packwood: The Public and Private Life, from Acclaim to Outrage* (New York: HarperCollins, 1995), 63–84.

3. "A Maverick Bows Out," *Washington Post*, January 1, 1969, A18.

4. Morse is quoted in "Recount Confirms Senator Morse Loss," *Washington Post*, December 22, 1968, D2. See also "Sen. Morse Concedes Election to Packwood," A4.

5. Kirchmeier, *Packwood*, 125–35.

6. Kirchmeier, *Packwood*, 119.

7. Kirchmeier, *Packwood*, 200.

8. Georgie Packwood is quoted in "'Shadow Life' Stuns Family," *New York Times*, September 11, 1995, B10.

9. Franklin is quoted in Graves and Shepard, "Packwood Accused of Sexual Advances," A26.

10. Packwood is quoted in Graves and Shepard, "Packwood Accused of Sexual Advances," A26.

11. Graves and Shepard, "Packwood Accused of Sexual Advances," A26.

12. Graves and Shepard, "Packwood Accused of Sexual Advances," A26.

13. The incident and quotes are found in Graves and Shepard, "Packwood Accused of Sexual Advances," A26. See also "Accuser of Packwood Says Friend of His Pressured Her for Silence," *New York Times*, November 29, 1992, 24.

14. The incident and the quotes are found in Graves and Shepard, "Packwood Accused of Sexual Advances," A26.

15. The incident and the quotes are found in Graves and Shepard, "Packwood Accused of Sexual Advances," A26.

16. Packwood is quoted in Graves and Shepard, "Packwood Accused of Sexual Advances," A27.

17. The incident and quotes are found in Graves and Shepard, "Packwood Accused of Sexual Advances," A26.

18. The incident and quotes are found in Graves and Shepard, "Packwood Accused of Sexual Advances," A27. See also Egan, "Packwood Is Leaving as a Pariah in His State," 8.

19. The quote is found in Graves and Shepard, "Packwood Accused of Sexual Advances," A26.

20. The quotes are found in "Sexual Harassment in the Senate," *New York Times*, November 24, 1992, A14. See also Timothy Egan, "Oregon Now Wonders Who Is Real Packwood," *New York Times*, December 8, 1992, B12.

21. Packwood is quoted in "Packwood: Behavior Was 'Wrong'; Senator Rejects Calls to Resign," *Washington Post*, December 11, 1992, A1. See also "The Packwood Problem," *New York Times*, December 11, 1992, A38.

22. Packwood is quoted in "Packwood: Behavior Was 'Wrong,'" A16. See also Clifford Krauss, "Drinking Might Have Prompted Sexual Advances, Senator Says," *New York Times*, November 28, 1992, 9; Clifford Krauss, "Senator Enters Alcohol Clinic for Evaluation," *New York Times*, December 1, 1992, A18; "Panel Gets a New Complaint on Packwood," *New York Times*, December 3, 1992, A17.

23. Eric Pianin, "Senate Inquiry on Packwood Signals Sea Change in Attitude; Conduct No Longer Seen 'Above the Law,'" *Washington Post*, December 7, 1992, A1.

24. Nancy E. Marion, *The Politics of Disgrace: The Role of Political Scandal in American Politics* (Durham, NC: Carolina Academic Press, 2010), 217. See also "Packwood Diaries: A Rare Look at Washington's Tangled Web," *New York Times*, September 10, 1995, 1.

25. Marion, *The Politics of Disgrace*, 217,

26. Marion, *The Politics of Disgrace*, 217.

27. "The Packwood Resignation," *New York Times*, September 8, 1995, A26.

28. McConnell is quoted in *CQ Press Guide to Congress*, 7th ed. (Thousand Oaks, CA: Sage, 2013), Vol. 1, 1138. See also Marion, *The Politics of Disgrace*, 217–18.

29. Marion, *The Politics of Disgrace*, 218.

30. The term "a spectral figure in Oregon" and the information are found in Egan, "Packwood Is Leaving as a Pariah in His State," 8.

31. The quotes are found in Egan, "Packwood Is Leaving as a Pariah in His State," 8.

32. Egan, "Packwood Is Leaving as a Pariah in His State," 8. See also "The Packwood Resignation," A26.

33. Packwood is quoted in Katharine Q. Seelye, "Packwood to Leave in 3 Weeks as Dole Fails to Buy More Time," *New York Times*, September 9, 1995, 8.

34. "The Packwood Resignation," A26.

35. "Democrat Wins Race in Oregon for Packwood's Seat in Senate," *New York Times*, January 31, 1996, A13.

36. The editorial is "The Packwood Resignation," A26. Roche is quoted in Egan, "Packwood Is Leaving as a Pariah in His State," 8.

CHAPTER 11

"I Did Not Have Sexual Relations with That Woman, Miss Lewinsky"

Bill Clinton and Monica Lewinsky

It was the most infamous sex scandal in American history, and it nearly toppled an American president from power. Bill Clinton, the forty-second president of the United States, engaged in a sexual relationship with a much younger woman, Monica Lewinsky, a White House intern. After initially denying the relationship, the president was forced to admit that he had had sex with the young woman. Some American presidents had cheated on their wives either before or during their time in office—Warren G. Harding, John F. Kennedy, and Donald J. Trump are the most famous examples—but Clinton's dalliance became part of an impeachment inquiry after he lied about the affair under oath.

His behavior with Lewinsky was reckless beyond belief. Throughout his public life, Clinton had been accused of extramarital episodes, some consensual and others not. When he entered the presidency in 1993, his life came under intense scrutiny unlike anything he had ever had before. To think that he could pursue a sexual relationship inside the White House and the affair would go undetected was simply unfathomable. Yet he did so, and as a result, he almost ruined his marriage and his political career.[1]

The affair came to light during Clinton's second term as president, at a moment when he was enjoying a public renaissance of sorts. The Clinton presidency had gotten off to a rocky start. He had served as governor of a small state, Arkansas, and had never served in Congress. Consequently, when Clinton and his advisers arrived in Washington, they were in for a rude awakening. They thought that his election victory granted them a mandate to improve on the old ways of doing business. They also believed they could reform the nation's dysfunctional health-care system. The Clintons soon learned otherwise. The president's health-care initiative, spearheaded by his wife, Hillary, was a debacle. A series of scandals over relatively minor issues generated innumerable negative headlines. Even the suicide of their good friend Vince Foster, who served in the White House counsel's office, generated news stories questioning whether Foster was the victim of foul play and whether the Clintons had something to do with his death.[2]

In 1994 the Republicans seized control of both houses of Congress with historic victories in the midterm elections. Dubbed the "Republican revolution," the Republican onslaught ensured that Clinton would experience difficulties shaping the policy agenda or seeing any of his legislative priorities enacted into law. For all intents and purposes, the Clinton presidency appeared to be dead on arrival. News stories questioned whether the young president was no longer relevant to the policy process, just a figurehead who would serve out his time in office until a more suitable replacement could be found.[3]

Yet he was down but not out. The man who once called himself the "comeback kid" did it again. He won a second term in office, and he mastered the art of triangulation, a process where the president learned how to compromise on crucial issues and deal with a Republican Congress to enact legislation. The 1996 Personal Responsibility and Work Opportunity Reconciliation Act of 1996 (PRWORA) was a prime example of Clinton's newfound success. By agreeing to reform a major part of the nation's social welfare programs, even to the point of removing some recipients from the welfare rolls, Clinton captured enough Republican support to pass the bill into law. Progressive Democrats were furious that they finally had someone from their party in the White House and yet he was willing to support a major Republican effort to trim the welfare rolls. For their part, conservative Republicans did not like or trust Bill Clinton. They believed that he would never support their policy initiatives and was just cynically using PRWORA to tally a legislative victory. Despite all the misgivings, though, Clinton convinced enough moderates in both political parties to support the bill. He had found an effective strategy for neutralizing extremists in both political parties.[4]

His resurgence occurred before the 1996 election cycle. A year earlier Clinton and congressional Republicans had been fighting over provisions in the federal budget. The two sides forced a government shutdown, which necessitated most of the White House staff leaving the premises until the impasse was resolved. One of the few workers who remained was a 22-year-old White House intern, Monica Lewinsky. Had the government shutdown not occurred, it is unlikely that she would have been able to approach President Clinton as she did in November 1995. A regular White House staffer probably would have blocked her access to the president.[5]

One evening Lewinsky brought a sheaf of papers to the Oval Office, where she found the president alone. According to Lewinsky, the two "made eye contact." The following evening she appeared again, and they exchanged glances. She smiled at him and made conversation. In a moment of candid flirtation, she lifted her skirt to show the president her thong underwear.

This was the pivotal moment. Clinton might have admonished her that she was in the White House and she must behave appropriately. Rebuffed, perhaps humiliated, she probably would have stayed away from Clinton. Alternatively, he could have said nothing and simply ignored the gesture. Instead, he was intrigued, and he responded to her overtures. The married president guided the young intern to a secluded doorway, and they kissed. Before the encounter ended, Lewinsky performed oral sex on him.[6]

For the next year and a half, Lewinsky visited the president in the White House on nine or ten occasions. It was important to keep the illicit relationship secret, and so the couple arranged the trysts late at night and on weekends when few people were around. Lewinsky later recalled performing oral sex on Clinton while the president spoke on the phone with a congressional leader. On another memorable occasion, he ate take-out pizza while she performed oral sex.[7]

Lewinsky believed that their relationship was more than simply a one-night stand, but she was fooling herself. Clinton repeatedly told her that their affair must remain secret. Months passed between their meetings. She and Clinton spoke on the phone, but always at his pleasure. He called her from the White House or when he was on the road and could find a quiet moment. Although he could be tender and solicitous, the calls sometimes slipped into steamy dirty talk that she thought of as phone sex. They also exchanged gifts. He gave her a copy of Walt Whitman's famous collection of poems, *Leaves of Grass*.[8]

The relationship remained secret for many months, undoubtedly longer than it would have under normal circumstances. The government shutdown allowed Lewinsky and Clinton to steal away for furtive encounters during the early weeks, but soon the White House staff returned. It became much more difficult for Clinton and Lewinsky to find time alone. By April several staffers expressed concern that the flirtatious Lewinsky was spending entirely too much time in the White House. Clinton's more cynical advisers worried that their man was too easily subject to "bimbo eruptions," or his willingness to seek sex from women he encountered.[9]

In April 1996, staffers transferred Lewinsky to another government job. Someone asked United Nations ambassador Bill Richardson to interview Lewinsky for a position on his staff. It was unusual for a lowly White House intern to meet with an ambassador, but Richardson agreed to the interview. He later offered Lewinsky a job, which she turned down. She eventually landed at the Pentagon, supposedly a well-deserved promotion. Lewinsky did not see it that way, of course. She correctly believed that the White House staff had banished her to the hinterlands in hopes of limiting her time with the president. She even complained to him about her situation.[10]

Had Clinton and Lewinsky broken off the relationship when she landed at the Pentagon and told no one of the episodes, the matter might have

Figure 11.1. Bill Clinton and Monica Lewinsky pose for a photograph in the Oval Office inside the White House. Courtesy of the Clinton Presidential Library.

concluded with no one else the wiser. Lewinsky was not easily dissuaded, however. She felt overcome by her feelings toward the handsome leader of the free world. She confided in her mother and as many as ten friends about her trysts with Clinton. It was one friend, however, who betrayed that confidence.

Linda Tripp was a longtime government employee, almost a quarter century older than Monica Lewinsky. They met at the Pentagon not long after Lewinsky started working at her new job, sometime during the summer of 1996. Tripp had worked in the White House during both the George H. W. Bush administration and the Clinton administration, but, like Lewinsky, she had been banished to the Pentagon. Although the move resulted in a salary increase, Tripp missed her time near the center of power. She and Monica Lewinsky shared their resentment of moving out of the White House and across the river to the Defense Department.[11]

The reasons they were moved, of course, were vastly different. As the pair talked about their experiences, Lewinsky let it slip that she had engaged in a sexual affair with a much older man. Tripp was intrigued. She encouraged her young colleague to talk, and soon the floodgates opened. The young woman confided her innermost secrets, describing in detail how, when, and under what circumstances she and Bill Clinton met. No lurid detail was omitted.[12]

Aside from talking at work, Linda Tripp and Monica Lewinsky talked on the phone. Typically, Lewinsky provided a running narrative with occasional prompts from Tripp. Unbeknownst to Lewinsky, Tripp began tape-recording the conversations. In all, the older woman captured more than twenty hours of their sometimes rambling exchanges. In moments of hurt and anger, Monica Lewinsky lashed out at Bill Clinton, referring to the man who jilted her as "the big creep." Whether this was self-awareness that the president had abused her by taking advantage of a much younger, lovesick woman or merely expressions of temporary pique was open to debate. What was clear, however, was Lewinsky's almost total recall of the episodes with Clinton.

Linda Tripp's motives for tape-recording the calls came under much subsequent scrutiny. She claimed that the recordings provided her with an insurance policy. Even in the early days of her relationship with Lewinsky, Tripp thought it was highly probable that the two women might have to testify about the Clinton affair. Linda Tripp had no firsthand knowledge of the affair; she had not witnessed the president and the intern in an uncompromising position. She would be testifying about what her young friend told her. The testimony would be based on hearsay. It would be easy to discredit her by insisting that she was mistaken or lying. With tape recordings in her possession, Tripp could corroborate any testimony with audio of Monica Lewinsky's words.[13]

Tripp's explanation sounds opportunistic, but it might have been plausible were it not for her other actions after she spoke with Lewinsky. Tripp had met a politically conservative literary agent, Lucianne Goldberg, in the early 1990s. The two women became friends. Goldberg was a self-styled activist and, like many conservatives, fiercely critical of Bill Clinton's administration as well as his personal life. After Lewinsky confided in her, Tripp discussed the admissions with Goldberg. Clinton's penchant for sexual escapades was well known, but Lewinsky's allegations were explosive because they had occurred while Clinton was president. The other episodes dated from the time before Clinton had moved to the White House.

Goldberg envisioned a tell-all book emerging from Lewinsky's conversations with Tripp, and so she encouraged her friend to tape-record the calls. Tripp lived in Maryland at the time, and Goldberg told her friend that tape-recording conversations was legal in Maryland if one party consented, even if the other party was unaware of the recording. That advice turned out to be incorrect. Nonetheless, Goldberg realized that she could use Lewinsky's allegations to harm Clinton—and perhaps remove him from office.[14]

The Lewinsky-Tripp conversations occurred while Clinton's life and career were being investigated on multiple fronts. One high-profile case involved a young Arkansas woman, Paula Corbin Jones, who was suing Clinton for allegedly sexually harassing and assaulting her in a Little Rock hotel room in 1991. Her case had been hanging over his head for years. It might have disappeared but for a group of zealous, politically conservative lawyers who seized on her allegations to score points against a president they despised. Clinton's defense team argued that a sitting president could not be sued while serving in office, but the US Supreme Court disagreed. The suit proceeded.[15]

Jones's legal team wanted to show a pattern of sexual abuse by Bill Clinton, especially when he was in a position of power over government employees. To demonstrate the pattern, they subpoenaed women they suspected Clinton had either harassed or had affairs with. Thanks to Linda Tripp and Lucianne Goldberg, Monica Lewinsky was on the list. On January 7, 1998, Lewinsky filed an affidavit with Jones's lawyers insisting that she had never had sexual relations with Bill Clinton. Ten days later Clinton provided a deposition that corroborated the information in her affidavit.

Jones's lawyers tried to pin down the president. One questioner asked, "Have you ever had sexual relations with Monica Lewinsky, as that term is defined in Deposition Exhibit 1, as modified by the Court?" The definition read, "a person engages in sexual relations when the person knowingly engages in or causes contact with the genitalia, anus, groin, breast, inner thigh, or buttocks of any person with an intent to arouse or gratify the sexual desire of any person." Using that definition, the president said that he had not had sexual relations with Monica Lewinsky. With both alleged participants presenting similar stories, in most cases the matter would have been concluded.[16]

Yet a wrinkle developed in the case. Even before the Jones lawsuit advanced through the courts, a special three-judge division of the District of Columbia Court of Appeals, acting on authorization provided by US Attorney General Janet Reno, appointed Kenneth Starr, a former solicitor general of the United States as well as former federal appellate court judge, to investigate the Whitewater affair, a failed real estate deal involving the Clintons in Arkansas. Independent counsel Starr and his investigative team had spent three years digging through Whitewater and associated matters. They had found a complex, unseemly web of activities that demonstrated the propensity of elected officials to enjoy perquisites unavailable to average people, but they had uncovered no hard and fast evidence of criminality. Several ancillary matters, such as the Clintons' decision to fire members of the White House Travel Office and the apparent suicide of the Clintons' close friend Vince Foster, had convinced right-wing ideologues that the president and his wife were involved in massive conspiracies, but Starr could offer no support.[17]

His investigation might have sputtered to an abrupt conclusion but for a telephone call that his office received on January 12, 1998. Linda Tripp called to tell the independent counsel that she possessed tapes of her conversations with a young woman who said she had engaged in a sexual affair with the president. This new information, if true, would breathe new life into a dying investigation. Within two hours of the call, six members of the independent counsel's office, accompanied by a Federal Bureau of Investigation (FBI) agent, arrived at Linda Tripp's house to nail down what she knew and the evidence she had.

Investigators gleaned from Tripp's tapes that Clinton and Lewinsky had had sexual relations, but they needed more information. Evidence of an affair between the president of the United States and a woman half his age in the White House would be politically explosive, but an affair by itself was not criminal conduct. Starr's people needed more information, especially about whether the president had instructed anyone to lie under oath about the affair. Perjury was a criminal offense, and it was possible that the president was guilty of such a crime.[18]

At the request of the Independent Counsel's Office, Tripp arranged to meet with Monica Lewinsky at the Ritz-Carlton hotel bar in Pentagon City, Virginia. To Lewinsky, it appeared to be an ordinary meeting between two friends. During their conversation, as they had discussed many times in the past, they spoke of the Lewinsky-Clinton affair. This time, however, Linda Tripp wore a wire that allowed the Office of Independent Counsel and the FBI to record the conversation. Their discussion that day confirmed what Tripp had told Starr: Monica Lewinsky had engaged in a sexual affair with the president of the United States.[19]

Far from being a naïve ingenue, Lewinsky understood the high-stakes game she was playing. Clinton was facing multiple threats regarding his sexual advances and conflicting accounts of his behavior. After the initial meeting in the Ritz-Carlton, Lewinsky supplied Tripp with a document titled "Points to Make in an Affidavit," apparently how-to advice on shading the truth without committing perjury. Investigators wondered whether President Clinton or someone on his staff had encouraged Lewinsky to prepare the talking points.[20]

Events moved quickly. Based on what he had learned from Tripp and the Lewinsky tapes, Starr contacted US Attorney General Janet Reno to request authorization to expand his probe. Presidents are reluctant to submit to independent investigations for exactly this reason. A probe that is initiated for one purpose—in this case, to chase down the details surrounding the Whitewater land deal—can expand to cover innumerable issues far beyond the original scope. Because the independent counsel had good reason to believe that subornation of perjury and obstruction of justice had occurred, Reno had few options but to submit the request to the three-judge panel of the District of Columbia Court of Appeals. The judges authorized the expanded purview.[21]

With legal authorization in hand, Starr and his team urged Linda Tripp to arrange a second meeting with Monica Lewinsky. They set it up for January 16, 1998. Once again the two friends met at the Ritz-Carlton. This time, however, they did not trade gossip about "the big creep." Instead, FBI agents and US attorneys confronted Lewinsky. With no advance warning, they whisked her away to a nearby hotel room for a twelve-hour interrogation.

Accounts differ as to what happened in the hotel room. The agents and attorneys claimed that they asked the questions they would ask any material witness in a federal investigation. Lewinsky screamed, cried, and threw a temper tantrum, they said. Monica Lewinsky claimed that she was badgered and forced to endure all manner of humiliation. When she asked to contact her mother, Lewinsky said that the agents belittled her, questioning why a woman her age would need to speak to her mother. Eventually, the agents relented, and Lewinsky placed the call.[22]

Marcia Lewis was savvy enough to know that her daughter needed a lawyer to represent her. Before taking a train to Washington, DC, to meet Lewinsky, Lewis contacted her ex-husband, Bernard Lewinsky, Monica's father, and asked for his assistance. In turn, Dr. Lewinsky, a physician, was friends with William H. Ginsburg, a lawyer who specialized in medical malpractice cases. The doctor reached out to his friend, who agreed to represent Monica Lewinsky.[23]

Back in the hotel room, the FBI and the US attorneys continued pressuring Monica Lewinsky to cooperate. They offered to grant her immunity if she would wear a wire and tape-record President Clinton. It was a tempting offer. If he asked her to lie in a deposition, investigators would have compelling evidence of an impeachable offense. The plan went awry when William Ginsburg called to tell the authorities that he represented Ms. Lewinsky, and he insisted that the interview end until he could confer with his client.[24]

Following Ginsburg's appearance in the case, Starr's office moved away from a full grant of immunity. The increasingly contentious negotiations dragged on for more than six months until the two sides reached a deal late in July 1998. Lewinsky would receive immunity in exchange for her grand jury testimony.[25]

Even as the legal maneuvering stretched across the months, news that the president had engaged in an affair with a White House intern leaked out and, predictably, generated numerous headlines. Journalists besieged the Clinton White House asking for the president's response. On January 26, 1998, in a soon to be infamous on-camera statement, Clinton appeared at the podium and wagged his finger at the press. "I did not have sexual relations with that woman, Miss Lewinsky," he righteously proclaimed as his wife, Hillary, looked on. Recognizing that an admission at this point might jeopardize his presidency, Clinton had resolved to issue a blanket denial and hope he could withstand the coming onslaught.[26]

And it was an onslaught. Clinton was a man who had made many enemies over the years. His politically conservative critics were delighted to find him in this predicament, and they intended to pursue the matter through the law courts, and in the court of public opinion as long and as loudly as they could. Appearing on television the day after Bill Clinton's comment, Hillary Clinton lashed out at the president's critics, noting that there was a "vast right-wing conspiracy that has been conspiring against my husband since the day he announced for president."[27]

Whether a genuine conspiracy existed seems unlikely, but even if it did, Bill Clinton certainly provided fodder for his enemies. One item especially sealed his fate. During their conversations Monica Lewinsky had revealed to Linda Tripp that Bill Clinton had stained her blue dress with semen. Tripp told her friend to preserve the dress, stains and all, in case she needed it to bolster her credibility in the future. It was good advice. Tripp also gleefully reported this fact to Lucianne Goldberg, who ensured that the story made the rounds in the tabloid press.[28]

The independent counsel, Kenneth Starr, understood that this piece of evidence, if he could find it, would be crucial in demonstrating the existence of a sexual affair between Clinton and Lewinsky. DNA evidence was virtually incontrovertible. If the independent counsel hoped to make a legal case against the president, he first needed to establish that the relationship had occurred. A search of Lewinsky's apartment failed to locate the dress.

The mystery was solved during Monica Lewinsky's grand jury testimony, when she revealed that she had given the stained dress to her mother for safekeeping. Starr quickly moved to obtain the dress. Afterward, he had it tested for DNA evidence. He also filed a motion to obtain a blood sample from Clinton so that he could compare the DNA from the blood with the DNA from the semen-stained dress. They matched. The prosecutors were elated. Although they believed that Linda Tripp and Monica Lewinsky had testified truthfully, both women had credibility problems. The DNA match corroborated their statements.[29]

Bill Clinton had dragged his feet for months, but he could not avoid testifying under oath. His lawyers worked out a compromise where the president would be questioned in the White House rather than the grand jury room inside the federal courthouse. Moreover, the testimony could not last more than four hours. The president was a busy man, as everyone knew.

On Saturday, August 15, 1998, Clinton told his wife that he had lied about his relationship with Lewinsky, and he would have to admit it when he testified before the grand jury lest he commit perjury. "She looked at me as if I had punched her in the gut," Clinton wrote in his autobiography, *My*

Life. The first lady was "almost as angry at me for lying to her in January as for what I had done." He would have to admit his deception to his daughter, Chelsea, his staff, and cabinet, and to the American people as well. The president had few options but to act contrite and seek forgiveness for his transgressions.[30]

He first had to get through his grand jury testimony. Two days after he confessed the affair to Hillary, President Clinton met interrogators in the Map Room of the White House while jurors watched the proceedings live on closed-circuit television. The Office of the Independent Counsel video-taped the testimony as well. Clinton kept his sometimes volcanic temper in check, but he was uncomfortable with the explicit nature of the questions. In the president's view, "Starr and his interrogators did their best to turn the videotape into a pornographic home movie, asking me questions designed to humiliate me and to so disgust the Congress and the American people that they would demand my resignation, after which he might be able to indict me."[31]

It was a predictably combative session as Clinton bobbed and weaved. Hoping to avoid a perjury charge, he repeatedly said he could not recall key facts. He acknowledged that his relationship with Lewinsky was improper, but he vehemently denied counseling anyone to lie. When pressed to explain why he concealed his relationship, he was blunt. "I did what people do when they do the wrong thing. I tried to do it when nobody else was looking."[32]

In the most famous exchange of that day, Starr's team of lawyers relentlessly tried to pin down Clinton on whether the president had committed perjury when he testified at his deposition in January 1998. If Clinton admitted that he had knowingly made a false statement under oath—the legal definition of perjury—the admission could serve as grounds for impeachment. Clinton, of course, knew exactly what Starr's prosecutors were driving at, and he could not admit to lying in his deposition if he hoped to escape from his predicament.

Deputy independent counsel Solomon "Sol" Wisenberg asked Clinton, "the statement of your attorney, Mr. Bennett, at Paula Jones's deposition, 'Counsel is fully aware'—it's page 54, line 5—'Counsel is fully aware that Ms. Lewinsky has filed, has an affidavit which they are in possession of saying that there is absolutely no sex of any kind in any manner, shape or form, with President Clinton.' That statement is made by your attorney in front of Judge Susan Webber Wright, correct?" Although Clinton's attorney Robert Bennett had made the statement, he was speaking on Clinton's behalf, and the president had not corrected him. Clinton admitted that Bennett had made the statement.

"That statement is a completely false statement. Whether or not Mr. Bennett knew of your relationship with Ms. Lewinsky, the statement that there was 'no sex of any kind in any manner, shape or form, with President Clinton,' was an utterly false statement. Is that correct?" Wisenberg had come to the heart of the matter. If Clinton admitted that it was a false statement, his legal woes would be compounded significantly.

In one of the most tortured constructions possible, Clinton parsed the words carefully to show that he was not responsible for any misinterpretations of his lawyer's statements. "It depends on what the meaning of the word 'is' is," he said. "If the—if he—if 'is' means is and never has been that is not—that is one thing. If it means there is none, that was a completely true statement. But, as I have testified, and I'd like to testify again, this is—it is somewhat unusual for a client to be asked about his lawyer's statements, instead of the other way around. I was not paying a great deal of attention to this exchange. I was focusing on my own testimony."[33]

Clinton was saying two things in his defense. First, he was arguing that he should not be held responsible for his attorney's statements. The president did not correct his attorney because he, the president, was focused on his own statement. Second, because Clinton was not presently involved in a sexual relationship with Lewinsky—it had occurred wholly in the past—it was not a lie to say that he is not in such a relationship.

The argument grew even more convoluted. "Now if someone had asked me on that day, 'Are you having sexual relations with Ms. Lewinsky?' That is, asked me a question in the present tense, I would have said, 'No.' And it would have been completely true."

Wisenberg was stunned at the patently ridiculous response. "Do you mean today, that because you are not engaging in sexual activity with Miss Lewinsky during the deposition that the statement of Mr. Bennett might literally be true?" Clinton had acquired the pejorative nickname "Slick Willie" for his evasive answers to uncomfortable questions in the past, and it was not difficult to see how he had earned that reputation. He was suggesting exactly what Wisenberg concluded.[34]

That night Clinton addressed the American public on television to prepare them for the news that he had misled the country. "This afternoon in this room, from this chair, I testified before the Office of Independent Counsel and the grand jury," he said at the outset of his four-and-a-half-minute speech. "As you know, in a deposition in January, I was asked questions about my relationship with Monica Lewinsky. While my answers were legally accurate, I did not volunteer information. Indeed, I did have a relationship with Miss Lewinsky that was not appropriate. In fact, it was wrong. It constituted a critical lapse in judgment and a personal failure on my part for which I am solely and completely responsible."

Having acknowledged his misconduct, the president insisted that he had never suborned perjury. "But I told the grand jury today and I say to you now that at no time did I ask anyone to lie, to hide or destroy evidence or to take any other unlawful action. I know that my public comments and my silence about this matter gave a false impression. I misled people, including even my wife. I deeply regret that."

The goal was to appear contrite and accept full responsibility for placing himself, his friends and family, and the American people in a terrible position, but Clinton could not leave it at that. He expressed his opinion that Kenneth Starr and his investigators were out of control. "The independent counsel investigation moved on to my staff and friends, then into my private life. And now the investigation itself is under investigation," he said. "This has gone on too long, cost too much and hurt too many innocent people."[35]

Reviews of the speech were mixed. Many Americans believed that a sign of contrition was the first step toward healing the nation's wounds, but others were put off by Clinton's attack on Starr and the Office of Independent Counsel. As Clinton later acknowledged, "I believed every word I said, but maybe anger hadn't worn off enough for me to be as contrite as I should have been."[36]

In the aftermath of the admission, it was unclear what would happen next. It was clear, however, that a single speech by the president was insufficient penitence, even if one believed that the president had not encouraged Monica Lewinsky to lie and even if he had not committed perjury during his original deposition. Starr and his deputies were laboring on a report to Congress, and the next moves would depend on what they recommended, if anything. Clinton's Republican critics were anxious to launch an impeachment inquiry, and they were confident that the Starr report would provide ammunition for the assault.[37]

A persistent question that arises whenever an elected official, especially a president, faces a scandal is whether the official can continue to fulfill his or her duties. Clinton did not intend to resign, so he would have to work through his ongoing problems with the Office of the Independent Counsel while he struggled to act as president. The answer to this question came three days after his grand jury testimony and his speech that evening.

On August 20, 1998, in a series of cruise missile attacks codenamed Operation Infinite Reach, the US Navy struck against the terrorist group al-Qaeda's bases in Khost, Afghanistan, and the Al-Shifa pharmaceutical factory in Khartoum, Sudan. The attacks were in retaliation for al-Qaeda's August 7 bombings of American embassies in Kenya and Tanzania. The operation missed killing the group's leader, Osama bin Laden, but Clinton believed the reprisals were necessary because bin Laden was "perhaps the preeminent organizer and financier of international terrorism in the world today." Critics doubted that bin Laden was as dangerous as Clinton suggested. Instead, they saw the operation as akin to *Wag the Dog*, a film in which a fictional president starts a phony war to distract the public from a sex scandal involving the president and a young woman in the White House.[38]

Less than three weeks later, Kenneth Starr delivered his 445-page report to Congress. The original area of inquiry, the Whitewater land deal, was barely mentioned. Instead, the independent counsel focused on Clinton's relationship with Monica Lewinsky, citing eleven possible grounds for impeachment involving perjury, obstruction of justice, witness tampering, and abuse of power.[39]

The report became the subject of intense partisan debate. The president's critics cited the lengthy summary of his behavior as evidence that he had engaged in impeachable conduct and cheapened the presidency. Clinton's supporters argued that Starr included unnecessary details aimed at humiliating the president. By going far beyond the scope of his initial inquiry, the independent counsel had engaged in a fishing expedition to assist the Republican Party in its political vendetta against a Democratic president.[40]

If Republicans hoped that the Starr report would assist them at the ballot box, they were in for a rude awakening. The Republican speaker of the House of Representatives, Newt Gingrich of Georgia, had predicted that his party would capture at least thirty House seats in the November 1998 midyear elections owing to voter outrage over Clinton's conduct. It was a safe bet; the party that does not control the White House typically picks up seats in Congress in off-year elections. To the surprise of many, Republicans lost five House seats in 1998. A chastened Gingrich, who was widely regarded as the source of much anti-Republican feeling, resigned his congressional seat in response to the disappointing election results. Many Republicans who had been especially vehement in investigating Clinton soon found their own marital infidelities exposed and exploited in the tabloid press. It was a season of ultra-political hypocrisy in Washington, DC.[41]

Despite his party's encouraging results at the ballot box, Bill Clinton was under no illusions. Republicans controlled the House of Representatives, and many Republicans detested him. The Starr report gave them the cover to institute impeachment proceedings, and that is exactly what they did, returning two articles of impeachment in December 1998. A simple majority of the House, 218 votes, was required to submit articles of impeachment to the United States Senate for adjudication.[42]

On December 11, 1998, the House Judiciary Committee voted on three articles of impeachment against Clinton—one for perjury in the grand jury proceedings, a second for perjury in the Paula Jones lawsuit deposition, and a third for obstruction of justice. The next day the committee added an article of impeachment for abuse of power.[43]

The full House voted down two articles. By a vote of 229 to 205, House members rejected the charge that Clinton had committed perjury in the deposition he gave in the Paula Jones sexual harassment lawsuit. The full

House also rejected the abuse of power article, this one by a 248 to 148 vote, with eighty-one Republicans crossing the aisle. That left two articles of impeachment to transfer to the Senate for trial.[44]

Article One found that "On August 17, 1998, William Jefferson Clinton swore to tell the truth, the whole truth, and nothing but the truth before a federal grand jury of the United States. Contrary to that oath, William Jefferson Clinton willfully provided perjurious, false and misleading testimony to the grand jury." It passed by a 228 to 206 vote, with five Democrats joining 223 Republicans in the final tally.[45]

The second article alleged that Clinton had obstructed justice by making false statements under oath and by allowing his attorney to make false statements without correcting the record. The charge outlined seven instances when the president provided an affidavit, provided false or misleading testimony during a deposition, or lied in his grand jury testimony. His efforts and the efforts of his colleagues "to secure job assistance to a witness [i.e., Monica Lewinsky] in a Federal civil rights action brought against him in order to corruptly prevent the truthful testimony of that witness in that proceeding at a time when the truthful testimony of that witness would have been harmful to him" also figured into the obstruction of justice article.[46]

Republicans controlled the Senate 55 to 45 when it took up the two articles of impeachment in January 1999. The US Constitution requires a two-thirds vote to convict a high-ranking federal official of an impeachable offense, which meant that sixty-seven or more senators would have to convict Clinton before he could be removed from office. The Founders deliberately made the bar high so that unpopular officials would not be chased from office for purely political reasons. Under this standard it appeared unlikely that Clinton would be convicted and forced to leave the presidency. Nonetheless, his legal team left nothing to chance.[47]

The impeachment managers, a dedicated group of Republican House members who had long opposed the president's personal conduct as well as his public policies, argued that Clinton should be removed from office owing to "willful, premeditated, deliberate corruption of the nation's system of justice through perjury and obstruction of justice." They carefully sifted through the misleading statements and inconsistencies in Clinton's public pronouncements about his relationship with Monica Lewinsky. Congressman Lindsey Graham of South Carolina offered perhaps the broadest view of impeachment: "You don't even have to be convicted of a crime to lose your job in this constitutional republic if this body determines that your conduct as a public official is clearly out of bounds in your role," he said. "Impeachment is not about punishment. Impeachment is about cleansing the office. Impeachment is about restoring honor and integrity to the office."[48]

Clinton's defenders contended that the grand jury testimony was replete with inconsistencies that muddied the waters, making a perjury case indefensible. The partisan wrangling had been so divisive that the case had been inalterably tainted. Accordingly, the impeachment managers had presented "an unsubstantiated, circumstantial case that does not meet the constitutional standard to remove the President from office." Article II, Section 4 of the US Constitution states that "the President, Vice President and all civil officers of the United States, shall be removed from office on impeachment for, and conviction of, treason, bribery, or other high crimes and misdemeanors." Although treason and bribery are not the only actions that constitute "high crimes and misdemeanors"—the text includes the word "other" to modify high crimes and misdemeanors—the implication is that the president's behavior must rise to a high level of malfeasance. In short, his misconduct must imperil the health and vitality of the republic. Even if President Clinton lied under oath about a sexual relationship with a young woman less than half his age, such action is not akin to treason or bribery.[49]

The Senate debated whether to call live witnesses for public testimony or opt for closed-door sessions sans eyewitness accounts. A majority eventually allowed for videotaped, closed-door depositions of Monica Lewinsky, Clinton's friend and confidant Vernon Jordan, who attempted to find Lewinsky a job, and White House aide Sidney Blumenthal, who allegedly assisted the president in covering up the affair. The Office of Independent Counsel had already conducted an exhaustive, multiyear investigation, and many senators on both sides of the aisle believed that nothing would be gained by drawing out the proceedings.[50]

On February 8, 1999, each side presented closing arguments. White House counsel Charles Ruff stressed the seriousness of removing a duly elected president from office based on anything other than a clear-cut case of malfeasance that threatened the health of the country. Speaking for the House impeachment managers, Congressman Henry Hyde emphasized that lying under oath is a serious offense. "We have reduced lying under oath to a breach of etiquette, but only if you are the President," he said. "And now let us all take our place in history on the side of honor, and, oh, yes, let right be done."[51]

The following day, the Senate sat in closed-door deliberations. The senators announced the final verdict on February 12, with the tally on the perjury charge 45 votes for conviction and 55 against. On obstruction of justice, the vote was 50 to 50. President Bill Clinton would not be removed from office.[52]

Two hours after the verdict announcement, the president walked into the Rose Garden and issued a short statement. He said he was "profoundly sorry" for his conduct. "Now I ask all Americans, and I hope all Americans here in Washington and throughout our land, will rededicate ourselves to the work of serving our nation and building our future together. This can be and this must be a time of reconciliation and renewal for America."

He took only one question: "In your heart, sir, can you forgive and forget?"

Evincing the contrition that sometimes caused skeptics to mock him with the wry comment "I feel your pain," Clinton responded that "I believe any person who asks for forgiveness has to be prepared to give it." He was ready to get back to work for the American people, he said. Following his acquittal, the forty-second president enjoyed some of the highest public approval ratings of his time in office.[53]

Yet he unquestionably tarnished his legacy. Clinton finished out his term of office, but his impeachment was a black mark against his name in the history books. He was the second president to be impeached by Congress, and the entire imbroglio was an unnecessary waste of his time in office and his political capital. Historians regard Bill Clinton as a man of tremendous political gifts as well as spectacular personal failings.[54]

As for Monica Lewinsky, she had been badly used by President Clinton, and she was badly used by the media. Her name elicited snickers and became synonymous with the ditzy young girl with low self-esteem who throws herself at a famous public figure. Women's rights advocates argued that the recurring story of a powerful, much older man who has an affair with an adoring subordinate, only to leave her vulnerable and empty-handed when the illicit relationship becomes public, must change. For far too long, famous men had taken it as a matter of right that they could use and abuse young women with impunity.

Seeking to turn her status in pop culture to her advantage, Lewinsky cooperated with celebrity biographer Andrew Morton on his book *Monica's Story*. She also granted an interview to television journalist Barbara Walters and appeared on several segments of the long-running comedy show *Saturday Night Live*, which had mercilessly mocked her during the height of the Clinton fiasco. Eager to capitalize on her infamy, she designed handbags for a company called The Real Monica Inc. and became a spokesperson for the diet company Jenny Craig. She showed her serious side when she earned a master's degree from the London School of Economics.[55]

Decades after its culmination the Clinton-Lewinsky affair remains the most infamous sex scandal in American history. Presidents had cheated on their wives in the past, but Clinton lied about the affair under oath, adding another layer to the scandal. In addition, the times they were a-changin'. So many presidents of the past had survived public disclosure of their peccadilloes because the press did not print stories about their escapades even when they were well known. By the 1990s the nature of the presidency—and the willingness of the press to turn a blind eye to presidential misbehavior—had changed. Whether the change is a positive or a negative feature of politics is open to debate. On one hand, if presidential character counts in the public's approval or disapproval of a president, knowing about the chief magistrate's extracurricular activities is vitally important. A man who recklessly cheats on his wife and hides other secrets may not be fit to hold high office. On the other hand, a person, even a president, should enjoy a measure of privacy. If he or she is not engaged in treason, bribery, or public malfeasance, the person ought not be answerable for private conduct. Perhaps the person should answer to a spouse or to God, but not to the public. Holding presidents to an impossibly high standard only ensures that the American people will be continually disappointed in the performance of presidents who are "all too human."[56]

NOTES

1. John F. Harris, *The Survivor: Bill Clinton in the White House* (New York: Random House, 2005), 220–22; Jules Witcover, *Party of the People: A History of the Democrats* (New York: Random House, 2003), 681, 683.

2. Ken Gormley, *The Death of American Virtue: Clinton vs. Starr* (New York: Crown, 2010), 66–75; Harris, *The Survivor*, 24–30, 34–40, 45–51, 55–61, 76–78, 85–87, 100–7, 108–117, 130–38.

3. Harris, *The Survivor*, 151–58; Witcover, *Party of the People*, 673.

4. Sidney Blumenthal, *The Clinton Wars* (New York: Plume, 2004), 146–48; Harris, *The Survivor*, 228–37; Witcover, *Party of the People*, 674–76.

5. Gormley, *The Death of American Virtue*, 236–37; Harris, *The Survivor*, 220–21; Michael Isikoff, *Uncovering Clinton: A Reporter's Story* (New York: Crown, 1999), 171; 757–68; William E. Leuchtenburg, *The American President: From Theodore Roosevelt to Bill Clinton* (Oxford and New York: Oxford University Press, 2015), 767–68.

6. Gormley, *The Death of American Virtue*, 237–38; Harris, *The Survivor*, 221–22; Jeffrey Toobin, *A Vast Conspiracy: The Real Story of the Sex Scandal That Nearly Brought Down a President* (New York: Random House, 1999), 85–86.

7. Gormley, *The Death of American Virtue*, 238–41; Isikoff, *Uncovering Clinton*, 171.

8. Leuchtenburg, *The American President*, 768–69; Toobin, *A Vast Conspiracy*, 111.

9. Leuchtenburg, *The American President*, 769.

10. Harris, *The Survivor*, 294; Isikoff, *Uncovering Clinton*, 212–13; Leuchtenburg, *The American President*, 769; Witcover, *Party of the People*, 686.

11. Gormley, *The Death of American Virtue*, 295–98; Harris, *The Survivor*, 293; Isikoff, *Uncovering Clinton*, 130–35; Leuchtenburg, *The American President*, 769.

12. Anita Gates and Katharine Q. Seelye, "Linda Tripp, Whose Secret Lewinsky Tape Led to Clinton, Is Dead at 70," *New York Times*, April 9, 2020, B11; Gormley, *The Death of American Virtue*, 298–300; Witcover, *Party of the People*, 686.

13. Harris, *The Survivor*, 293.

14. Gates and Seelye, "Linda Tripp," B11; Gormley, *The Death of American Virtue*, 301–3; Isikoff, *Uncovering Clinton*, 191–93.

15. Gormley, *The Death of American Virtue*, 115–17, 122–28, 183–84, 140; Harris, *The Survivor*, 288, 289, 291; Isikoff, *Uncovering Clinton*, 20–23, 82–118.

16. Harris, *The Survivor*, 298–300.

17. Toobin, *A Vast Conspiracy*, 70–75.

18. Gormley, *The Death of American Virtue*, 304–6, 307–8; Witcover, *Party of the People*, 686.

19. Gates and Seelye, "Linda Tripp," B11; Gormley, *The Death of American Virtue*, 292–94; Toobin, *A Vast Conspiracy*, 195–96.

20. Gormley, *The Death of American Virtue*, 330–34.

21. Gormley, *The Death of American Virtue*, 329–30; Leuchtenburg, *The American President*, 770.

22. Toobin, *A Vast Conspiracy*, 204–6.

23. Gormley, *The Death of American Virtue*, 369–71; Toobin, *A Vast Conspiracy*, 236–38.

24. Gormley, *The Death of American Virtue*, 362–74.

25. Gormley, *The Death of American Virtue*, 514–16, 520–22; Toobin, *A Vast Conspiracy*, 304.

26. Bill Clinton is quoted in Witcover, *Party of the People*, 685. See also Gormley, *The Death of American Virtue*, 417–18; Leuchtenburg, *The American President*, 771–72.

27. Hillary Clinton is quoted in Witcover, *Party of the People*, 685. See also Gormley, *The Death of American Virtue*, 418–19.

28. Gormley, *The Death of American Virtue*, 517–18; Isikoff, *Uncovering Clinton*, 221–24, 312, 324.

29. Gormley, *The Death of American Virtue*, 522–24.

30. Bill Clinton, *My Life* (New York: Knopf, 2004), 800. See also Hillary Rodham Clinton, *Living History* (New York: Simon & Schuster, 2003), 465–66; Gormley, *The Death of American Virtue*, 542–43.

31. Clinton, *My Life*, 801. See also Toobin, *A Vast Conspiracy*, 312–15; Witcover, *Party of the People*, 686–87.

32. Clinton is quoted in "Testimony Excerpts from the President," *Chicago Tribune*, September 22, 1998, n.p. See also Leuchtenburg, *The American President*, 774–75.

33. The quote is found in many sources. See, for example, Michael Takiff, *A Complicated Man: The Life of Bill Clinton as Told by Those Who Know Him* (New Haven, CT, and London: Yale University Press, 2010), v. See also Gormley, *The Death of American Virtue*, 344–52; Harris, *The Survivor*, 336–38.

34. Gormley, *The Death of American Virtue*, 548–50.

35. The quotes can be found in many sources. See, for example, Toobin, *A Vast Conspiracy*, 344. See also Gormley, *The Death of American Virtue*, 553; Harris, *The Survivor*, 339–41; Witcover, *Party of the People*, 687.

36. Clinton, *My Life*, 803. See also Clinton, *Living History*, 468; Leuchtenburg, *The American President*, 775.

37. Gormley, *The Death of American Virtue*, 553–54; Don Van Natta Jr. and Richard L. Berke, "Lewinsky Again Faces Jurors as Starr Seeks to Compare Accounts," *New York Times*, August 21, 1998, A1, A20.

38. Gormley, *The Death of American Virtue*, 558; Harris, *The Survivor*, 341–42; Witcover, *Party of the People*, 687.

39. Harris, *The Survivor*, 346–47; Witcover, *Party of the People*, 688.

40. Clinton, *Living History*, 475–76; Isikoff, *Uncovering Clinton*, 351–53; Leuchtenburg, *The American President*, 776.

41. Gormley, *The Death of American Virtue*, 587–88; Leuchtenburg, *The American President*, 779; Witcover, *Party of the People*, 689.

42. Gormley, *The Death of American Virtue*, 3–8.

43. Blumenthal, *The Clinton Wars*, 498–537; Gormley, *The Death of American Virtue*, 603–4; Harris, *The Survivor*, 353.

44. Blumenthal, *The Clinton Wars*, 537–43; Clinton, *My Life*, 834–38; Harris, *The Survivor*, 353.

45. The charge is quoted in Nancy E. Marion, *The Politics of Disgrace: The Role of Political Scandal in American Politics* (Durham, NC: Carolina Academic Press, 2010), 165. See also Clinton, *My Life*, 834; Witcover, *Party of the People*, 691.

46. The quote is found in Marion, *The Politics of Disgrace*, 165–66. See also Witcover, *Party of the People*, 691.

47. Toobin, *A Vast Conspiracy*, 369–70.

48. Graham is quoted in *Cong. Rec.*, 106th Cong., 1st Sess., 1999, Vol. 145, no. 7: S-290. Graham's views on impeachment evolved over time. Twenty years later, when a president from his own party was impeached, Graham, who had become a US senator, voted against impeachment, arguing against a broad interpretation of the constitutional requirement—a direct contradiction of his 1999 argument. See Gormley, *The Death of American Virtue*, 614–16, 625–29; Larry F. Murphy, *Trump and Congressional Republicans Must Go!* (Bloomington, IN: AuthorHouse, 2019), 18.

49. Toobin, *A Vast Conspiracy*, 333–34, 371.

50. Blumenthal, *The Clinton Wars*, 554–62, 587–98; Toobin, *A Vast Conspiracy*, 371–72.

51. Hyde is quoted in *The Impeachment and Trial of President Clinton: The Official Transcripts from the House Judiciary Committee Hearings to the Senate Trial* (New York: Times Books, 1999), 431. See also Gormley, *The Death of American Virtue*, 641–42.

52. Blumenthal, *The Clinton Wars*, 622–23; Clinton, *My Life*, 845; Gormley, *The Death of American Virtue*, 643–46; Harris, *The Survivor*, 356–57, 373; Isikoff, *Uncovering Clinton*, 354; Leuchtenburg, *The American President*, 784; Witcover, *Party of the People*, 694.

53. The exchange can be found in several sources. See, for example, Blumenthal, *The Clinton Wars*, 623; Witcover, *Party of the People*, 694.

54. Gormley, *The Death of American Virtue*, 559; "Drawn Out Impeachment Battle Dealt Its Meager Spoils to All Sides," *New York Times*, February 14, 1999, 1, 29; Witcover, *Party of the People*, 696–97.

55. Andrew Morton, *Monica's Story* (New York: St. Martin's Paperbacks, 1999). See also Michael D'Antonio, *Hunting Hillary: The Forty-Year Campaign to Destroy Hillary Clinton* (New York: Thomas Dunne Books, 2020), 290; Herbert N. Foerstel, *From Watergate to Monicagate: Ten Controversies in Modern Journalism and the Media* (Westport, CT: Greenwood Press, 2001), 124; Vanessa Grigoriadis, "Monica Takes Manhattan," *New York* (March 19, 2001), n.p.

56. This was the title of a memoir by Clinton adviser George Stephanopoulos. George Stephanopoulos, *All Too Human* (Back Bay Books, 2000). See also Gormley, *The Death of American Virtue*, 559; Leuchtenburg, *The American President*, 796–802.

CHAPTER 12

"Out of Respect for My Family, and Out of a Specific Request from the Levy Family, I Think It's Best That I Not Get Into Those Details"

Gary Condit and Chandra Levy

Congressman Gary Condit was a conservative "Blue Dog Democrat" from California when he became involved with a young intern thirty years his junior. Chandra Ann Levy, the intern, hailed from Condit's district. She met him in the fall of 2000, not long after she moved to Washington, DC, to pursue an internship with the US Bureau of Prisons. A student in the Master of Public Administration (MPA) program at the University of Southern California (USC), Levy was 23 years old when she stepped into the married congressman's office. Within a few weeks they became lovers.

The congressman might have kept the affair secret, but Levy disappeared seemingly without a trace on May 1, 2001, as she prepared to return to California for her USC graduation. Frantic, her parents contacted the police to report a missing person. Investigators discovered that she had not taken her phone, computer, clothes, or personal effects with her. It was unlikely that she had disappeared of her own free will. As they examined her electronic devices, they discovered one number that she had called repeatedly. Police officers dialed the number and found that it belonged to Congressman Gary Condit.

When he was questioned about his relationship with Levy, Condit admitted that he knew her, but he denied that they were anything more than friends. It was a lie. Family members told police that the congressman had been meeting with her in secret, and that Chandra Levy was in love. Forced to admit that he had lied, Condit soon found himself engulfed in a scandal that generated headlines across the country and around the world. If he had lied about the relationship, he might have lied about other things. Perhaps he knew who had taken Chandra Levy. Perhaps he had kidnapped and/or killed her. With no clues about what had happened, who could say?

The months rolled by, and no one knew where Levy had gone. Finally, police identified her remains after a man walking his dog on May 22, 2002, made a grisly discovery in Rock Creek Park, less than four miles from her home. Although Condit was never formally a suspect in Levy's death, his acknowledgment of the affair after she had disappeared effectively destroyed his political career. An illegal immigrant who was arrested, tried, and convicted of her murder later won a retrial. Prosecutors chose not to pursue a second trial after evidence indicated that the man was not guilty. As of this writing, no one else has been charged with the young woman's murder.[1]

In reconstructing Chandra Levy's life to determine if they could find out what happened, investigators learned few details from the congressman. Levy's family members provided more assistance. Her introduction to Washington, DC, was so ordinary and commonplace that it bordered on the cliché. She arrived in the fall of 2000, excited at the prospect of interning at the Bureau of Prisons. Like many young people, she found her proximity to the corridors of power intoxicating. She was not at the top of the echelon, to be sure—interns in the White House or in one of the high-profile agencies could claim to be closer to the centers of authority—but it was close enough to suit her.

One day in October 2000, she and a friend from USC, Jennifer Baker, marched up to Capitol Hill. To earn an MPA degree, a student needed to complete an internship. Although Levy had already snagged a position, Baker had not. The plan was to make the rounds and see if they could find an internship for Baker. The logical place to start was in the offices of the California senators and congressmen who represented them.

Normally, a low-level staffer meets with constituents who drop in at a representative's office. Sometimes the staffer can provide tickets to upcoming events at the Kennedy Center or offer access to the gallery when the House of Representatives or the Senate is in session. On this day, however, Congressman Gary Condit was in the office. He stepped out to greet the two fresh-faced, excited young women.

If Condit had left it at that, the meeting would have been the standard, run-of-the-mill five-minute encounter between a congressman and two constituents. Yet he took time to escort the young ladies around the building, even showing them the House chamber. When Jennifer Baker mentioned that she needed an internship, Condit immediately offered her a job. He also agreed to pose for a photograph, a common occurrence. Members of Congress enjoy meeting with constituents. Photographs for the folks back home encourage voters to remember their elected official at election time.[2]

Baker was happy to find a job on Capitol Hill, but that was the extent of her reaction. Chandra Levy, however, felt something different. She thought that Congressman Condit was charming and handsome. In her view he resembled the actor Harrison Ford, one of her favorite Hollywood celebrities. A few days later, after she had stopped in at the office to see how Baker's internship was working out, Levy again encountered Congressman Condit. They spoke briefly before exchanging phone numbers and email addresses.

Several days later the smitten young intern called the congressman. They exchanged small talk and Condit offered career advice. At the end of the call, Condit gave Levy his private phone number. Their relationship, such as it was, might have ended there.

Shortly before Thanksgiving, however, they took the next step. Levy called Condit and he invited her to his condominium in the posh Adams Morgan neighborhood of Washington, DC. Condit's wife mostly stayed at their home in California while the congressman lived alone in his chic fourth-floor apartment overlooking Rock Creek Park. She accepted the invitation and they fell into bed together.[3]

It became more than a one-night stand as the couple settled into a routine. Levy spent the night with Condit two or three nights a week. The Bill Clinton–Monica Lewinsky affair was still fresh in everyone's mind, and Condit knew he was running an enormous risk. If anyone found out about the affair, his career would be over. To avoid publicity, Levy rode the train from her apartment to the Woodley Park–Zoo metro station. From there, she walked to Condit's condominium. She told no one of her plans, and she slipped into his condo with a ball cap pulled low over her face, creeping in as quietly and surreptitiously as possible.

Condit and Levy did not go out in public. Instead, they ordered take-out food and cuddled up to watch movies on HBO. Condit continually admonished his young lover to tell no one of the affair, and she mostly complied. When Jennifer Baker repeatedly asked her friend to go out on the town, Levy invented excuses. She eventually said that she was dating an FBI agent.[4]

Chandra Levy confided in only one person, her aunt Linda Zamsky. Whether Gary Condit loved her remains a mystery, but Levy certainly loved him. She told her aunt how much she cared for "her man," the Harrison Ford look-alike who had changed her life. Condit had promised to leave his wife and make a new life with Chandra. The young lady knew the promises might be false, and she knew that she could get hurt, but it was a risk she was willing to take. She swore her aunt to secrecy, and Zamsky agreed. She honored her promise until her niece disappeared under suspicious circumstances.[5]

The affair continued for approximately five months. In April 2001 Chandra Levy learned that her internship was ending earlier than she had expected. With graduation day approaching, she decided to return to California to attend her USC commencement ceremony. Ideally, she would return to Washington afterward, diploma in hand, to find a permanent job and continue her relationship with Gary Condit. She last spoke to him on April 29, when she told him of her plans.[6]

After Condit did not hear from her for a few days, he called and left two messages on her answering machine. He said she should call him when she arrived in California. He never heard from her again. On May 6 her father, Robert Levy, called to say that Chandra was missing and to ask if the congressman had heard anything from her. It was unnerving to receive a call from his young girlfriend's father. Even more unnerving was the next call he received. A detective from the Washington Metropolitan Police Department had a few questions about the missing intern.

Reconstructing her steps, investigators found that Chandra had emailed her landlord on April 28 to say that she would vacate her apartment on May 5 or 6. On May 1 she signed on to her computer and searched for flights home. She also searched hiking trails in Rock Creek Park. She signed off at 12:24 p.m. and disappeared into thin air.[7]

By May 6, when no one had heard from Chandra Levy in days, her father called the Washington police. The department dispatched an officer to her apartment. The manager opened the door and let him inside. Nothing seemed out of place except that her wallet was still there. He also found two open suitcases, but there was no sign of Chandra Levy.

Robert Levy called the Bureau of Prisons, where his daughter had been working, but no one had seen her since the internship had ended. Desperate for information, he called Washington-area hospitals, but no patients answering her description had been admitted. The Levy family normally paid Chandra's cell phone bills. Anxious to find her, they thought they could uncover clues in her phone records. Robert and his wife, Susan, divided up the list of callers and combed through the frequently called numbers.[8]

When Susan Levy called a frequently dialed number and reached an answering machine for Congressman Gary Condit, she felt sick to her stomach. Her husband was unaware of a deeply disturbing incident that had occurred three weeks earlier. Susan Levy had been talking with Otis Thomas, a Pentecostal minister who operated a groundskeeping business. As Thomas was working in her yard, Susan Levy struck up a conversation. She and Thomas traded information about their children. When Susan mentioned that her daughter had made friends with a congressman, Thomas told her a troubling story. Seven years earlier, Thomas said, his 18-year-old daughter had dated Congressman Gary Condit. At Thomas's insistence, his daughter broke off the relationship. Thomas wondered if Condit was Chandra Levy's "friend." If so, Thomas said, she should intervene.

Susan Levy did exactly that. After that conversation she marched inside, picked up the phone, and called her daughter. As soon as Chandra answered, her mother blurted out her suspicions. "Are you involved in a relationship with Gary Condit?"

Chandra was stunned. "How did you know?"

With her worst suspicions confirmed, Susan Levy told her daughter about the conversation with Otis Thomas. "Chandra," she pleaded, "I'm concerned for your safety."

Chandra told her mother not to be concerned. As a grown woman, she insisted that she could decide for herself who she would date. She also implored her mother to keep the relationship a secret. Against her better judgment, Susan Levy agreed to do so.

"Be careful," she said as she and Chandra ended the call. "You could get hurt."

Susan Levy remained true to her word. She did not tell her husband, or anyone, about her daughter's affair with the congressman. She remained deeply troubled, though.

The next time she saw Chandra, about a week later, on April 14, 2001, her daughter mentioned Otis Thomas's comments. Chandra said that she had discussed the matter with Condit, and he "explained it all." How the congressman had explained the earlier affair was unclear.

Now, two weeks after she had last seen her daughter, Susan Levy wondered what Condit had said to explain his behavior. She also wondered if Condit had been angry at having to explain himself or fearful that Chandra might reveal the affair. Could he have hurt or killed her to keep her quiet?

Desperate times call for desperate measures. Burdened with the secret as well as her daughter's unexplained disappearance, Susan Levy realized she could no longer remain silent. She told her husband about the affair and the troubling phone conversation with Chandra in April.

Having learned of his daughter's affair with the much older congressman, Robert Levy shared his wife's concern. He found a phone book, looked up Condit's home number, and dialed the man's residence. The congressman was not home, but his wife, Carolyn, answered. Robert Levy said that he needed Condit's help to find his missing daughter. Carolyn said she would pass along the message.

Condit called shortly thereafter. "Do you know my daughter?" Robert Levy asked. His voice trembled. "Where is she? Do you know where she went?"

Condit assured the frantic father that he did not know where Chandra was. He said he knew her in passing, and that he had given her career advice. He promised to call the police and urge them to continue their investigation.

Robert Levy was upset with Condit's lie, but Susan Levy was incensed. She knew that her daughter and Condit were involved in an intimate relationship. If he would lie about the affair, he probably would lie about other things, too, such as what had happened to Chandra.[9]

As for Gary Condit, he had carefully crafted a secret life over many years. Chandra Levy was not his first affair with a much younger woman. Whenever he took a lover, he instituted clear ground rules. No one must know. They must meet far away from prying eyes. Nothing must interfere with his political career, for Gary Condit's star was ascending. He was a man who might have a truly stellar career as a Washington mover and shaker—provided that his private life remained private. With the young intern's disappearance, his career was jeopardized.[10]

On the day that Gary Condit spoke with Robert Levy in early May 2001, the congressman's career was on an upswing. He could cite his rise through the ranks as an American rags-to-riches story, the sort of narrative that all elected officials love to tout. He was born in Salina, Oklahoma, on April 21, 1948, the son of a Baptist minister. Growing up in the Sooner State, Condit attended high school in Tulsa. He worked for several summers as a roustabout in the Oklahoma oil fields.

At age 18, on January 18, 1967, he married his high school sweetheart, Carolyn Berry. Even at that young age, he had discovered the advantages of lying. Under Oklahoma law, males under 21 needed parental consent to marry. Condit simply supplied an inaccurate birth date to avoid an inconvenient legal requirement. Their son, Chad, was born the summer after he and Carolyn married. A daughter, Cadee, followed.

Condit's father headed to Ceres, California, to become the pastor of a Baptist church there. Gary and his wife followed him. The small town was not far from Modesto, a prominent agricultural city known for its vineyards. Gary Condit attended California State University at Stanislaus, thirteen miles away, during the day. At night he worked for Norris Industries, a munitions factory. He earned a bachelor of science degree in 1972.

As a college senior, he decided to run for the Ceres city council. He was charming, handsome, and charismatic. People who saw him campaigning believed that he had a way with words. His conservative philosophy of less government and lower taxes reflected the core beliefs of most people in Ceres. At the age of 24, he won the election, much to everyone's surprise, including his own. Two years later the voters elected him mayor.

Condit's career kept advancing as his political skills grew. He served on the Stanislaus County Board of Supervisors before winning election to the California State Assembly in 1982. There he joined a group of conservatives known as the "Gang of Five" in a politically liberal state. The gang resolved to oust the longtime assembly speaker, Willie Brown, a legend in California politics. Brown was gracious and well-mannered in public—and his dapper suits, flamboyant hats, and colorful silk pocket handkerchiefs made him a hard-to-miss showman during his public appearances—but behind the scenes, the speaker was an old-school politician who held a grudge. When the Gang of Five failed to secure the requisite votes to defeat Brown, the speaker stripped all of them, including Condit, of their committee chairmanships. The move hobbled Condit's career in state politics, but it made him a conservative hero back home among his like-minded constituents.

Condit feared that he had destroyed his political career, but an unexpected opportunity arose in 1989. House Majority Whip Tony Coelho, the third-highest-ranking member of the House of Representatives, was the congressman representing Condit's district. Coelho had invested $100,000 in high-yield junk bonds through a firm, Drexel Burnham Lambert, that provided him with a sweetheart deal. When the deal became public, a firestorm erupted. The House was prepared to launch a lengthy, detailed ethics investigation. To avoid a protracted scandal, Coelho resigned from Congress. The vacancy created an opportunity for Condit to move from Sacramento, where he had gone as far as he could in the wake of the Willie Brown imbroglio, to Washington, DC, where the slate was clean.

As a high-profile conservative Democrat, Condit threw his hat into the ring in a special election for Coelho's seat. He won. Departing for Washington in 1989, Condit vowed to wow his constituents and learn the lessons from his dustup with Speaker Brown. In the House, Condit quietly learned his place and played the game, never taking on the leadership. At home he courted his constituents, sending them cards and flowers on special occasions such as graduations, marriages, birth announcements, and funerals. He flew home often to meet voters. He was lean, fit, charismatic, attentive, and down-to-earth. When he met the men and women of his district, he insisted that they call him "Gary." He became the epitome of the open, honest, roll-up-your-sleeves-and-get-it-done elected official who cares about the folks back home. He was a kinder, gentler Marlboro man, a rugged individualist who never forgot his roots and who was uncorrupted by Washington.

He may have been a good Democrat, but he was not a liberal, or even a progressive. At his core, Gary Condit was a conservative, completely in line with his district. When Bill Clinton became president in 1993, Condit frequently voted against his party's standard bearer. The California congressman eventually joined the coalition of Blue Dog Democrats, who argued for lower taxes and less intrusive government. He was not a Republican—Condit still believed that some social welfare programs were valuable—but he championed fiscal responsibility and tighter controls over federal spending than liberals in his party supported. His ability to straddle the line between dyed-in-the-wool Democrats and reactionary Republicans ensured that he would win his reelection bids in 1990, 1992, 1994, 1996, 1998, and 2000. He did not face even a token Republican challenger during the general election in 1992 and 1998.

In keeping with his conservative persona, and perhaps to boost his right-leaning bona fides, Condit became known as a "pro-family" politician. When news of President Clinton's affair with a young White House intern, Monica Lewinsky, broke, Condit was among the critics who urged the president to "come clean" about the relationship. Considering the adage about people living in glass houses not throwing stones, the congressman might have assumed a less public role during the Clinton debacle.

Because Carolyn Condit lived back in California, her husband's life in Washington, DC, allowed him to enjoy his privacy during most evenings. He occasionally attended official receptions and dinners, but otherwise he was free to pursue his personal interests. Condit's personal interests involved other women. Once upon a time, he had romanced another intern, Otis Thomas's daughter, Jennifer, and more recently a 39-year-old flight attendant named Anne Marie Smith. For a man who touted his family values, Condit's willingness to engage in reckless sexual behavior was remarkably hypocritical, even by Washington standards.[11]

As unnerving as Robert Levy's call was for the seemingly strait-laced congressman, he was especially perturbed when a District of Columbia missing persons detective, Ralph Durant, called to inquire about the vanished intern. Condit repeated the same story he had given Chandra's father. Durant arranged to meet with Condit on May 9 at the latter's Adams Morgan condominium to take a formal statement.

Durant and a police sergeant, Ronald Wyatt, arrived at the condominium at 9:55 p.m. on May 9. Condit welcomed them into his home and repeated his original story. He added that Chandra had not appeared nervous or upset when they had last spoken. After he explained how he had met Chandra and hired her friend, Jennifer Baker, the two investigators pushed for more details. It was clear that the congressman had not been completely forthcoming. Durant had spoken to Levy's aunt Linda Zamsky before the May 9 appointment, so he knew more than he initially revealed.

When Condit finally admitted that Chandra Levy had spent the night at his condominium on numerous occasions, Sergeant Wyatt's patience was almost exhausted. "Did you have an intimate relationship with Ms. Levy?" he asked. The officers wanted to see how Condit answered the question.

The congressman knew that his secret was out, but he remained reluctant to speak about the matter. "I don't think we need to go there," he said, "and you can infer what you want with that." Durant and Wyatt understood the inference. They also knew that it was only a matter of time before the press got wind of a scandal. Gary Condit's privacy would soon be a thing of the past.[12]

The first news story, buried in the back of the Metro section of the *Washington Post* on May 11, 2001, mentioned the missing woman and asked for tips, but it refrained from discussing Congressman Condit. A second story, published on May 16, referred to Condit and contained a quote from him expressing his hope that Chandra, "a great person and a good friend," would be found safe and sound. The affair was not mentioned.[13]

Unfortunately for Condit, reporters were working their police sources, and by May 16 they believed that the congressman had been involved in a sexual relationship with the missing intern. In response to a flood of media inquiries, Condit's chief of staff in Modesto, California, Michael Lynch, told reporters from the *Washington Post* that the notion of an affair was preposterous. "Totally did not occur," he said without hesitation or equivocation. "It's really distressing that a lot of people are focusing on that issue when the focus should be on finding where Chandra is."[14]

It was too late to stem the tide. Suddenly, Gary Condit, who had not been a household name, was linked to Chandra Levy, the missing intern. Whether he had been responsible for her disappearance to cover up an affair was the subject of intense speculation. The police never formally charged him as a suspect, but their investigation became almost beside the point. The media could not resist the story of the playboy congressman who claimed to be a family values man, but who had carried on multiple affairs during his time in Washington. The tape of Condit urging Bill Clinton to come clean about Monica Lewinsky surfaced, and reporters loved the juicy irony of hoisting another two-faced politician on his own petard. Chandra's parents were convinced that Gary Condit had done something to their daughter, or, at the very least, he knew more than he was saying about her whereabouts.[15]

Finding Chandra was the priority, but the police made innumerable mistakes in their investigation. The missteps undoubtedly complicated the task. Sergeant Wyatt searched the laptop in Chandra's apartment, but he was not trained in computer forensics, and he corrupted the data. Moreover, neither he nor Detective Durant checked the surveillance cameras in Chandra Levy's apartment building to see when she left and if she left alone. The videotapes were erased every seven days. By the time anyone thought to review them, the footage from May 1 was gone.[16]

In the meantime Gary Condit's life was consumed by the growing scandal. News media followed him everywhere he went, frequently calling out "where's Chandra?" The congressman tried to go about his business, but night after night lurid tales of the missing intern and her powerful lover dominated the headlines. Robert and Susan Levy ratcheted up the pressure when they went on television on June 14, 2001, begging Condit to reveal what he knew. They were convinced that Condit had had an affair with their daughter and that he knew where she had gone.[17]

Realizing that the relentless negative publicity was not his worst problem, Condit hired a lawyer to defend him. Abbe Lowell was a prominent defense attorney who specialized in representing powerful clients who had fallen from grace. His list of clients reads like a who's who of infamous political figures charged with corruption and self-dealing: Bob Menendez, John Edwards, Jared Kushner, Jim Wright, Dan Rostenkowski, Charles Keating, Joseph McDade, Joe Bruno, and Jim Gibbons. Condit feared that police investigators were focusing exclusively on him and not pursuing other leads that might eventually lead them to Chandra Levy and end the nightmare for everyone involved.[18]

Lowell navigated his client through a series of grueling meetings. First, they met with Chandra's mother, Susan Levy, and Condit told her emphatically that he did not know what had happened to her daughter. Lowell and Condit also met several times with police detectives to try and satisfy their seemingly insatiable desire for more information about Condit's relationship with Levy. By this time, a flight attendant, Anne Marie Smith, had come forward with details about her sexual relationship with Condit. The airwaves were inundated with speculation about Condit's multiple affairs.[19]

Lowell and Condit eventually convinced the police that they had the wrong man. Condit had not killed Chandra Levy, and he did not know where she was. Avoiding prosecution was a major victory for the embattled congressman, but it did nothing for his reputation, which was in tatters. He and Lowell decided that he should launch a public relations offensive to rehabilitate his media image and possibly resuscitate his political career.[20]

Connie Chung, a correspondent for ABC Television's *Primetime Live*, was one of many media personalities anxious to land an exclusive interview with Gary Condit. The congressman selected her because he thought that a woman interviewer might be a bit softer in her questioning than some of the male anchors known for roughing up their subjects. He sat down with her for an on-camera interview on August 23, 2001. He soon learned the error of his ways.

Chung opened with blunt questions that got to the heart of the matter. "Congressman Condit," she asked, "do you know what happened to Chandra Levy?"

"No, I do not," he said.

"Did you have anything to do with her disappearance?"

"No, I didn't."

"Did you say anything or do anything that could have caused her to drop out of sight?"

"You know, Chandra and I never had a cross word."

When she asked whether their relationship was sexual, Condit gave her an evasive answer that satisfied no one. He repeated it almost verbatim several times throughout the interview. "Well, Connie, I've been married for 34 years, and uh, I've not been a . . . a perfect man, and I've made my share of mistakes. But um, out of respect for my family, and out of a specific request from the Levy family, I think it's best that I not get into those details uh, about Chandra Levy."

If Condit had expected Connie Chung to treat him with kid gloves, he was sorely disappointed. She grilled him like a veteran prosecutor trying to pin a mafia don. Why had he thrown away a wristwatch box shortly before the police searched his condominium? Was Chandra Levy pregnant? What was his relationship with Anne Marie Smith, the flight attendant who publicly acknowledged an affair with the married congressman? Why wouldn't he submit to a police polygraph? On and on it went for thirty-one agonizing minutes.

The interview was an unequivocal victory for Connie Chung and ABC. The ratings went through the roof. The interview was the most watched television program of the summer of 2001. It was the biggest television audience for an interview since Barbara Walters had interviewed Bill Clinton's lover, Monica Lewinsky.

For Gary Condit the interview was an unmitigated disaster. He had harbored misgivings about the public relations offensive from the outset, worrying that by taking to the airwaves, he was only prolonging the story—giving it "legs," as journalists call it. He had finally relented because he wanted to do something proactive to stop the ceaseless television coverage. Yet the interview had the opposite effect from what he had intended. Rather than demonstrating his openness and his willingness to cooperate with investigators, Condit appeared evasive and shifty. He seemed to be hiding something. By repeating his mantra about not being a perfect man and "out of respect for my family, and out of a specific request from the Levy family, I think it's best that I not get into those details," he seemed robotic and unconcerned about the disappearance of this young lady. He probably would not have been reelected to Congress even before the interview aired, but afterward it was a foregone conclusion that Gary Condit's congressional career was all but over.[21]

Watching the interview on television, the Levys were outraged. Condit kept insisting that he would not answer questions "out of a specific request from the Levy family," but they had made no such request. Once again he was lying. More than ever, Robert and Susan Levy believed that the congressman knew more than he was saying about their daughter's disappearance. They were frustrated that no one could break through the facade and find out what he knew.[22]

Nineteen days after the Connie Chung interview, the ongoing Chandra Levy media saga abruptly ended. The television trucks that had been parked outside of Gary Condit's condominium swiftly packed up and raced away from the premises. Susan Levy had planned to fly to Chicago to appear on the popular *Oprah* television program, followed by a trip to New York for an appearance on the *Today* show, but she did not go to the airport. The terrorist attacks in New York and Washington, DC, on September 11, 2001, changed the world forever. As the media focused on wall-to-wall coverage of the worst terrorist attacks in American history, the story of a missing intern and her congressman lover quickly became yesterday's news.[23]

It wasn't yesterday's news to Gary Condit. He still hoped to salvage his career in Congress. On December 7, 2001, he announced that he would seek reelection. He knew he faced an uphill battle, but Condit believed that he should be judged on his entire record representing his constituents in the House, not on the Levy scandal.

He faced a former aide, Dennis Cardoza, then serving as a California assemblyman, in the Democratic primary in March 2002. Condit was bitter because he had helped Cardoza earlier in his career, and now a former friend and subordinate was challenging him for the congressional seat. He was right to be worried. When the votes came in, Condit lost with 37.5 percent of the vote to Cardoza's 55.3 percent. Gary Condit's public service career had ended. He tried to be sanguine about it. "Things happen in life that you can't explain," he mused. "Whatever happens, happens. I'll do something else."[24]

Of course, Chandra Levy's disappearance also wasn't yesterday's news to Robert and Susan Levy. They were desperate for information on their daughter. Even as stories faded from the headlines, they pushed authorities to continue the search. Police had combed through sections of Rock Creek Park, but it was a lot of ground to cover. The area was twice the size of New York's Central Park. Repeated searches found no sign of her.

It wasn't until a 42-year-old furniture maker, Philip Palmer, was walking his dog near the Western Ridge Trail in Rock Creek Park on May 22, 2002, that the authorities found out where Chandra Levy was. Palmer came upon upon a decomposed body and immediately alerted the police. It was a trail that had been searched, but this area off the trail was well hidden.[25]

As soon as police determined that the bones were human, word circulated around Washington. The news media descended on the scene. They asked the question that everyone who heard the story pondered: Had Chandra Levy been found? Jonathan L. Arden, the DC medical examiner, examined the skull and compared its teeth to Chandra Levy's dental records, which the family had supplied the previous year. It did not take long to reach his grisly conclusion. Chandra Levy had been found. This was her body. Arden concluded that she died from a homicide, but the cause was undetermined. "There's less to work with here than I would like," he said. "It's possible we will never know the specific injury that caused her death."[26]

The case had been dormant for months, but now it suddenly reappeared in the headlines. Every detail, no matter how minute, was grist for the mill. The bones had been scattered around the site, which suggested that animals had gotten to them, although some observers wondered if the location and condition of the remains were related to how she died. A minor scandal occurred after private investigators hired by the Levy family scoured the crime scene and discovered Chandra's shin bone about twenty-five yards away from the other remains. Greatly embarrassed, Police Chief Charles H.

Figure 12.1. Congressman Gary Condit (left), pictured here with his son, Chad, addresses reporters in 2002. He was a suspect in the disappearance of intern Chandra Levy, although he insisted that he knew nothing about it. Courtesy of Zuma Press, Inc./Alamy Stock Photo.

Ramsey admitted that his team should have found the shin bone and other remains.[27]

DC police investigators felt enormous pressure to solve the homicide case, but they had few clues. The body was so badly decomposed that determining a cause of death or finding physical evidence was impossible. If a stranger had come out of the woods and attacked Chandra while she was walking or jogging, any evidence of that encounter was long gone after exposure to the elements for a year. Despite the investigators' best efforts, the search for a killer was stalled.

Eight months earlier a lawyer for Ramón Alvarez, an inmate in the DC jail, had called the US attorney in Washington to tell an interesting story. The lawyer said that Alvarez had spoken with another inmate, 20-year-old El Salvador native Ingmar Adalid Guandique, and the inmate claimed to have killed Chandra Levy. According to Alvarez, Guandique said that Gary Condit had paid him $25,000 to murder the young woman. Guandique had ambushed Levy while she was jogging on a path in Rock Creek Park. After stabbing her in the neck and stomach with a knife, Guandique supposedly dug out a small hole in the woods and buried her body under leaves and tree branches.

The story sounded farfetched, especially the tale about Condit's involvement. Police had combed through the congressman's life with a fine-tooth comb. They had found no suspicious financial transactions suggesting that Condit had accessed a large amount of cash. Nonetheless, with few credible tips to guide their investigation, detectives met with Guandique and showed him a photograph of Chandra Levy. He denied having ever seen her other than in news reports on television.

Information provided by jailhouse snitches is notoriously unreliable. Alvarez might have lied, or perhaps Guandique had said something after all. Either Guandique or Alvarez possibly embellished the tale. On November 28, 2001, police administered a polygraph to Alvarez. He failed. Guandique sat for his polygraph on February 4, 2002. The examiner rated the results as inconclusive, although in his opinion Guandique was "not deceptive." Alvarez and Guandique spoke little English, and the examiners were not bilingual, which further complicated the results.[28]

Guandique's record suggested that he might have attacked and killed Chandra Levy. He had been implicated in assaults on two other women in Rock Creek Park. On May 14, 2001, a strange man wielding a knife had attacked 30-year-old journalist Halle Shilling as she jogged in the park. After a brief physical altercation, she escaped and alerted the US Park Police. The man disappeared before the police could find him.[29]

Six week later, on July 1, 2001, a man matching the same description as the attacker in the Shilling case—a Hispanic man wearing baggy pants, a T-shirt, and sneakers—attacked another jogger, 25-year-old Christy Wiegand, who was running with her fiancé in Rock Creek Park. As the couple became separated, a man came out of the brush with a knife and forced Wiegand into a ravine. She fought him off, flagged down a passing motorist, and they located her fiancé. This time, however, when the Park Police received the report, they found the man and took him into custody. He was Ingmar Guandique.

Faced with strong evidence against him in the Shilling and Wiegand cases, Guandique agreed to plead guilty. He may have been involved in two other assaults on women as well, but those cases were not before the court. Based on the defendant's guilty plea, Judge Noel Anketell Kramer sentenced him to serve ten years in prison.[30]

Shortly before the sentencing, US attorney Kristen Ament informed the judge about Guandique's possible involvement in the Levy disappearance. Prosecutors told Judge Kramer that Guandique had cooperated in the Levy case, and had even consented to take a polygraph test, which he passed. Based on the record, the judge concluded that "this is such a satellite issue. To me it doesn't have anything to do with this case." Consequently, Chandra Levy's disappearance did not factor into the judge's sentence.

Ingmar Guandique headed off to prison. Authorities transferred him from facility to facility as he caused trouble with fellow inmates and prison guards. He started serving time in the Rivers Correctional Institution in Winton, North Carolina, before heading to the United States Penitentiary near Inez, Kentucky, and eventually the Victorville Federal Correctional Institution in California. He remained safely tucked away, all but forgotten until the dog walker discovered Chandra Levy's remains in May 2002. The breaking story that the missing intern had been found in Rock Creek Park, not terribly far from where similar attacks on women had occurred, renewed interest in this strange Hispanic immigrant with a penchant for wielding a knife and prowling that area.[31]

Even with the heightened interest in the case, investigators did not aggressively follow up with Guandique. A year after they found Chandra's bones, the police released her remains to her family. The Levys held a private graveside service for her on May 27, 2003. Again, the case triggered headlines briefly, but the world—and the ever fickle news cycle—moved on. It might have become just another unsolved homicide but for several events that occurred beginning in 2006.[32]

First, an inmate named Armando Morales had shared a cell with Guandique, and Morales claimed that his roommate confessed to murdering Chandra Levy. This was the second time that an inmate had snitched on Guandique. The information was surprisingly detailed and believable.[33]

Another factor was a change in police personnel. Chief Ramsey had moved on to the Philadelphia police force. His successor, Cathy L. Lanier, believed that it was time to revisit the case. She met with Susan Levy in 2007 and pledged to reexamine the evidence with new detectives at the helm and a fresh perspective on the case. Chief Lanier assigned three experienced homicide investigators to take the lead.[34]

The third occurrence involved reporters at the *Washington Post*. A new team of reporters began to examine the original police investigation. In a series of long newspaper articles that ran in the *Post* beginning on Sunday, July 13, 2008, the reporters outlined numerous police errors. Some mistakes, such as failing to secure surveillance videotapes in Chandra Levy's apartment building and corrupting her computer files, were already known, but other errors had only recently been discovered. The error that garnered the most attention was the failure to investigate Ingmar Guandique's connection to Chandra Levy or to interview the two women he confessed to attacking in Rock Creek Park.[35]

The new detectives—Kenneth Williams, Anthony Brigidini, and Emilio Martinez—dug into the case and planned to re-interview key witnesses. On September 8, 2008, they met with Guandique. Martinez spoke Spanish, so he translated the conversation. Although Guandique never confessed, he made several incriminating statements. While he spoke with the detectives, prison authorities searched his cell and discovered a picture of Chandra he had ripped from a magazine. They also learned that Guandique had confessed to several people, including Armando Morales, that he had killed Levy. Although there was no smoking gun, so to speak, investigators believed they had built a strong case based on circumstantial evidence.[36]

On March 3, 2009, the District of Columbia Superior Court issued an arrest warrant for Ingmar Guandique. He remained incarcerated in the Victorville facility in California, and so authorities knew where to find him. After he was transferred back into the custody of the DC Department of Corrections, Guandique was indicted by a grand jury on six counts: kidnapping, first-degree murder committed during a kidnapping, attempted first-degree sexual abuse, first-degree murder committed during a sexual offense, attempted robbery, and first-degree murder committed during a robbery. He pleaded not guilty.[37]

The trial commenced on October 4, 2010. Halle Shilling and Christy Wiegand testified about their terrifying experiences with Guandique, and prosecutors noted the similarities in circumstances and locations between those attacks and the Chandra Levy attack. Coupled with Armando Morales's testimony, it was a persuasive case. The trial lasted a month. On November 22, 2010, the jury convicted Guandique of first-degree murder. On February 11, 2011, Judge Gerald Fisher sentenced him to sixty years in prison.[38]

"Today's verdict sends a message that it's never too late for justice to be served," said Ronald C. Machen Jr., US attorney for the District of Columbia. Susan Levy was relieved that her daughter's killer had been tried, convicted, and sentenced to a lengthy prison term. Still, it did not represent closure. "The result of this verdict may be guilty," she said, "but I have a life sentence of a lost limb missing from our family tree."[39]

That should have been the end of the matter. Ingmar Guandique was a bad actor, an illegal immigrant with a history of attacking women. He had repeatedly flouted the rules in prison. He appeared to be a member of M-13, a notorious criminal gang of brutal Salvadoran immigrants. Police and prosecutors were confident that they had convicted the correct defendant. The Levy case had already had its share of twists and turns, but it seemed to be over.

It was not over. Defense attorneys had always argued that the informant, Armando Morales, was unreliable. In their view he had fabricated the information about the defendant to curry favor with prosecutors. That suggestion was borne out by a series of events that came to light years after Guandique's conviction.

In May 2015 defense attorneys succeeded in convincing Judge Fisher that the defendant deserved a new trial. After much back and forth between prosecutors and defense attorneys, the date was set for October 11, 2016. As in the first case, the verdict would depend largely on Morales's credibility.[40]

The retrial was in trouble almost from the beginning. Prosecutors are required by law to reveal possibly exculpatory evidence to the defense, but they had not done so during Guandique's first trial. When the defense attorneys learned of this failure, they filed motions to dismiss the case.

Even more troubling for the prosecution was new information about Armando Morales's veracity. During a seemingly routine pretrial hearing on July 21, 2016, a prosecutor divulged that a part-time actress named Babs Proller had contacted his office and said that she had information about Morales concerning the Levy case. According to Proller, she had become acquainted with Morales, who had been released from prison and was living in Maryland, on July 6 of that year. During their discussions Morales threatened Proller's ex-husband. Fearful of what might happen, Proller tape-recorded their conversation. Morales admitted on tape that he had lied about Guandique's confession to improve his standing with prosecutors and secure an earlier release from prison.

Proller contacted Susan Levy and told her about the recording. Levy told Proller to contact prosecutors, but she declined to listen to the recordings. "I can't believe we are going through this all over again," Susan Levy later remarked.[41]

After hearing the recording, prosecutors conceded that their case against Ingmar Guandique had collapsed. Morales had no credibility whatsoever. Without his testimony, the case against Guandique could not proceed.

On July 28, 2016, the US Attorney's office in Washington, DC, issued a brief statement: "Today, in the interests of justice and based on recent unforeseen developments that were investigated over the past week, the office moved to dismiss the case charging Ingmar Guandique with the May 2001 murder of Chandra Levy. The office has concluded that it can no longer prove the murder case against Mr. Guandique beyond a reasonable doubt."[42]

Even without the conviction for Chandra Levy's murder hanging over his head, Guandique was not a free man. He had illegally entered the United States, and he had committed other crimes while in the country. Prosecutors turned him over to US Immigration and Customs Enforcement (ICE). After exhausting his hearings and appeals, Guandique could not remain in the United States. On May 5, 2017, ICE deported him to El Salvador.[43]

Robert Levy, among others, was outraged by the prosecutors' decision to dismiss the case. He was adamant that Guandique had murdered his daughter. "Who is this woman?" he asked during a telephone interview, referring to Babs Proller. "What is her motivation for doing this? Maybe she tricked him into saying these things." Of course, a distraught family member is seldom a good judge of guilt or innocence in a murder trial. Robert Levy had once been just as adamant that Gary Condit had killed his daughter.[44]

As for Condit, after he lost his reelection bid for his congressional seat, he moved to Arizona and faded from the public spotlight. He operated two Baskin-Robbins ice cream stores with his wife and son until he became embroiled in a franchise dispute with the company. Later, he lost his breach-of-contract lawsuit. Searching for employment, Condit registered as a lobbyist with the state of California.[45]

He filed a lawsuit against *Vanity Fair* writer Dominick Dunne, who had published unsubstantiated rumors about Condit's involvement in affairs with prostitutes at Middle Eastern embassies. Dunne also had detailed Condit's search for someone to kill Chandra Levy. Condit received an undisclosed amount as part of a settlement in that case. He also settled a case against the tabloid the *National Enquirer*.[46]

Gary Condit never publicly admitted to having an affair with Chandra Levy, but his refusal to deny the existence of a sexual relationship strongly suggests that they were involved. He suffered the grave misfortune of becoming a suspect in her death. To this day some observers believe that he was involved in her disappearance and murder. As one of Condit's lawyers, Bertram Fields, put it after the police had eliminated the congressman as a suspect, "Who gives him his career back? That career has been destroyed and his life turned upside down, and that will never change."[47]

As of this writing, Chandra Levy's murder remains unsolved.

NOTES

1. James Risen, "Fourth Condit Interview Is Possible, Washington Police Say," *New York Times*, July 24, 2001, A16; Katharine Q. Seelye, "Body of Intern Found in Park in Washington," *New York Times*, May 23, 2002, A1, A28.

2. Scott Higham and Sari Horwitz, *Finding Chandra: A True Washington Murder Mystery* (New York: Simon & Schuster, 2010), 41–43.

3. Higham and Horwitz, *Finding Chandra*, 43–44.

4. Higham and Horwitz, *Finding Chandra*, 43–44.

5. Higham and Horwitz, *Finding Chandra*, 44, 56.

6. Todd S. Purdum, "Condit Denies Any Knowledge of Levy's Fate," *New York Times*, August 24, 2001, A116.

7. Raymond Bonner, "Police Focusing on Voluntary Absence or Foul Play in Intern Case," *New York Times*, July 6, 2001, A10.

8. Higham and Horwitz, *Finding Chandra*, 27.

9. Higham and Horwitz, *Finding Chandra*, 29–30.

10. Higham and Horwitz, *Finding Chandra*, 29–30, 39–40.

11. Condit's background is outlined in Higham and Horwitz, *Finding Chandra*, 28–29, 93–103; See also Risen, "Fourth Condit Interview Is Possible," A16.

12. The quotes are found in Higham and Horwitz, *Finding Chandra*, 57.

13. Higham and Horwitz, *Finding Chandra*, 58–59. See also Bonner, "Police Focusing on Voluntary Absence or Foul Play in Intern Case," A10.

14. Lynch is quoted in Higham and Horwitz, *Finding Chandra*, 59.

15. Felicity Barringer, "The Lost Privacy of Gary Condit," *New York Times*, July 15, 2001, WK3; Bonner, "Police Focusing on Voluntary Absence or Foul Play in Intern Case," A10.

16. Higham and Horwitz, *Finding Chandra*, 57–58.

17. Lanny J. Davis, "Public Candor and Gary Condit," *New York Times*, July 12, 2001, A23.

18. Bonner, "Police Focusing on Voluntary Absence or Foul Play in Intern Case," A10.

19. Higham and Horwitz, *Finding Chandra*, 88–90, 93–103, 142.

20. Davis, "Public Candor and Gary Condit," A23.

21. Condit is quoted in Higham and Horwitz, *Finding Chandra*, 184. See also Purdum, "Condit Denies Any Knowledge of Levy's Fate," A1, A16.

22. Higham and Horwitz, *Finding Chandra*, 192.

23. Higham and Horwitz, *Finding Chandra*, 192.

24. Condit is quoted in Higham and Horwitz, *Finding Chandra*, 207. See also Mike Sager, "The Final Days of Gary Condit," *Esquire* 138, no. 3 (September 2002): 180–90.

25. Higham and Horwitz, *Finding Chandra*, 208–13; Seelye, "Body of Intern Found in Park in Washington," A28.

26. Arden is quoted in Sari Horwitz and Allan Lengel, "Chandra Levy Ruled a Homicide Victim; D.C. Police Ask FBI Lab's Help in Learning How Ex-Intern Died," *New York Times*, May 29, 2002, A1.

27. Higham and Horwitz, *Finding Chandra*, 214–15; Horwitz and Lengel, "Chandra Levy Ruled a Homicide Victim," A1; Seelye, "Body of Intern Found in Park in Washington," A28.

28. Higham and Horwitz, *Finding Chandra*, 196–99.

29. Higham and Horwitz, *Finding Chandra*, 109–11, 196, 219–20.

30. Higham and Horwitz, *Finding Chandra*, 107–9, 196, 199–204, 209–10, 219.

31. Higham and Horwitz, *Finding Chandra*, 216, 234.

32. Higham and Horwitz, *Finding Chandra*, 228. See also Keith L. Alexander and Lynh Bui, "Secret Recordings Emerged and the Chandra Levy Case Rapidly Unraveled," *Washington Post*, July 30, 2016, n.p.

33. Sabrina Tavernise, "Salvadoran Convicted of Killing Intern Chandra Levy," *New York Times*, November 23, 2010, A18.

34. Higham and Horwitz, *Finding Chandra*, 233–34.

35. The stories ran in the *Washington Post* from July 13 to 27, 2008. See, for example, Sari Horwitz, Scott Higham, and Sylvia Moreno, "Who Killed Chandra Levy?" *Washington Post*, July 13, 2008, A1; Sari Horwitz, Scott Higham, and Sylvia Moreno, "Chandra's Secret," *Washington Post*, July 14, 2008, A1. See also Higham and Horwitz, *Finding Chandra*, 231–34.

36. Higham and Horwitz, *Finding Chandra*, 234–39.

37. Tavernise, "Salvadoran Convicted of Killing Intern Chandra Levy," A18.

38. Sabrina Tavernise, "Chandra Levy's Killer Gets 60 Years for Murder, Ending Case That Chilled Capital," *New York Times*, February 12, 2011, A12. See also Higham and Horwitz, *Finding Chandra*, 240–44; Tavernise, "Salvadoran Convicted of Killing Intern Chandra Levy," A18.

39. The quotes are found in Tavernise, "Salvadoran Convicted of Killing Intern Chandra Levy," A18.

40. Chris Harris, "A Murder Case Crumbles: Who Killed Chandra Levy?" *People* 86, no. 7 (August 15, 2016): 56–57; Richard Perez-Pena, "Man Accused in Levy Killing Is Cleared of All Charges," *New York Times*, July 29, 2016, A15.

41. The quote is found in Alexander and Bui, "Secret Recordings Emerged and the Chandra Levy Case Rapidly Unraveled," n.p. See also Harris, "A Murder Case Crumbles," 57.

42. The quote is found in Perez-Pena, "Man Accused in Levy Killing Is Cleared of All Charges," A15.

43. Maria Sacchetti and Keith L. Alexander, "Ex-Suspect in Chandra Levy Slaying Is Deported," *Washington Post*, May 9, 2017, B5.

44. Alexander and Bui, "Secret Recordings Emerged and the Chandra Levy Case Rapidly Unraveled," n.p.

45. Michael Doyle, "Baskin-Robbins Found It Hard to Get Scoop on Condit; Trial Transcript Reveals Court Costs, Son's Book," *Modesto Bee* [Modesto, CA], January 3, 2009, B1.

46. James Barron, "Gary Condit Strikes Back," *New York Times*, December 17, 2002, B2; "Condit Settles Suit Against Tabloids," *Oakland Tribune* [Oakland, CA], September 10, 2004, 1; Michael Doyle, "Condit, Author Settles Lawsuit; Ex-Congressman Avoids Deposition, Gets Apology," *Modesto Bee* [Modesto, CA], March 15, 2005, A1.

47. The quote is found in Tavernise, "Salvadoran Convicted of Killing Intern Chandra Levy," A18.

CHAPTER 13

"If Only He'd Hired a Hooker Like a Normal Congressman"

Anthony Weiner

Anthony Weiner was a seven-term US congressman when his political career was engulfed by a controversy of his own making. He used his Twitter account in May 2011 to send a sexually explicit photograph of himself to a woman who followed him on social media. It was not his first episode of "sexting," nor would it be his last. Even after he resigned from Congress in June 2011, Weiner would not or could not prevent himself from self-destructing. Two years later, as he was campaigning for mayor of New York City, he sent a sexually explicit photograph of himself to another woman using the *nom de guerre* "Carlos Danger." In 2016 he did it again, this time showing himself lying in bed with his young son. He also sent a sexually explicit photograph to a 15-year-old girl, which earned him a twenty-one-month sentence in prison. Although many of the political figures profiled in this book acted in risky ways that all but ensured that they would be caught, these men typically attempted to gratify their sexual urges and cover them up. Anthony Weiner's actions are far more inexplicable, strongly suggesting that he wanted to be caught. Perhaps his acts of self-flagellation reinforced long-held feelings of self-loathing.[1]

Before he became a national punchline for comedians and cynical observers who delighted in commenting on the peccadilloes of elected officials, Anthony Weiner was a young man who held great promise. He was born on September 4, 1964, to a lawyer, Mort Weiner, and his wife, a high school math teacher, Frances, in Brooklyn, New York. Anthony was the middle son. He was raised in the Jewish faith.

After graduating from Brooklyn Technical School in 1981, he attended the State University of New York at Plattsburgh. He spent his junior year at the College of William & Mary, where he met the future comedian Jon Stewart. During his college years Weiner immersed himself in student government, even earning an award as the most effective state senator. He earned a bachelor of arts degree in political science in 1985.

Like many young people interested in politics, Weiner gravitated to Washington, DC. He worked in the office of Congressman Charles "Chuck" Schumer, who later became a US senator and eventually Senate majority leader. After three years working in Washington, Weiner transferred to Schumer's district office in Brooklyn. Schumer was aware of the young man's interest in politics and encouraged Weiner to consider running for elective office.

After the New York City Council expanded from thirty-five to fifty-one seats in 1991, Weiner spied an opportunity to realize his ambitions. He threw himself into a campaign to join the city council, but he was considered a longshot. His opponents in the primary race enjoyed higher name recognition and had more funding. Despite the long odds, Weiner eked out a narrow victory, defeating his opponent, Adele Cohen, by fewer than two hundred votes. The closing weeks of the campaign were especially acrimonious as Weiner's campaign workers disseminated leaflets tying Cohen to civil rights activist Jesse Jackson and Mayor David Dinkins, two black political figures who were viewed as antagonistic to Jewish residents during the August 1991 Crown Heights riots. It was an ugly smear tactic that demonstrated Weiner's willingness to play ruthless, hardball politics.

Because of the overwhelmingly Democratic character of the district, when he won the primary race, Weiner was a shoo-in for the general election. At 27 he was the youngest councilman in the city's history. He wasted no time in making his mark. Weiner's abrasive personality and sharp elbows could be off-putting to some critics, but he established a reputation as a relentless, driven, and effective councilman.

He set out to address his constituents' quality-of-life concerns. One initiative aimed to put troubled, at-risk children and teenagers to work cleaning up graffiti. He also supported efforts to revive Sheepshead Bay, a prominent historic area that had fallen into ruin.

Weiner's mentor, Chuck Schumer, decided to run for a seat in the Senate in 1998. With Schumer's House seat vacant, Weiner filed to run for the post. He won the primary race in a heavily Democratic district that included a portion of southern Brooklyn as well as south and central Queens. In November 1998 he won the general election. At age 34 he was on his way to Washington, DC, as a member of Congress.[2]

In a House career that spanned a dozen years, Anthony Weiner became known as an outspoken, fiery, combative political liberal. He supported pro-choice issues, Medicare health coverage for all Americans, and unwavering assistance to Israel. He occasionally adopted positions out of line with his party—such as voting to grant President George W. Bush authorization to use military force in Iraq—but for all intents and purposes, he was proudly a traditional liberal Democratic Jewish politician from New York. Unlike some politicians who establish a conciliatory public persona to smooth over rough edges, Weiner enjoyed politics as a blood sport. He was unafraid to use angry, intemperate language, and his in-your-face rants delighted leftists as it angered right-wing politicians.[3]

By the early 2000s he was already thinking about advancing his political career. As a member of the House of Representatives, Weiner was one of 435 lawmakers in a body that rewarded seniority. It would be many years before he would be a mover and shaker. He wanted to make an impact sooner rather than later, and Weiner thought he could do that by becoming mayor of New York City. He believed that his passion and energy, not to mention his take-no-prisoners style of bare-knuckle politics, would propel him to the front of a crowded field.

He sought the Democratic nomination for mayor in 2005 with a three-part strategy. First, he criticized the incumbent mayor, Michael Bloomberg, as too imperious and wedded to top-down management to allow for all voices to be heard. Weiner pledged to be more democratic in his administration. Second, he believed that the mayor's office had been too passive in securing federal funding for New York City. With his typically aggressive approach, Weiner promised results in the competition for federal dollars. Finally, he promoted a book of fifty "real solutions" for improving city hall and its operations, including a neighborhood cleanup program dubbed "Weiner's cleaners."

He appealed to a variety of voters, but the opposition was steep. Weiner came in second in the primary balloting, conceding to the top vote getter, former Bronx borough president Fernando Ferrer, for the sake of party unity. Weiner might have forced a runoff, but he resolved to be a team player in hopes that Democratic Party leaders would remember the gesture in future contests.[4]

Weiner considered another mayoral campaign in 2009, but he chose not to run after the New York City Council modified the term limits so that Bloomberg could run again. Anticipating a race in 2013, Weiner began collecting funds. In July 2010 he had $3.9 million on hand, and by March 2013, he had $5.1 million in his war chest, second only to Christine Quinn, speaker of the New York City Council.[5]

Weiner's name recognition steadily increased during these years, and it rose markedly after he married Huma Abedin, Hillary Clinton's chief assistant, on July 10, 2010. Former president Bill Clinton officiated at their wedding. Commenting on her closeness to Abedin, Hillary Clinton offered this insight at her aide's wedding. "I have one daughter. But if I had a second daughter, it would [be] Huma." In December 2011 Weiner and Abedin celebrated the birth of their son.[6]

Figure 13.1. Congressman Anthony Weiner marches in a Gay Pride parade in 2009, two years before his first sex scandal ended his political career. Courtesy of Thomas Good, NLN, Creative Commons Attribution.

Anthony Weiner seemed to have it all. He was a well-known member of Congress, a perennial favorite to win the New York City mayoral election in 2013, and husband to the chief assistant of the powerful Clinton family. He appeared to live a storied life.

Yet all was not well. From his earliest days in Congress, troubling stories circulated about Weiner's behavior with subordinates. A driven workaholic, he expected the same devotion from his staffers. He had a volcanic temper, which often erupted when he was unhappy with how a task had been handled. Shouting at staff members and throwing office furniture during his frequent tirades made Weiner a nightmare boss, and his behavior led to one of the highest turnover rates on Capitol Hill. Critics suggested that these episodes raised unresolved questions about his temperament and maturity.[7]

Aside from emerging as one of Congress's worst bosses, Weiner also enjoyed the dubious distinction of amassing numerous unpaid parking tickets. He might have been forgiven such relatively minor offenses, but Weiner had been a loud, shrill voice against United Nations diplomats failing to pay their parking tickets in New York City. Critics charged him, rightly, with hypocrisy.[8]

These actions, while distasteful, were minor transgressions and undoubtedly would not have been remembered but for Weiner's unsavory activities on social media. The first public episode began on Friday, May 27, 2011, when a young woman received a sexually provocative photograph sent from Weiner's Twitter account. The photograph was quickly deleted. The next day another Twitter user who saw the photograph shared it with friends and alerted Andrew Breitbart, a notorious ring-wing ideologue who operated a website devoted to attacking politically liberal politicians. Weiner took to Twitter and insisted that his Facebook account had been hacked. Despite this plausible explanation, Breitbart posted the photograph on his website, BigGovernment.com.[9]

For the next ten days, Weiner and his staff fielded numerous inquiries about the photograph. The congressman initially stuck to his "I was hacked" story. A spokesman indicated that Weiner was consulting a lawyer to determine whether any criminal laws had been violated. Yet his story also began to change, which worried people who knew him. In response to one query, he admitted that he could not "say with certitude" that he was not pictured in the photograph.[10]

Finally, the congressman called an extraordinary twenty-seven-minute press conference on June 6, 2011. Weeping and at times stammering, he admitted that he had snapped racy photographs of himself in various states of undress and had shared them with a multitude of women. "Over the past few years, I have engaged in several inappropriate conversations conducted over Twitter, Facebook, email and occasionally on the phone with women I met online," he said. He had never met the women, nor had he planned to meet them. Something about the virtual nature of the sexual contact gratified him. "I don't know what I was thinking," he confessed. In a stunning understatement, he conceded that this "was a destructive thing to do. I apologize for doing it."[11]

It was a political bombshell. A man who had been a rising star in the Democratic Party suddenly became a laughingstock. He had humiliated himself, to be sure, but he had also hurt his wife and, by extension, the Clintons. He acknowledged that Huma Abedin was hurt by his actions. "We have been through a great deal together, and we will—we will weather this," he predicted. "I love her very much, and she loves me."[12]

Pressed to resign from Congress, he was adamant. He would seek treatment, he said, but he would not resign his seat. The disease or addiction he would be treated for was not clear, but it was clear, at least at the outset, that he would not give up his political standing without a fight. He was a man accustomed to a political brawl, and he appeared to be ready to face whatever assaults came his way.

Public reactions were predictably withering. Republicans and many members of the public howled in protest. This abrasive liberal Democrat who had for so long railed against conservatives was now vulnerable—a victim of his own inexplicable, self-destructive tendencies—and the criticism was unrelenting. "There is zero chance today of a Mayor Weiner," veteran political analyst Hank Sheinkopf predicted. "Mayors don't do these things. It's too much already." One constituent who turned out to protest Weiner's decision to stay in office, Kevin Hilton, spoke for many voters: "I don't want my congressman sending pictures of his genitals," he said. "It's disgusting."[13]

Democrats were left to clean up the mess, and they were furious at Weiner for placing them in an untenable position. Senator Chuck Schumer, Weiner's political mentor, would only say that "those of us who have been longtime friends of Anthony are heartbroken." New York Governor Andrew Cuomo sought to distance himself from the affair. "It's basically a federal matter, so I don't know that my involvement would be helpful or relevant," he said. "Whether or not he should resign, that's up to him, his constituents, and the Democratic leadership."[14]

The Democratic House leadership understood that Weiner faced a long, possibly drawn-out ethics investigation if he stayed in office. It would distract from the party's agenda and provide Republicans with months' worth of fodder for the cable news talk shows, to say nothing of the fundraising opportunities for conservative "family values" candidates.

Faced with this stark choice, Minority Leader Nancy Pelosi of California urged Weiner to resign, as did Steny Hoyer of Maryland, the number-two Democratic leader in the House. "All his colleagues agree that this process—a judicial process through the Ethics Committee—is going to take time," Hoyer said. "I really don't know that we have that time, and I would hope that Mr. Weiner would use this opportunity to reflect upon whether or not he can effectively proceed. I don't see how he can, and I hope he would make that judgment."[15]

Recognizing that he could not stay in office under the circumstances, Weiner scheduled a press conference for June 16, 2011. "I am here today to again apologize for the personal mistakes I have made and the embarrassment I have caused," he said. Hecklers called him a pervert and other unflattering names as he addressed the crowd of reporters along with a smattering of constituents.

"I am announcing my resignation from Congress, so my colleagues can get back to work, my neighbors can choose a new representative and most important so that my wife and I can continue to heal from the damage I have caused," he said. His wife, Huma Abedin, was not at his side as he faced the crowd.[16]

The press conference marked the end of Weiner's congressional career, but it did not end the public fascination with his case. Pundits endlessly debated his reasons for acting so recklessly. Late-night comedians mocked his actions, and voters wondered how they could have misjudged him so badly. Ginger Lee, an exotic dancer and former pornographic film actress, had called for the congressman to step down, leading one Twitter correspondent to comment, "Hey Ginger Lee! Glad to hear you think Weiner should resign for lying. Now how about you resign that pink lip gloss? Just a thought." Comedian John Fugelsang commented that "Anthony Weiner resigns after no sex, no crimes, no complaints. If only he'd hired a hooker like a normal congressman."[17]

Weiner left the public stage. A Republican captured his House seat, but Democratic leaders were pleased that they did not have to defend the indefensible in a public forum. Huma Abedin remained a high-profile assistant to Hillary Clinton, but she refused to answer questions publicly about her husband other than to say that he was seeking treatment, and that she loved him and supported him. In a strange way, Abedin's predicament brought her closer to Hillary Clinton, who had suffered her own share of indignities when her husband Bill's sexual scandal became a public matter in 1998.[18]

Two years after the 2011 scandal, Weiner announced another run for mayor of New York City. It was a long-shot effort, but he assured former supporters and constituents that he had learned much from his wilderness years and he was ready to lead. F. Scott Fitzgerald claimed that there are no second acts in American lives, but Weiner was banking on the equally plausible notion that citizens allow repentant sinners a chance at redemption.[19]

Redemption, however, requires genuine penitence, and Weiner failed to clear that bar. In July 2013, Dirty, a website that posts gossip and satire about public figures, revealed that Weiner had been sexting with a woman beginning in 2012, the year after he resigned from Congress. The website did not reveal her name, but resourceful reporters tracked her down anyway. She was 23-year-old Sydney Leathers of Princeton, Indiana. A few days before the story broke, Leathers had sent a series of screenshots to Nik Richie, host of the Dirty website, showing her online exchanges with a character who styled himself "Carlos Danger."[20]

Carlos told the woman in explicit detail the sexual acts he had fantasized performing with her. Describing himself an "argumentative, perpetually horny middle-aged man," he sent along a picture of his penis as well. He had never met her, but Señor Danger told "the walking fantasy" that he loved her. He wanted to meet for sex. As an afterthought, Carlos asked her to "do me a solid. Could you hard delete all our chats?"[21]

Alas, Leathers did not do him the solid; she kept the messages and images. As soon as they became public, it was clear that Carlos Danger's alter ego was Anthony Weiner. A firestorm erupted, a repeat of the outrage and disbelief of 2011. After initially resisting her turn in the spotlight, Leathers threw herself into the arena with gusto. She appeared on the tabloid television program *Inside Edition* and parlayed her notoriety into a budding pornographic film career.[22]

As for Carlos Danger, it became Weinergate, the sequel. Just when you thought it was safe to go back into politics . . . along comes this Latin American social media alter ego, Señor Danger. In a hastily called news conference on July 23, 2013, a chagrined Anthony Weiner acknowledged that he was guilty as charged. He insisted that his social media adventures were "in our rearview mirror . . . but it's not that far."[23]

He confessed that Sydney Leathers was not his only correspondent, but he could not provide a fixed number. "There were more than—there are a few," he said. "I don't have a specific number for you. Sometimes they didn't go consistently. Whatever." He estimated that he had sent messages to at least ten women.[24]

Huma Abedin stood by her man. She had been invisible during his 2011 troubles, but she appeared at the 2013 press conferences by his side. She admitted that staying with him after he revealed his proclivity for sexting was "not an easy choice." "Anthony's made some horrible mistakes, both before he resigned from Congress and after," she said. Nonetheless, she supported him and his political ambitions without reservation. "We discussed all of this before Anthony decided he would run for mayor, so really what I want to say is, I love him, I have forgiven him, I believe in him."[25]

It was a heartfelt admission by a humiliated woman who seldom revealed her private thoughts and emotions. If Abedin had been absent from his side or had expressed reservations about his ability to govern, his campaign would have ended immediately. With his wife standing by him steadfastly, Weiner hoped he could weather the crisis.

A few constituents were willing to give him the benefit of the doubt. One letter to the editor observed that "we already knew that Mr. Weiner was not the most affable politician New York had to offer, and the revelation that he sent more lewd messages than we thought is not particularly surprising. Surely it raises questions regarding his marriage and personal life, but it does nothing to inform voters about his ability to lead." Even with all his flaws, "voters have found that Mr. Weiner has something important to offer, and there is no reason to deprive them of their choice."[26]

Judging by the volume of letters to the editor in the *New York Times*, this tolerant approach—allow the voters to decide whether they want to elect Anthony Weiner, warts, flaws, and all—was a minority view. Far more prevalent was the opinion of a woman who concluded that "Anthony D. Weiner is a sick man. His intellectual abilities and emotional self-awareness are at war. New York City cannot be the forum for his struggle." Another correspondent asked, "How can we elect someone like this to public office with total assurance that his sexual need to do what he did will not be repeated? There is no proof that Anthony D. Weiner's behavior has been, should we say, cured?" Another writer agreed with the candidate's policies but could not accept his behavior. "Politically, I am in sync with most of Mr. Weiner's positions. But do I see in him the integrity and stability I want in a candidate? Not even close."[27]

Columnist Maureen Dowd suggested that it was "time to hard-delete Carlos Danger." In her view a voter might weigh a politician's transgressions against his or her public service, but "there's nothing in Weiner's public life that is redeeming. In twelve years in Congress, he managed to get only one minor bill passed, on behalf of a donor, and he doesn't work well with people. He knows how to be loud on cable and wave his Zorro sword in their faces." Referring to the governor of South Carolina, who confessed to an affair with his mistress, Dowd pointed out that "some sex scandals, like Mark Sanford's, fall into the realm of flawed human nature, and some, like Weiner's, fall into the realm of 'Seriously, what is wrong with you?'"[28]

On and on it went. The overwhelming consensus was that Weiner must drop out of the mayoral race and forget about pursuing a career in elective office. Many commentators saw his predicament as part of a larger narrative about the coarsening of public discourse and the willingness of public figures to engage in outrageous behavior in the belief that their behavior will become acceptable. Columnist Frank Bruni lamented the new reality of "superficiality trumping substance, of fame rather than accomplishment being the aim of too many people in politics these days." He contended that Weiner was "the poster boy for a subspecies of lawmakers who are really noisemakers, maestros of the cable-ready kerfuffle, their sights set on MSNBC or Fox News or Politico, their need for notice constant." Bruni could see no value to Weiner's candidacy. "He's a fun house mirror of narcissism in politics, and his demand that total strangers ogle his anatomy in cyberspace was in some sense a sick-joke version of other politicians' thrill at the sounds of their voices and their addiction to applause."[29]

Weiner resolved to stay in the race despite the controversy. He had been leading in the polls before the Sydney Leathers revelations, but his support plummeted in the wake of the latest scandal. On primary election night, September 10, 2013, he placed fifth, earning just shy of 5 percent of the vote.[30]

Three years passed before Anthony Weiner appeared in the headlines again. On August 28, 2016, the *New York Post* reported that the incorrigible sexter was at it again. This time he posed in photographs with his 4-year-old son lying next to him. This time it was too much for Huma Abedin to take. She announced that she was separating from her husband. "After long and painful consideration and work on my marriage, I have made the decision to separate from my husband," she said in a statement released to the press. "Anthony and I remain devoted to doing what is best for our son, who is the light of our life. During this difficult time, I ask for respect for our privacy."[31]

It was Weiner's third sex scandal in five years. Most Democratic leaders and many constituents expressed disgust at his actions and exhaustion at the number of incidents. "It's sad and a little bit ironic that a guy who understood the intersection of politics and technology and media better than anyone and exploited it better than anyone to fuel his rise, fell because of it," said Stu Loeser, who had worked with Weiner on Schumer's staff during the early 2000s. "Removing himself from the public conversation, he's taking himself out of the part of the equation that has proven again and again to be part of his downfall."[32]

As bad as the 2011 and 2013 incidents were, the 2016 incident was worse. By involving his 4-year-old son in the photographs, Weiner raised questions of whether child abuse had occurred. The New York City Administration for Children's Services launched an investigation into the matter to determine whether the child had been endangered.[33]

Even more damaging was the revelation that one of Weiner's correspondents was a 15-year-old girl from North Carolina. According to the girl, whose identity was withheld because she was a minor, they met online. During their initial chat Weiner told her she was "kinda sorta gorgeous." They agreed to speak during a Skype call. Their initial conversation was not overtly sexual, consisting mostly of idle chitchat. He asked her where she went to school, and she told him the name of the high school, indicating that he knew she was not an adult. The conversations stretched across several months. They even joked about his Carlos Danger persona. His online alias this time around was "T Dog."

After a few months T Dog could no longer control himself. He told the girl about his rape fantasies and urged her to wear "schoolgirl" outfits. While his son was being bathed downstairs, Weiner gave in to his id. The girl recalled that "he asked me to take my clothes off and just started saying these really sexual things. He would tell me to say his name as I was touching myself." He sent her a photograph of himself, shirtless, with his hands placed on his genitals.

During one exchange that Weiner sent using an encryption app, Weiner promised the girl that if they had a sexual encounter, she would "limp for a week." In another message he wrote, "I thought of you this morning. Hard." The teenage girl said that he sent her nude photographs of himself using a confidential message that deleted the file as soon as it was read. He also sent her pornographic videos and provided explicit commentary on scenes in the video.[34]

Because he had been exchanging sexually explicit material with a minor child across state lines, T Dog's behavior was a federal criminal matter. The Federal Bureau of Investigation (FBI) opened a criminal probe. As investigators sifted through Weiner's emails and electronic communications, they discovered a laptop containing Weiner's private messages as well as emails between Huma Abedin and her boss, Hillary Clinton.[35]

Weiner's actions affected Abedin, of course, but they also involved Clinton. By 2016 Hillary Clinton was campaigning for the presidency, and Abedin remained her closest aide. As secretary of state, Clinton had mixed personal and private emails, and the FBI had logged months trying to ascertain whether she had compromised any classified material. The bureau had decided that Clinton had been reckless in the way she handled State Department emails, but she had not violated the law. Clinton was relieved when the FBI closed its file on what she saw as a minor matter.

With the revelation that Weiner's laptop contained some of Clinton's emails, however, FBI Director James Comey announced that he was directing his agents to reexamine the Clinton case. Although the bureau decided that nothing on the laptop changed the initial assessment that the former secretary of state had not broken the law, the decision to reopen the case eleven days before the 2016 presidential election—which amounted to the proverbial "October surprise" that every candidate fears—probably contributed to Clinton's loss to Republican Donald J. Trump in the Electoral College.[36]

Clinton's loss could not be laid completely at Weiner's feet, but he played a part. His antics had destroyed his life and the lives of his loved ones. By 2017 he was facing criminal liability as well. Sending sexually explicit materials to a child violated federal law. Rather than subject his family, friends, and Democratic Party colleagues to a lengthy trial, Weiner waived his rights and agreed to plead guilty. On Friday, May 19, 2017, he surrendered to the FBI. Agents transported him to federal court, where he formally pleaded guilty to one count of transferring obscene material to a minor. The offense carried a maximum term of ten years in prison.[37]

As he stood weeping before the judge, Weiner admitted that "I knew this was morally wrong as well as unlawful. I have a sickness, but I do not have an excuse." Prosecutors asked for a sentence of between twenty-one and twenty-seven months.[38]

Judge Denise Cote of the US District Court for the Southern District of New York remarked that "this was a serious crime and it's a serious crime that deserves a serious punishment." Although she understood defense counsel's plea that Weiner avoid prison and be required to undergo extensive treatment, the judge concluded that Weiner had a history of this behavior. He had caused irreparable damage to an adolescent girl. "She was a minor. She was a victim. She's entitled to the law's full protection." Judge Cote sentenced Weiner to serve twenty-one months in prison, beginning on November 6, 2017. He would be supervised for three years following his release.[39]

Huma Abedin was noticeably absent from his side during his sentencing hearing. She had separated from her husband when the third scandal became public in August 2016. Shortly after he appeared in court on May 19, she filed for divorce. In January 2018, however, she withdrew the petition, saying that she and Weiner would resolve their differences privately to avoid further public embarrassment for their son.[40]

In the meantime Anthony Weiner served fifteen months of his sentence at the Federal Medical Center, Devens, a facility in Ayer, Massachusetts, for male inmates who require specialized or long-term medical or mental health treatment. During the last three months, Weiner lived in a halfway house in Brooklyn. With three months shaved off his sentence for good behavior, the former congressman was released from custody on May 15, 2019.[41]

Facing reporters following his release, Weiner said that he was a changed man. "It's good to be out. I hope to be able to live a life of integrity and service. I'm glad this chapter of my life is behind me."[42]

It was unclear exactly what life of integrity and service Weiner meant, but his priority was to earn a living. He shopped a book proposal to New York publishers in 2019, but no one seemed interested. Sex scandals sometimes sell books, but Weiner's story appeared pathetic and perverted—as opposed to daring and salacious—hardly the type of book that flies off the shelves.[43]

He had already entered popular culture. In 2016 two filmmakers, Josh Kriegman and Elyse Steinberg, produced a "fly on the wall" documentary, *Weiner*, about the 2013 mayoral race. Kriegman had served as Weiner's chief of staff for some of his years in Congress, and he hoped to chronicle the candidate's return to electoral politics. For a brief time it appeared that the documentary would capture one of the greatest comebacks in American political history. With the revelations about Weiner's 2013 behavior, the film became a behind-the-scenes story of a deeply flawed candidate with a seriously disturbed psyche.[44]

Aside from the documentary, Weiner enjoyed cameo roles in the campy film *Sharknado 3: Oh Hell No*, where he played the head of the National Aeronautics and Space Administration, as well as a short-run television program, a political satire created by cartoonist Gary Trudeau, that ran in 2013 and 2014. A 2013 theater production, *The Weiner Monologues*, examined media coverage of Weiner's 2011 sexting scandal.[45]

Despite his remarks upon leaving prison, Weiner's contribution to political discourse is not about living a life of integrity and service but providing a cautionary tale for public figures. People who thrust themselves into the limelight, and especially those politicians who seek elective office to effect public policy, must establish a brand that reflects the values and beliefs of their constituents, assuming they want to succeed and make a good name for themselves. Public figures who gratify their own interests and desires at the expense of the common good risk becoming, like Weiner, a punchline to a sick, sad joke.

NOTES

1. Amy Chozick and Patrick Healy, "Weiner's Texts Cast Shadow on Campaign; Wife, Top Clinton Aide, Decides to Separate," *New York Times*, August 30, 2016, A1, A15; Jennifer Fermino, Jason Silverstein, and Larry McShane, "Sick Wein and Teen; Girl: He Said Be 'Mine,' and Sent Crotch Pictures; New Low Could Turn Pervert into Prisoner," *New York Daily News*, September 22, 2016, 4.

2. For information on Weiner's background, see, for example, Daphna Berman, "Live from New York, It's Anthony Weiner," *Moment Magazine* 36, no. 3 (May/June 2011): 28–36; Jennifer Monroe, "Anthony Weiner," in *Our States* (New York: History Reference Center, 2020), 3.

3. Berman, "Live from New York," 30–32; Shane Dixon Kavanaugh, "Weiner's Gift to His Mayoral Rivals," *Crain's New York Business* 27, no. 23 (June 6, 2011): 1; Monroe, "Anthony Weiner," 3.

4. Berman, "Live from New York," 35–36; Monroe, "Anthony Weiner," 3; Jamal E. Watson, "Despite Polls, Weiner Looks Ahead," *New York Amsterdam News* 96, no. 32 (August 4–10, 2005): 1.

5. Berman, "Live from New York," 36.

6. Clinton is quoted in Berman, "Live from New York," 35. See also Vivian Yee, "Weiner Confirms City Agency Is Investigating How He Treats His 4-Year-Old Son," *New York Times*, September 2, 2016, A17.

7. Berman, "Live from New York," 32.

8. "Weiner Roasted as Capitol Scofflaw King," *New York Post*, March 30, 2011, 2.

9. Michael Barbaro, "Tearful Weiner Admits Sending Explicit Picture; Says He Won't Resign; Asserts No Crime Was Committed—Pelosi Calls for Inquiry," *New York Times*, June 7, 2011, A1, A28; J. Scott Smith, "With a Little Help from My Wife: An Examination of Anthony Weiner's Image Repair Discourse Through Third-Party Defense and a Postcrisis Discourse of Renewal," *Northwest Journal of Communication* 44, no. 1 (Spring 2016): 42–43.

10. Barbaro, "Tearful Weiner Admits Sending Explicit Picture," A1, A28; Kavanaugh, "Weiner's Gift to His Mayoral Rivals," 1; Smith, "With a Little Help from My Wife," 42–44.

11. Weiner is quoted in Barbaro, "Tearful Weiner Admits Sending Explicit Picture," A1.

12. Weiner is quoted in Barbaro, "Tearful Weiner Admits Sending Explicit Picture," A28.

13. The Hank Sheinkopf "zero chance" quote is found in Barbaro, "Tearful Weiner Admits Sending Explicit Picture." The Kevin Hilton quote "pictures of his genitals" is found in Raymond Hernandez, "Despite Plan to Enter Rehab, Weiner Still Faces Calls to Resign," *New York Times*, June 13, 2011, A18.

14. The quotes are found in Hernandez, "Despite Plan to Enter Rehab," A18.

15. Hoyer is quoted in Hernandez, "Despite Plan to Enter Rehab," A18.

16. Weiner is quoted in Raymond Hernandez, "In Chaotic Scene, Weiner Quits Seat in Scandal's Wake; Vulgar Shouts During Announcement in Brooklyn—Relief for Democrats," *New York Times*, June 17, 2011, A1. See also "Anthony Weiner Resigns," *New York Times*, June 17, 2011, A34.

17. The quotes are found in "Anthony Weiner Resigns After No Sex, No Crimes, No Complaints," *New York Times*, June 19, 2011, NJ3.

18. David W. Chen and Javier C. Hernandez, "Weiner Admits Explicit Texting After House Exit," *New York Times*, July 24, 2013, A1, A21.

19. Chen and Hernandez, "Weiner Admits Explicit Texting After House Exit," A1, A21. See also Javier C. Hernandez and Michael Barbaro, "Weiner Admits to More Lewd Exchanges but Denies an Addiction," *New York Times*, July 26, 2013, A18.

20. Chen and Hernandez, "Weiner Admits Explicit Texting After House Exit," A21; Maureen Dowd, "Time to Hard-Delete Carlos Danger," *New York Times*, July 28, 2013, SR11.

21. The quote about an "argumentative, perpetually horny middle-aged man" is found in Dowd, "Time to Hard-Delete Carlos Danger," SR11. Señor Danger's quote "do me a solid" is found in Chen and Hernandez, "Weiner Admits Explicit Texting After House Exit," A21.

22. Hernandez and Barbaro, "Weiner Admits to More Lewd Exchanges but Denies an Addiction," A18.

23. Weiner's quote is found in Chen and Hernandez, "Weiner Admits Explicit Texting After House Exit," A1.

24. Weiner is quoted in Hernandez and Barbaro, "Weiner Admits to More Lewd Exchanges but Denies an Addiction," A18.

25. Abedin is quoted in Chen and Hernandez, "Weiner Admits Explicit Texting After House Exit," A21.

26. Jess Coleman, "To the Editor," *New York Times*, July 25, 2013, A26.

27. The quote "Anthony D. Weiner is a sick man" is found in Isidore Shapiro, "To the Editor," *New York Times*, July 25, 2013, A26. The quote "How can we elect someone like this to public office" is found in Robert Bernstein, "To the Editor," *New York Times*, July 25, 2013, A26. The quote "Politically, I am in sync with most of Mr. Weiner's positions" is found in Mary H. Brown, "To the Editor," *New York Times*, July 25, 2013, A26.

28. Dowd, "Time to Hard-Delete Carlos Danger," SR11.

29. Frank Bruni, "The Freak Show as Fable," *New York Times*, August 4, 2013, SR3.

30. Ginia Bellafante, "A Candidate Eclipse," *New York Times*, July 28, 2013, LI1, LI6; Chozick and Healy, "Weiner's Texts Cast Shadow on Campaign," A15.

31. Abedin is quoted in Chozick and Healy, "Weiner's Texts Cast Shadow on Campaign," A15.

32. Loeser is quoted in Vivian Yee, "After His Latest Scandal, Weiner Avoids Spotlight," *New York Times*, September 1, 2016, A22.

33. Yee, "Weiner Confirms City Agency Is Investigating How He Treats His 4-Year-Old Son," A17.

34. T Dog is quoted in Fermino and McShane, "Sick Wein and Teen," 4. See also "It Gets Worse for Weiner; Embroiled in Sexting Trouble with Teen," *Toronto Sun*, September 22, 2016, A10.

35. Chozick and Healy, "Weiner's Texts Cast Shadow on Campaign," A1, A15.

36. Hillary Rodham Clinton, *What Happened* (New York: Simon & Schuster, 2017), 314; Erica Orden and Nicole Hong, "Anthony Weiner Pleads Guilty Following Sexting Probe; Many Democrats Say the Case Involving the Former Lawmaker Contributed to Hillary Clinton's Defeat," *Wall Street Journal*, May 19, 2017, n.p.

37. Orden and Hong, "Anthony Weiner Pleads Guilty Following Sexting Probe," n.p.

38. Weiner is quoted in "The Wreckage of Anthony Weiner," *New York Times*, September 26, 2017, A26.

39. Judge Cote is quoted in Benjamin Weiser, "Weiner, Teary and Chastened, Is to Serve 21 Months for Lewd Texts," *New York Times*, September 26, 2017, A1.

40. "Huma Abedin Decides to Withdraw Divorce from Weiner," *News India Times*, January 19, 2018, 8.

41. Emily Heil, "Anthony Weiner Finishes His Prison Term," *Washington Post*, May 15, 2019, C2; Tyler Pager, "Weiner Is Out of Prison and Living in Brooklyn," *New York Times*, February 18, 2019, A16.

42. Weiner is quoted in Heil, "Anthony Weiner Finishes His Prison Term," C2.

43. Heil, "Anthony Weiner Finishes His Prison Term," C2.

44. Tatiana Siegel, "The Hillary Mystery at the Center of the Anthony Weiner Movie," *Hollywood Reporter* 422, no. 3 (2016): 72.

45. Michael M. Grynbaum, "A Greek Tragedy with Elements of Danger. Carlos Danger," *New York Times*, October 8, 2013, A20; "Hey, It's Our Ol' Chum! Weiner Fish Food in *Sharknado 3*," *New York Post*, July 12, 2015, 3.

CHAPTER 14

"Who Would Have Thought That 90 Seconds with Donald Trump Would Turn Into 90 Percent of My Life?"

Donald Trump's Sex Scandals

Donald J. Trump, forty-fifth president of the United States, became arguably the most divisive figure in American political history. A shamelessly self-promoting real estate developer and reality television show host, Trump launched his improbable bid for the presidency in June 2015 with provocative and derogatory comments about Mexican immigrants—"They're bringing drugs. They're bringing crime. They're rapists. And some, I assume, are good people"—that would have destroyed any other candidate's chances at capturing the White House. Worse was yet to come. He questioned whether Barack Obama was born in the United States and was therefore constitutionally eligible to serve despite overwhelming evidence that the forty-fourth president was born in Hawaii in 1961. He called women childish, profane names, often related to their weight or appearance. He ridiculed a Gold Star family because their son, who died in the line of duty, was Muslim. He denigrated a federal judge, questioning the man's ability to remain impartial because he was "of Mexican heritage." He bragged about his superior intellectual and sexual prowess. He professed his love for authoritarian political and military figures. For any reason or no reason at all, he lied about virtually everything, whether he benefited or not. Lying seemed to be the hallmark of his candidacy, the sine qua non of the Trump brand. Incredibly, the more outlandish, incendiary, rude, insulting, profane, or cartoonish his behavior, the more Trump attracted a segment of right-wing voters, mostly older whites who seethed with resentment at a variety of real and imagined ills supposedly perpetrated by non-whites with different values, customs, traditions, and religious affiliations. He succeeded in winning the presidency not despite his boorish behavior, but because of it.[1]

He was perhaps the first postmodern president in American history. Trump rejected traditional norms and customs. He did not concern himself

with facts or efforts to unite disparate Americans to achieve a common purpose. He was not interested in listening to intelligence briefings, mastering
the arcane details of governance, or reassuring the public that his administration would provide at least minimal technical competence. He was
single-mindedly devoted to self-aggrandizement, which became the foundation of Trumpism. Say anything on a whim, no matter how audacious,
contradictory, or inaccurate, if it cast The Donald in the best possible light.[2]

For these reasons, Trump became a kind of Rorschach test in American
politics. Almost no one agreed on anything about him. He was refreshingly
authentic or intolerably crude; a savvy tycoon who would shake up busi-
ness-as-usual in dysfunctional Washington or a malignant narcissist and
bully who had destroyed every business he ever touched and would do the
same for the American republic if he became grifter-in-chief. He was an
unbought, politically incorrect outsider who would drain the swamp, or a
racist, misogynistic, incompetent, hopelessly corrupt con man who *was* the
swamp.

One thing everyone agreed on was that he was far from conventional.
Trump brought with him much baggage—a slew of failed marriages; bank-
rupt businesses; racial discrimination in his properties; incendiary, outlandish evidence-free claims about all manner of public issues; promises
made and promises broken; and charges of sexual harassment and assaults,
among other things—but his admirers overlooked his innumerable shortcomings. He was their guy, a straight-shooting, foulmouthed, tough-talking
wise guy who would stick it to elites and "own the libs," those effete, insuf-
ferable, politically and culturally liberal snobs who looked down on ordinary, hardworking Americans eking out a living in the Heartland.

Many Trump supporters joyfully and unabashedly joined his personality
cult. They were with him no matter how crazy his claims. In fact, when
"lamestream" political figures derided the Trump cult, the attacks further
endeared the faithful to the Chosen One. The viciousness of the Never
Trumpers' assaults propelled the true believers together into a tight-knit
circle of brotherhood. Just as they felt they had been assailed by the elites
throughout their lives, so, too, was their beloved leader. The vehemence
of the criticism demonstrated that Trump was onto something. The elites
would not be so upset if the great man weren't about to knock them off
their high horses.

Donald Trump never met a conspiracy theory he could not embrace—the
zanier, the better. His followers accepted everything that he said, even the
far-fetched conspiracies. Who cared how many demonstrably false claims
Trump uttered? His assertions could defy all logic, evidence, and common
sense, but it mattered not to his legion of devotees. All criticism of his behavior was the product of fake news—a hoax, a witch hunt—and a political
establishment that was out to get their guy. He could do no wrong. Trump

was anointed by God, a messianic figure who would fix the deficiencies in the American republic or otherwise burn it all down. His admirers seemed not to care which. He was the ultimate warrior in the culture wars, a man who never apologized, backed down, or accepted responsibility. He stood up for his supporters and did what his base wished they could do. He was the epitome of what they hoped to be: unbowed, unapologetic, rich, savvy, and tough. When he was campaigning for president early in 2016, Trump boasted that "I have the most loyal people—did you ever see that? I could stand in the middle of Fifth Avenue and shoot somebody, and I wouldn't lose any voters, okay?"[3]

Admirers saw a man who was not a career politician. In fact, Trump had never held any elective office, nor had he served in the military. The first forty-four men who served as president of the United States could boast of one or both qualifications, but Trump made it clear that he was a new kind of man. He did not need experience to fix the problems of American government. In fact, political experience only corrupted a president, hindering his ability to shake up the establishment. "I alone can fix it," he promised. The normal rules of campaigning and governance did not apply to him. In fact, no rules seemed to apply to him. He was a figure without precedent or peer. He was a *sui generis* candidate for high office. Responding to criticism, he described himself as "a very stable genius."[4]

Despite his success in flouting the normal rules of political behavior during the 2016 presidential contest, the very stable genius knew that his string of sex scandals could hurt him with voters outside the cult. His behavior played well to his base of supporters no matter what he did, but the candidate needed to appeal to potential voters outside the cult. Suburban soccer moms and young professionals might not cast their ballots for Trump if they knew of his marital infidelity or his string of alleged sexual assaults.

A month after he officially captured the Republican presidential nomination, Trump authorized his personal lawyer and "fixer," Michael Cohen, to pay $150,000 in hush money to Karen McDougal, a former *Playboy* Playmate, who alleged a ten-month affair with Trump that originated in the summer of 2006. According to McDougal, she met Trump during a filming of his television show *Celebrity Apprentice* at the Los Angeles Playboy Mansion three months after his youngest son, Barron, was born. He asked for her phone number. Shortly thereafter, they began talking on the phone. She eventually joined him for dinner at a bungalow in Beverly Hills. As McDougal wrote in her journal, "We talked for a couple of hours—then, it was 'ON'! We got naked + had sex." He offered her money after the encounter, but she declined. "You are special," Trump told her.[5]

The couple met for sex "many dozens of times" during the ensuing ten months. Whenever he could slip away, Trump met McDougal in hotels, at

Trump golf clubs, and in the Trump Tower apartment he shared with his third wife, Melania. Trump was seen in public with her, even allowing himself to be photographed with her and his family. Paying her the ultimate compliment, Trump told McDougal that she was "beautiful like her," referring to his elder daughter, Ivanka, whom he adored.[6]

McDougal said that she fell in love with Trump. "There were real feelings between the two of us," she insisted. Unlike the brutish lout that he portrayed on television, Trump was kind and gentle with her. "He's so sweet," she observed, a "very respectful, very loving, very kind and caring man."[7]

By April 2007 Karen McDougal had broken off the relationship with this very kind and caring man. She later claimed that she felt guilty about the affair when she thought about Trump's wife, Melania. She also felt offended by some of Trump's comments.[8]

Trump never appeared to worry about the McDougal affair until he launched his presidential bid. In August 2016 he authorized Michael Cohen to "fix" the problem. Cohen did. Karen McDougal agreed to accept $150,000 in "hush money" to remain silent about their affair a decade earlier. The arrangement followed a similar deal that Cohen had brokered to buy the silence of Stormy Daniels, a pornographic film actress who claimed to have had sex with Trump on one occasion in July 2006. In October 2016 Daniels agreed to accept $130,000 for her silence.[9]

The money was supposed to conceal an incident that allegedly occurred at the Edgewood Tahoe Golf Course at Lake Tahoe, Nevada. The American Century Golf Championship had attracted numerous celebrities during a July weekend in 2006, including pornographic actresses Jessica Drake and Stormy Daniels. The women were staffing a booth for Wicked Pictures in the Hospitality Room when Donald Trump appeared. Trump went for a walk with Drake on the golf course, but their interaction never went further. He invited Daniels to have dinner with him, however, and they wound up in the Harrah's hotel penthouse, where Trump was staying.[10]

When Daniels arrived at the penthouse to meet Trump for dinner, he greeted her in black silk pajamas. Daniels was surprised. She thought they were going to eat in a restaurant. He said they would eat in his room. It was clear that Trump wanted sex. Daniels, who was 27 years old at the time, told the 60-year-old Trump to put on his clothes.

Trump was self-impressed and assumed that others would be impressed with him, too. He showed Daniels a magazine with his photograph on the cover. She did not swoon. "I was like, 'Does this—does this normally work for you?'" she asked. Trump was taken aback. "Like, I was, 'Does, just, you know talking about yourself normally work?' And I was like, 'Someone should take that magazine and spank you with it.'"

Daniels did exactly that. She snatched the magazine and ordered him to "Turn around, drop 'em." He lowered his pants slightly and Daniels swatted him on the behind. "And from that moment on he was a completely different person," Daniels recalled. They talked normally. He was pleasant enough even though she knew that he still expected to have sex with her.

Daniels claimed that she was worried about being alone with Trump. She telephoned and texted friends, but they would not come to the penthouse. Eventually, Daniels and Trump had sex—"one position, no condom," she said—and she left soon after.[11]

Stormy Daniels saw Trump again a few times, but they never again had intercourse. He invited her to a bungalow at the Beverly Hills Hotel, where they ate dinner in his room and watched *Shark Week* on television. Trump wanted to have sex, but Daniels claimed to be menstruating. She left shortly thereafter and never met with him again.[12]

Like Karen McDougal, Stormy Daniels signed a nondisclosure agreement (NDA) in exchange for hush money in 2016. After news reporters uncovered the arrangement early in 2018, Daniels sought to abrogate the NDA. She soon found herself at the center of a media storm. The story of a pornographic film actress having sex with a man who went on to become president of the United States and bought her silence was too good to pass up.

"Who would have thought that 90 seconds with Donald Trump would turn into 90 percent of my life?" Daniels asked.[13]

In March 2018 Daniels hired an aggressive media-savvy lawyer, Michael Avenatti, to file a lawsuit seeking to invalidate the NDA. Daniels also filed a related defamation lawsuit against President Trump for publicly calling her a liar—he also labeled her "Horseface" in one tweet—in response to her allegations. The court dismissed the defamation lawsuit as frivolous and ordered Daniels to pay Trump's attorney fees. She later had a falling out with her attorney. For his part, Avenatti was later arrested and charged with wire fraud, identity theft, and embezzling almost $300,000 from Daniels.[14]

Stormy Daniels was a clear-eyed realist. She knew that her reputation as a pornographic film actress alleging an affair against the president of the United States placed her in a vulnerable position. Along with the enormous media attention, she received death threats as well as a barrage of news stories assessing her place in American culture. For some Americans, she was a "dirty porn star" who deserved all manner of vitriol. Others saw her as a feminist heroine, a woman who refused to be cowed or apologize for her life and actions. To capitalize on her fifteen minutes of fame, she published a memoir, *Full Disclosure*, in 2018. The book, which provided details on Trump's actions and described his penis, became a *New York Times* best seller.[15]

Karen McDougal and Stormy Daniels were the most high-profile affairs that Trump allegedly pursued, but they were only two among many. More troubling than his consensual escapades, however, were Trump's sexual assaults against unwilling women. He outlined his strategy for assaulting

Figure 14.1. Stormy Daniels, pictured here in 2015, was a pornographic film actress who alleged that she had a sexual relationship with Donald Trump in 2006. Courtesy of Glenn Francis, www. PacificProDigital.com, Creative Commons Attribution.

women during a conversation shortly before he appeared on the television show *Access Hollywood* in 2005. Speaking to the show's host, Billy Bush, Trump confessed that, "you know, I'm automatically attracted to beautiful—I just start kissing them. It's like a magnet. I just kiss. I don't even wait. And when you're a star, they let you do it. You can do anything." Lest the subtlety of the message escaped Bush's notice, Trump clarified his meaning. "Grab 'em by the pussy. You can do anything."[16]

Trump struggled mightily to live up to his creed. His record of sexual assault was long. His first wife, Ivana, alleged during the couple's divorce proceedings in 1989 that he had been violently abusive and raped her. Years later, Ivana recanted, claiming that she and Trump were the best of friends.[17]

The dark side of Donald Trump's sexual appetite comes through court filings against him dating back to the 1990s. In one instance a makeup artist named Jill Harth recounted an all-too-familiar tale of her run-in with the New York real estate tycoon. In December 1992 she and her boyfriend, George Houraney, scheduled a business meeting with Trump in New York. Harth and Houraney operated a small company, American Dream Enterprises, that staged events such as beauty contests, automobile shows, and music competitions. The couple hoped to persuade Trump to allow them to stage events at his Atlantic City casinos to raise their company's profile.

Trump listened to their spiel, but he was not as interested in the business opportunity as he was in Jill Harth. He considered himself a connoisseur of beautiful women, and Trump thought that Jill Harth was a beautiful woman. He wanted to enjoy a sexual relationship with her. It never occurred to him that a woman would resist his advances. During the initial meeting, he uttered inappropriate comments about Harth's sexual relationship with Houraney. He even bluntly told George Houraney that they could have a problem because he, Trump, was attracted to Houraney's girlfriend.

The next evening, as the couple met with Trump for follow-up discussions, the matter escalated. Trump ran his hands over Harth's body and, as she later alleged in a lawsuit, he tried to touch "her intimate private parts." She resisted, but Trump was adamant. In the days and weeks that followed, he called her repeatedly, admitting that he wanted to sleep with her even though he was married to his second wife, Marla Maples, at the time.

Despite the aggressive advances, Jill Harth continued talking with Trump. She was desperate to engage in a business relationship that could benefit her company. During a visit to Trump's Florida estate, Mar-a-Lago, Harth accompanied him on a grand tour of the property. When they entered his daughter Ivanka's bedroom, Trump pinned her to the wall and kissed her repeatedly, "touching her intimately," as she later recalled.

"I pushed him off me," Harth stated in a subsequent lawsuit. "And I was, I said to him, 'What are you doing? Why are you doing this?'"

According to Harth, Trump seemed shocked that she would push him away. She was worried that he might rape her. Feeling "degraded and humiliated as a female," Harth began vomiting, which may have saved her from an additional assault.

She, Houraney, and several "Calendar Girls" who had joined them for the trip, were supposed to spend the night at Mar-a-Lago, but she convinced her boyfriend to leave immediately. Even after she had fled, Trump continued to call, chiding her to leave Houraney— "that loser"—and "step it up to the Big Leagues" with Trump. He assured her that "I'm going to be the best lover you ever had."

Harth's dealings with Trump did not end there. Trump had agreed to a business relationship, but he subsequently walked away from the arrangement. In 1995 Houraney and Harth were married. That same year Houraney filed suit against Trump for breach of contract. In 1997 Harth sued Trump for sexual harassment. She withdrew the sexual harassment suit as a condition of settlement for the breach-of-contract suit.

Later, after Harth and Houraney divorced, she dated Trump. If it seemed strange that a woman would date a man who sexually assaulted her, Harth explained, "I was scared, thinking, 'what am I going to do now?'" When Trump called her, she agreed to see him. He was separated from Marla Maples, and Harth thought, "maybe I should give this rich guy a chance." She found Trump to be insensitive to her needs, always glued to the television and emotionally distant.[18]

E. Jean Carroll's experience with Trump was similar to Harth's, but the assailant went one step further than merely pursuing her. Carroll said that Trump raped her. An advice columnist, Carroll encountered the real estate developer as she left the Bergdorf Goodman department store on Fifth Avenue in New York City sometime late in 1995 or early the next year. She found him good-looking and charismatic. When he asked her to help him buy a present for someone, she readily agreed.

Browsing in the lingerie section, Trump insisted that she try on a lilac-gray lace bodysuit. The two bantered back and forth, with Carroll telling him that he should try it on. They eventually went to the dressing room, and the playful jokes grounded to an abrupt halt.

As Carroll later described the scene, the "moment the dressing-room door is closed, he lunges at me, pushes me against the wall, hitting my head quite badly, and puts his mouth against my lips." Stunned by the ferocity of the attack, Carroll did not know how to respond. Despite the shock, she still thought they were joking with each other. She laughed.

Trump removed all doubt about his intentions when he unzipped his pants. "The next moment," she recalled, "still wearing correct business attire, shirt, tie, suit jacket, overcoat, he opens the overcoat, unzips his pants, and, forcing his fingers around my private area, thrusts his penis halfway—

or completely, I'm not certain—inside me." Carroll continued to resist, and Trump eventually fled.[19]

When she told this story years later, Trump dismissed her allegations out of hand. "She's not my type," he remarked. It was Trump's way of trivializing her complaints, and Carroll would have none of it.[20]

In November 2019 Carroll filed a defamation lawsuit against Trump. He was serving as president of the United States by this time. According to Carroll, Trump's dismissal of her claims harmed her reputation and livelihood. As was customary with Trump and his advisers, they responded to the claims by attacking the woman. The White House press secretary, Stephanie Grisham, condescendingly commented that the lawsuit was frivolous and the story was fake, "just like the author."[21]

In September 2020 the Department of Justice filed a motion in court to assume Trump's defense from his private lawyers, arguing that Trump had been acting "within the scope" of his presidency when he allegedly defamed Jean Carroll. Moreover, federal employees enjoy limited immunity from defamation suits. As of this writing, the case remains active in court. The Justice Department under Trump's successor, Joseph Biden, remained steadfast in defending the former president in the defamation suit.[22]

Another woman, Summer Zervos, also sued Trump for defamation when he claimed that her charges were false. Zervos was a contestant on the fifth season of Trump's reality television show *The Apprentice*, which was filmed in 2005 and aired the following year. In 2007 she contacted Trump to ask for career advice. During their meeting Trump repeatedly kissed her on the lips without her consent.

As he did with so many other women, Trump phoned her several times following that initial encounter. Zervos understood that his intentions were far from altruistic, but she needed Trump's help in pursuing business opportunities. Despite his unwanted advances, she ignored the inappropriate behavior in hopes that he would help her career. At a meeting at the Beverly Hills Hotel, Trump kissed her again. He also "thrust his genitals" at her. When Zervos went public with the allegations years later, Trump branded her a liar and emphatically denied the charges. Zervos filed a defamation lawsuit against him. After much legal wrangling about whether Trump was immune from the suit because he was president, the courts agreed that the case could proceed, although she later dropped the suit.[23]

Another woman, Alva Johnson, also sued Trump, although the suit was dismissed. According to Johnson, she worked on the candidate's 2016 presidential campaign as director for outreach in Alabama. Before a rally in Florida on August 24, 2016, Trump was posing for photographs with volunteers. When he passed her on his way from his vehicle, Johnson spoke with him. "I've been on the road for you since March, away from my family," she told him. "You're doing an awesome job. Go in there and kick ass."

In response, according to Johnson, the candidate "grasped her hand and did not let go." He leaned "close enough that she could feel his breath on her skin" and kissed her on the corner of her mouth when she turned her head. "Then he walks out," Johnson recalled. The entire exchange was brief, but it left her feeling humiliated and vulnerable. Her mother recalled talking to Johnson shortly thereafter. "She was hysterical."

Johnson said that at least two other people witnessed the incident, including Pam Bondi, who was serving as the attorney general of Florida at the time. The supposed witnesses denied seeing anything untoward. Johnson remained at her post, working for the campaign. She eventually attended the inaugural ball and even applied unsuccessfully for two positions within the Trump administration. She later filed suit against the president, but a federal judge dismissed the case. Sarah Huckabee Sanders, Trump's press secretary, remarked that the lawsuit was "absurd on its face."[24]

These were only the legal proceedings stemming from Trump's sexual escapades. Many other women alleged that Trump had assaulted them and was a sexual predator, but they did not seek legal redress. Many of these women came forward in 2016, when it appeared likely that Trump would become the Republican presidential nominee and possibly the next president of the United States. Owing to the timing, Trump and his allies dismissed the claims as politically motivated and completely fabricated.[25]

Jessica Leeds became one of the most prominent of these accusers. She recalled that when she was traveling on an airplane to New York City sometime in 1979, she was upgraded from the coach section to first class. When she entered first class, she sat next to Donald Trump. She did not know who he was at the time, but the two engaged in small talk. They did not flirt. After the meal ended, Trump suddenly groped her and started kissing her without a word. His hands were everywhere. When he tried to reach under her skirt, Leeds stood, grabbed her things, and fled to the last seat in coach. After the plane landed, she waited to ensure that she was the last person to leave the airplane. Trump had departed when she finally crept down the jet bridge.[26]

"I was completely shocked and felt very vulnerable," she recalled. She told no one, not even her family, about the incident at the time. "When it originally happened, I didn't complain to the airlines," she said in 2016. "I didn't tell my boss. You didn't make a big deal about it." The reaction of many people, especially men, in that era was to brush off such complaints. Sexual harassment was to be expected when a woman worked in a man's world. "Boys will be boys" was the feeling.[27]

That might have been the end of her encounters with Donald Trump, but it was not. Leeds encountered Trump at a gala held at Saks Fifth Avenue a few years later. By that time she had left her previous employer and relocated to New York City. She was working for the Humane Society of

New York, and she was staffing a table where she handed out seating assignments. When she saw the real estate mogul arrive with his wife, Ivana, she immediately recognized him as the man who had groped her on the airplane two years earlier. During the 1979 incident, she had not known who he was. Now, living in New York, she was aware of Trump and his penchant for publicity.

It was not surprising that Jessica Leeds recognized Donald Trump, but it was astonishing that he recalled the incident. "I remember you," he said, nonchalantly, as they came face to face. "You're the cunt from the airplane." He uttered the remark without any apparent vitriol, as though he were speaking about a mundane matter. With that, he snatched up the chip showing his seat and sauntered away, leaving Leeds feeling devastated and vulnerable.[28]

Trump's predilection for groping women without their consent and denying any wrongdoing became an integral part of the Trump brand. He kept doing it because he never faced serious consequences. As he bragged in the *Access Hollywood* tape in 2005, famous people can do whatever they want. Most of the reported incidents occurred beginning in the 1990s, especially at times when he was experiencing marital difficulties or between marriages.[29]

Although this chapter does not present an exhaustive list of Trump's alleged sexual assaults, it presents representative cases. His interaction with a young model, Kristin Anderson, at a New York City nightspot, the China Club, in the early 1990s typified Trump's approach. The assaults often proceeded with little dialogue or explanation. Trump simply placed his hands wherever he wanted on anyone whom he deemed to be attractive. In Anderson's case she was sitting on a velvet couch in the club when a man sitting next to her slid his hand beneath her skirt and touched her vagina through her panties. She had not been conversing with the man, and she was unaware of his presence before the assault.[30]

Whipping her head around, she saw that Donald Trump was her assailant. She and her friends were "very grossed out and weirded out" by the thought that a much older, obese man would so brazenly snake his hand beneath her dress without her consent. "It wasn't a sexual come-on," Anderson concluded. "I don't know why he did it. It was like just to prove that he could do it and nothing would happen. There was zero conversation. We didn't even really look at each other. It was very random, very nonchalant on his part."[31]

Such encounters with a brazen Trump became commonplace. He often assaulted a young woman regardless of whether he knew her. A case in point: Sometime in 1996 Lisa Boyne, an entrepreneur, accepted an invitation from a friend, Sonja Morgan—who was then Sonja Tremont, and who later went on to fame on the television show *The Real Housewives of New*

York—to have dinner with Donald Trump and prominent modeling agent John Casablancas. Five or six models joined them as well.

Boyne recalled that she was put off by Trump from the moment he picked her up in his limousine. "He was a douche bag," she said. "He took all the air out of the limo. He wouldn't let anyone talk."

They arrived at Raoul's, a trendy New York restaurant, to meet Casablancas. Trump was in rare form, asking Boyne who he should sleep with and how she would rate the models. Boyne was astonished at his juvenile behavior. "This is a conversation I felt like I was having with a twelve-year-old boy," she said. Worse than the sexually suggestive talk were Trump's and John Casablancas's actions. When the women wanted to leave the booth, the men made them walk across the table.

As soon as a woman stepped up onto the table, Trump "stuck his head right under the women's skirts" and commented on their underwear and their genitalia. Boyne was disgusted. "It was the most offensive scene I've ever been a part of. I wanted to get the heck out of there." She left before the appetizers arrived.[32]

Cathy Heller's encounter with a randy Donald Trump occurred in 1997. She arrived at Trump's Mar-a-Lago estate with her husband, three children, and in-laws for a Mother's Day brunch. Trump came to the table to greet the guests, as he had done with others. Heller intended to shake his hand, but the big man had other plans. Trump "took my hand, grabbed me, and went for the lips." She turned her head at the last moment so that he kissed the side of her mouth. Angry at the exchange, Trump stomped away. "I remember she was really freaked out," a relative recalled of Heller's reaction. Trump was "very forceful" when he lunged at Heller.[33]

Temple Taggart (later McDowell) was 21 years old and serving as Miss Utah USA in 1997 when she met with Trump in his office. He peppered her with unwanted kisses and embraces. Trump's behavior upset one of the pageant chaperones so much that the chaperone wisely insisted that Taggart not be left alone with Trump again.[34]

Amy Dorris and her boyfriend, Jason Binn, attended the 1997 US Open with Trump. According to Dorris, while they were there, Trump groped and kissed her without her consent. She told her mother and a friend about the assault shortly thereafter. Trump, of course, denied the attack.[35]

In 1998 27-year-old Karena Virginia was waiting for a ride after the US Open tournament in Queens, New York. While she waited, Donald Trump approached her with a group of men. She had never met any of the men before. "Hey, look at this one," Trump said to his associates as he pointed out Virginia. "We haven't seen this one before."

Trump reached out and grabbed her arm. "Then his hand touched the right side of my breast," Virginia recalled at a 2016 press conference. "I was in shock. I flinched. 'Don't you know who I am? Don't you know who I am?'—that's what he said to me. I felt intimidated and I felt powerless." This behavior was consistent with Trump's insistence that "when you're a star, they let you do it. You can do anything."[36]

Karen Johnson reported a similarly aggressive Trump tactic. During a New Year's Eve party at the Mar-a-Lago estate in the early 2000s, she encountered Trump. Her husband, who was suffering from multiple sclerosis, was with her at the party. Johnson was familiar with the club, having held her wedding reception there a few years earlier. As she later recalled in an interview, she did not know Trump before her wedding reception. She said that he had "chased some of my bridesmaids around," but he treated her well during the reception.

The New Year's Eve party was a different story. After balloons fell to celebrate the midnight hour, Johnson's husband said that he did not feel well. The couple decided to leave, but Johnson ran to the restroom before their departure.

She had not seen Trump that evening, but as Johnson made her way across the room, "I was grabbed and pulled behind a tapestry, and it was him." Trump forcibly and repeatedly kissed her. He did not ask for, nor apparently desire, consent. "I was scared because of who he was," Johnson confessed. "I don't even know where it came from. I didn't have a say in the matter."

Trump grabbed her hand and told her that she needed to help him bid farewell to his guests. Still in a state of shock, she complied with his request. She tried not to alert anyone to the awkward situation but stood next to Trump and said goodbye to the departing guests.

In the ensuing days Trump relentlessly pursued her. The phone rang, and when she picked up, a voice intoned, "Do you know who this is?" She instantly recognized his voice and grew frightened.

Unfamiliar with Trump's trademark brand of narcissism, his callousness left her flabbergasted. When he urged her to fly up to New York for the day to see him, she explained that she was caring for her ailing husband. Trump brusquely dismissed her concerns. "Don't worry about it," he assured her. "He'll never know you were gone." The entreaties persisted for weeks before Trump ceased calling. Johnson told a relative about the episodes, but she never told her dying husband.

When she first heard Trump's confession of sexual assaults on the *Access Hollywood* tape, Johnson was stunned. His description of forcing himself on women with impunity because he was famous was exactly what he had done to her. She immediately recognized Trump's modus operandi.[37]

Mindy McGillivray and Rachel Crooks endured similar episodes with Trump. As with all of Trump's accusers, their accounts were dismissed as untrustworthy. In McGillivray's account she was 23 years old and working as a photographer's assistant for a friend, Ken Davidoff, at a Ray Charles concert held at Mar-a-Lago in January 2003. Standing backstage with friends after the concert, the "next thing you know I feel a grab." Donald and Melania Trump were standing with the group. She realized that Trump had reached out and clutched her behind. "To see someone who resembled my father grab me like that was just deplorable," she said.[38]

McGillivray never reported the incident to authorities, although she told family members and friends. Immediately after the incident, she told Ken Davidoff and exclaimed, "Donald just grabbed my ass!" She came forward shortly before the 2016 presidential election to tell her story after she heard Trump publicly deny numerous reports of his sexual assaults.[39]

Not everyone believed her. Ken Davidoff's brother, Darryl Davidoff, was present when the assault allegedly occurred. He was skeptical of McGillivray's story. "I do not believe it really happened," he said. "Nobody saw it happen and she just wanted to be in the limelight."[40]

Similarly, Rachel Crooks's story was met with skepticism. She said that the attack occurred in 2005, when she was working as a receptionist at the Bayrock Group, a real estate and development company, in the group's Trump Tower offices. Twenty-two years old, Crooks recently had moved to New York from Green Springs, Ohio, and was still naïve about the ways of certain men. "I didn't have any notion of him being the womanizer that he is," she admitted. "I just thought he was a successful New York businessman."

Crooks spied Donald Trump many times as he walked past the glass doors of the office. They occasionally made eye contact. Once or twice she even waved. One day she decided to introduce herself.

While they waited at the elevator, Crooks extended her hand. She expected him to shake, but suddenly Trump grabbed her hand and pulled her toward him. He kissed her on one cheek, then the other. He asked her where she was from. Without listening to her answer, he told her that she should be a model. "I have my own modeling agency," he bragged.

"It happened so quickly. I was just so surprised," Crooks explained later. "I didn't understand what he was trying to do. Ultimately, he pulled me in and kissed me on the lips, and I was very upset. The only thing I can think that ended the encounter was that his elevator arrived, thankfully."

She told her sister about the assault, but Crooks did not know how to respond. When Trump saw her sometime later, he asked for her phone number so the modeling agency could call her. "That was the last time I personally interacted with him," Crooks said. She gave him the phone number. Not surprisingly, no one from the modeling agency ever contacted her. In the meantime whenever Rachel Crooks saw Trump walk past her office window, she fled into a nearby kitchen area or hid behind her desk.

When Crooks's account surfaced before the 2016 presidential election, Trump denied her story, attributing it to a politically motivated hit job.

"Who would do this in a public space with live security cameras running?" he asked on Twitter.[41]

Natasha Stoynoff's story was one of the most widely publicized examples of Donald Trump's sexual predation that emerged in 2016. A Canadian author and journalist, Stoynoff arrived at Mar-a-Lago in December 2005 on assignment from *People* magazine to write a story about Donald and Melania Trump on their first wedding anniversary. Melania was visibly pregnant.

Stoynoff snapped several photographs of the couple. When Melania left to change into a new outfit for additional photographs, Donald Trump offered to show Stoynoff a "tremendous" room in the mansion. She followed him into a room and Trump closed the door. "I turned around, and within seconds he was pushing me against the wall and forcing his tongue down my throat." She was only saved, she believed, when a butler entered the room to inform Trump that Melania was on her way.

Still shocked at the sudden and unexpected encounter, Stoynoff followed the couple onto an outdoor patio. "In those few minutes alone with Trump, my self-esteem crashed to zero," Stoynoff remarked. "How could the actions of one man make me feel so utterly violated?"

As always, Trump apparently did not know nor care how his actions made anyone else feel. "You know we're going to have an affair, don't you?" he said when he and Stoynoff were alone. "Have you ever been to Peter Luger's for steaks? I'll take you. We're going to have an affair, I'm telling you." The audacity of the claim was breathtaking. After Melania returned, Trump acted as though nothing had happened. He played the role of the loving and dutiful husband to perfection.[42]

Trump had a particular type of woman he preferred—usually young, blonde, and white. Beauty pageant contestants especially interested him. On July 26, 2006, Ninni Laaksonen, Miss Finland 2006, appeared on the *Late Show with David Letterman* along with Trump and several Miss Universe contestants. As the women were being photographed before the show, Trump groped her. Laaksonen recounted that "Trump stood right next to me and suddenly he squeezed my butt. I don't think anybody saw it, but I flinched and thought: 'What is happening?'"[43]

Cassandra Searles, Miss Washington USA in 2013, charged that Trump treated the Miss USA contestants "like cattle." He often required the pageant contestants to line up "so he could get a closer look at his property." On a Facebook post in 2016, Searles wrote, "He probably doesn't want me telling the story about the time he continually grabbed my ass and invited me to his hotel room." Another contestant, Paromita Mitra, Miss Mississippi USA, commented, "I literally have nightmares about that process."[44]

Most of the women who experienced Trump's sexual predations left the encounter deeply disturbed, but not everyone. Jennifer Murphy and Juliet Huddy both reported that Trump had kissed them on the lips, but they were not upset. Murphy, a former beauty pageant competitor and a contestant on Trump's reality television show *The Apprentice*, was in Trump's office for an interview in 2005 when he kissed her without her consent. Nonetheless, Murphy said that the incident "didn't really bother me." Juliet Huddy, a former *Fox News* anchor, ate lunch with Trump sometime in 2005 or 2006. While they were on the elevator with Trump's security guard accompanying them, he kissed Huddy goodbye on the lips. "I wasn't offended," she insisted.[45]

Numerous other stories have circulated about Trump's escapades throughout the years, many illustrating the same theme. If the stories are credited, Donald Trump has been a sexual predator for much of his life, seldom if ever worried about the repercussions of his actions. After all, famous people can do virtually anything they desire.

In his capacity as a beauty pageant owner and judge, Trump sometimes entered women's dressing rooms to gawk at the young ladies while they dressed or undressed. Tales of Trump's enthusiasm for rating the "hotness" of women were rife among beauty pageant participants. As his television show *The Apprentice* became more popular and his public profile increased, however, Trump apparently curbed his behavior. At the very least, stories of his assaults on women diminished, although as Alva Johnson's and Cassandra Searles's allegations suggest, the behavior did not change. It just went underground.[46]

The question naturally arises as to how and why Donald Trump's public career survived in an era when so many powerful men were held at least partially accountable for their misbehavior. Forced resignations, tearful apologies, official investigations, and public humiliation for everyone concerned have become the order of the day. Yet somehow Donald Trump has escaped the consequences. The answer to this question is not altogether clear, although several factors likely played a part.

First, although the #MeToo movement predated Trump's political ascendancy, the movement did not attract widespread media attention until the charges against Hollywood producer Harvey Weinstein garnered media coverage late in 2017. By that time Donald Trump was already serving as president of the United States. As with so much of Trump's life, he had skated past allegations that probably would have destroyed any other politician's career.

Second, because many of the allegations surfaced in the media in the weeks and months leading up to the 2016 presidential election—even though the incidents sometimes occurred more than a decade earlier—Trump and his team dismissed the charges as factually inaccurate and politically motivated. The timing suggested to Trump that these were fake news fabricated to harm his candidacy. A significant number of voters apparently agreed.

Even in the wake of the *Access Hollywood* revelations, Trump insisted that he was innocent of all sexual assault allegations. Although many Trump detractors viewed his admissions on the tape as incontrovertible evidence of his long history of sexually assaulting women, Trump downplayed the remarks, explaining that his comments were little more than "locker room talk." In a rarity for Trump, he apologized for the comments, although he later suggested that he did not say those words. Instead, the tape must have been doctored to cast him in the worst possible light.

Finally, the #MeToo movement and other actions designed to take powerful men to task assume that assailants will bow to political pressure when they are cornered. The story line follows a typical pattern. A woman alleges that she was sexually harassed and assaulted by an influential political figure. The figure denies that the incident occurred. Sometimes the denial is robust, and the public figure aggressively insists on a political motivation for the supposedly unsubstantiated allegation. On other occasions the denial is fervent but does not cast aspersions on the claimant. Instead, the woman is portrayed as decent and well-meaning but ultimately mistaken. Often, although not always, Republicans choose the former approach while Democrats rely on the latter.[47]

If the political figure is fortunate, no additional allegations surface and the negative headlines soon disappear. In some cases, however, multiple accusers come forward, inundating the airwaves with tearful stories of unbridled malfeasance. The overarching narrative that emerges from the pattern of assaults is of a powerful man who has become arrogant and entitled, believing that he has a right to use his superior position to gratify his urges. He forces himself on a woman who is in a less powerful, often vulnerable position. The woman is frightened, for both her physical safety as well as her financial livelihood. She might confide in a close friend or family member, but sometimes her feelings of shame, guilt, and humiliation prevent her from speaking out publicly or to the police. When she finally comes forward, her tale convinces other women to speak, and a torrent of accusations flows.

Faced with a flood of negative stories, the political figure initially resists. He soon drowns in a sea of accusation and innuendo. If videos, tape recordings, letters, texts, social media posts, or emails exist, he soon exhausts his options. Faced with a barrage of negative press, the political figure resigns his position. Sometimes he is defiant to the bitter end, and sometimes he is contrite, vowing to spend more time with his family and promising to listen to women in the future so that he can be a better man moving forward.

Donald Trump bucked this trend. His strategy in his business and political careers was always to deny any allegation, regardless of how well founded or how thoroughly documented. He crafted his own reality, and he simply denied any facts or allegations that impinged on that reality. No matter how many women came forward, no matter how credible their stories, and no matter how well documented the claims, he unequivocally denied them all. He refused to listen to any news that contradicted his carefully constructed narrative. Any news or charges that cast him in a poor light were dismissed as fake news, lies told by the liberal elite to besmirch the good name of Trump and, by inference, attack his faithful supporters. In short, Donald Trump never exhibited shame. He would not be brought down by public shaming because he was immune to such feelings. He was the ultimate narcissist—unwilling or unable to feel anyone's pain but his own.

It is regrettable that a strategy of denying all allegations and aggressively attacking the accusers was so successful, but Trump was an unusual public figure. Many public figures seek the approbation of their fellow man. Much of Donald Trump's career suggested that he also sought that approbation, yet he frequently acted in ways that all but guaranteed he would not gain the respect he apparently craved. Always divorced from public approval except among his faithful core of supporters who would support him no matter what he did, Trump simply acted as he pleased and avoided responsibility. That was the Trump brand: Do as you will, and the consequences be damned. It is hardly a sterling credo for an honorable public life, but as of this writing, it is a reasonably effective means of surviving multiple sex scandals.

NOTES

1. See, for example, Philip Rucker and Carol Leonnig, *A Very Stable Genius: Donald J. Trump's Testing of America* (New York: Penguin Press, 2020), 23–24. Trump's quote about rapists from Mexico is quoted in many sources. See, for example, Mark D. Ramirez and David A. M. Peterson, *Ignored Racism: White Animus Toward Latinos* (Cambridge and New York: Cambridge University Press, 2020), 4.

2. On this point, see, for example, George Packer, "The Legacy of Donald Trump: His Reign of Lies Poisoned Our Mind and Our Politics, with Effects that Will Long Linger. But Democracy Survived," *Atlantic* 327, no. 1 (January/February 2021): 9–12.

3. Trump is quoted in Harold Holzer, *The Presidents vs. the Press: The Endless Battle Between the White House and the Media from the Founding Fathers to Fake News* (New York: Dutton, 2020), 414.

4. Holzer, *The Presidents vs. the Press*, 410–16. Journalists Carol Leonnig and Philip Rucker named their first book after Trump's self-description "a very stable genius." Their second book was titled *I Alone Can Fix It*. See Carol Leonnig and Philip Rucker, *I Alone Can Fix It: Donald J. Trump's Catastrophic Final Year* (New York: Penguin Press, 2021).

5. The quotes and information are found in Barry Levine and Monique El-Faizy, *All the President's Women: Donald Trump and the Making of a Predator* (New York: Hachette Books, 2019), 154. See also Brian Bennett, Teresa Berenson, Massimo Ca-

labresi, Philip Elliott, W. J. Hennigan, and Susanna Schrobsdorff, "Perfect Storm," *Time* 191, no. 5 (April 23, 2018): 25; Jim Rutenberg, "Former Playboy Model Tells of Affair with Trump That Lasted 10 Months," *New York Times*, March 23, 2018, A19.

6. Rutenberg, "Former Playboy Model Tells of Affair with Trump . . .," A19.

7. McDougal is quoted in Levine and El-Faizy, *All the President's Women*, 155.

8. Levine and El-Faizy, *All the President's Women*, 155. See also Rutenberg, "Former Playboy Model Tells of Affair with Trump . . .," A19.

9. Bennett, et al., "Perfect Storm," 23. In June 2021 the sensationalistic tabloid the *National Enquirer* agreed to a $187,500 fine from the Federal Election Commission (FEC) for paying $150,000 to McDougal as part of a "catch and kill" scheme to assist Trump in the 2016 presidential election. In 2016 the publication paid McDougal for a tell-all exposé on her affair with Trump. David Pecker, the *Enquirer* publisher, supported Trump's candidacy. Accordingly, he simply declined to run the story after he had bought the rights. The FEC determined that the $150,000 payment was an illegal campaign contribution. See, for example, Shane Goldmacher, "A Tabloid Publisher Will Pay $187,500 FEC Penalty for Its Trump Hush-Money Payment," *New York Times*, June 1, 2021, n.p.

10. Levine and El-Faizy, *All the President's Women*, 156–57.

11. Daniels is quoted in Levine and El-Faizy, *All the President's Women*, 160.

12. Levine and El-Faizy, *All the President's Women*, 161–62.

13. Daniels is quoted in Susanna Schrobsdorff, "Provocateur Stormy Daniels Takes an Unexpected Turn in the National Spotlight," *Time* 192, no. 17 (October 29, 2018): 12.

14. Schrobsdorff, "Provocateur Stormy Daniels Takes an Unexpected Turn in the National Spotlight," 13. See also Teresa C. Kulig, Francis T. Cullen, and Murat Haner, "President or Predator? The Social Construction of Donald Trump in a Divided America," *Victims & Offenders* 14, no. 8 (November 2019): 942; Michael D. Shear and Eileen Sullivan, "'Horseface,' 'Lowlife,' 'Fat, Ugly': How President Demeans Women," *New York Times*, October 17, 2018, A1.

15. Stormy Daniels, *Full Disclosure* (New York: St. Martin's 2018).

16. Trump is quoted in Kulig, et al., "President or Predator?" 942.

17. See, for example, Ruthann Robson, "The Sexual Misconduct of Donald J. Trump: Toward a Misogyny Report, *Michigan Journal of Gender & Law* 27, no. 1 (2020): 117–18.

18. The quotes and descriptions are found in Levine and El-Faizy, *All the President's Women*, 74–77. See also Robson, "The Sexual Misconduct of Donald J. Trump," 116–17.

19. The quotes and descriptions are found in Levine and El-Faizy, *All the President's Women*, 77–78. See also Kulig, et al., "President or Predator?" 941; Robson, "The Sexual Misconduct of Donald J. Trump," 123–24.

20. Trump is quoted in Robson, "The Sexual Misconduct of Donald J. Trump," 123.

21. El-Faizy, *All the President's Women*, 77–78. White House press secretary Stephanie Grisham is quoted in Lindsey Ellefson, "White House Calls Trump Assault Accuser E. Jean Carroll's New Defamation Suit a 'Fraud—Just Like the Author,'" *The Wrap*, November 4, 2019, accessed on September 3, 2021, www.thewrap.com/white-house-calls-trump-assault-accuser-e-jean-carrolls-new-defamation-suit-a-fraud-just-like-the-author/.

22. Alan Feuer and Benjamin Weiser, "Biden's Justice Dept. Backs Trump in Defamation Case," *New York Times*, June 9, 2021, A17.

23. Jonah E. Bromwich, "Legal Setback for Trump as 'Apprentice' Star Suit Is Cleared to Proceed," *New York Times*, March 31, 2021, A19; Robson, "The Sexual Misconduct of Donald J. Trump," 103–7. See also Jonah E. Bromwich, "Apprentice Contestant Ends Trump Defamation Lawsuit," *New York Times*, November 14, 2021, A18.

24. The information and quotes are found in Niraj Chokshi, "Former Staffer Claims Trump Forced Kiss," *New York Times*, February 26, 2019, A17.

25. Kulig, et al., "President or Predator?" 941.

26. Kulig, et al., "President or Predator?" 940–41. See also Megan Twohey and Michael Barbaro, "Two Women Say Trump Made Unwanted Advances Long Ago," *New York Times*, October 13, 2016, A1.

27. Leeds is quoted in Levine and El-Faizy, *All the President's Women*, 71.

28. The information and quotes are found in Levine and El-Faizy, *All the President's Women*, 71–72. See also Kulig, et al., "President or Predator?" 940–41; Robson, "The Sexual Misconduct of Donald J. Trump," 119.

29. See, for example, Lindsey E. Blumell, "She Persisted . . . and So Did He. Gendered Source Use During the Trump Access Hollywood Scandal," *Journalism Studies* 20, no. 2 (February 2019): 273.

30. Jessica Bennett, "'Strange Sorority' Bids Farewell to Trump," *New York Times*, January 24, 2021, ST4; Levine and El-Faizy, *All the President's Women*, 73–74; Robson, "The Sexual Misconduct of Donald J. Trump," 120.

31. Anderson is quoted in Levine and El-Faizy, *All the President's Women*, 73–74.

32. Boyne's story and the quotes are recounted in Levine and El-Faizy, *All the President's Women*, 78–79.

33. The quote is found in Levine and El-Faizy, *All the President's Women*, 79. See also Robson, "The Sexual Misconduct of Donald J. Trump," 121.

34. Michael Barbaro and Megan Twohey, "Crossing the Line: Trump's Private Conduct with Women," *New York Times*, May 15, 2016, 1; Robson, "The Sexual Misconduct of Donald J. Trump," 122.

35. Jodi Kantor, "Friends Recall Trump Accuser's Claims from 1997," *New York Times*, October 9, 2020, A25.

36. The information and quotes are found in Levine and El-Faizy, *All the President's Women*, 79–80. See also Robson, "The Sexual Misconduct of Donald J. Trump," 120; Trip Gabriel, "A 10th Woman Accuses Donald Trump of Inappropriate Touching," *New York Times*, October 20, 2016, n.p.

37. The information and quotes are found in Levine and El-Faizy, *All the President's Women*, 80–82.

38. The information and quotes are found in Levine and El-Faizy, *All the President's Women*, 82.

39. The information and quotes are found in Levine and El-Faizy, *All the President's Women*, 82. See also Robson, "The Sexual Misconduct of Donald J. Trump," 120.

40. The information and quotes are found in Meghan Keneally, "List of Trump's Accusers and Their Allegations of Sexual Misconduct," ABC News, Septem-

ber 18, 2020, accessed on September 3, 2021, https://abcnews.go.com/Politics/list-trumps-accusers-allegations-sexual-misconduct/story?id=51956410.

41. The information and quotes are found in Levine and El-Faizy, *All the President's Women*, 82–83. See also Twohey and Barbaro, "Two Women Say Trump Made Unwanted Advances Long Ago," A1.

42. The information and quotes are found in Levine and El-Faizy, *All the President's Women*, 84–85. See also Bennett, "'Strange Sorority' Bids Farewell to Trump," ST4; Robson, "The Sexual Misconduct of Donald J. Trump," 121.

43. The information and quotes are found in Levine and El-Faizy, *All the President's Women*, 85. See also Robson, "The Sexual Misconduct of Donald J. Trump," 122.

44. The information and quotes are found in Levine and El-Faizy, *All the President's Women*, 132–33.

45. The information and quotes are found in Levine and El-Faizy, *All the President's Women*, 84.

46. Barbaro and Twohey, "Crossing the Line," 1; Shear and Sullivan, "'Horseface,' 'Lowlife,' 'Fat, Ugly,'" A1.

47. The argument is that Democrats claim to be the party of women, people of color, and the disenfranchised. Casting aspersions on a claimant violates party norms.

Afterword

Sex scandals, as opposed to political corruption scandals, are relatively easy for the public to understand. Corruption cases can be convoluted and complex. The paper trail and circumstantial evidence of malfeasance can be opaque for anyone not immersed in the minutiae of the transactions. Had the Watergate investigation not produced tape recordings of President Richard Nixon discussing bribery and cover-up activities, the outcome might have been different. Ronald Reagan escaped impeachment for Iran-Contra because his participation in the scheme was not clear and definitive. Warren G. Harding's legacy was not tainted by Teapot Dome until after his death. Even then, he was not seen as an active conspirator but as a passive, disengaged administrator.

Sex scandals usually possess a narrative clarity lacking in corruption cases. When the secretary of the treasury fell into the embrace of a comely but manipulative woman in the heat of passion and sought to conceal evidence of the affair, his motives were not difficult to fathom. When the president of the United States engaged in sexual relations with an intern half his age and lied about it, everyone could understand what happened and why. When an aging, avuncular congressman lurked around town in the company of a much younger stripper, his desires were apparent. These men behaved badly, cheating on their wives and using their powerful positions to assist in achieving sexual gratification. Confronted with evidence of their behavior, they lied and attempted to cover up their actions to avoid public embarrassment. Anyone watching the scenario could understand even if they disapproved of the behavior.

Public figures are sometimes held accountable for sex scandals because the public can discern cause and effect. Critics argue that a political figure who surrenders to temptation does not possess the character and judgment necessary to conduct the public's business. Supporters observe that although such behavior is not to be encouraged, it does not constitute an irredeemable violation of the public trust.

Whether a public figure can survive a sex scandal depends on several factors. As discussed within the book, the salience of a sex scandal varies across the span of American history, acting as a metaphorical pendulum of societal mores. During the first hundred years of the republic, private affairs affected the public's opinion of whether an elected official could be trusted to transact public affairs. From the 1880s until the 1970s, standards changed. The private lives of public figures were mostly off-limits. From the latter half of the twentieth century and into the twenty-first century, sexual conduct—or, more appropriately, misconduct—again became relevant to the evaluation of public figures.

Even in eras when sexual impropriety captures headlines, outcomes vary, depending on circumstances. A sex scandal wrecked Gary Hart's presidential bid, Bob Packwood's Senate career, Gary Condit's House career, and Anthony Weiner's House career. Yet Grover Cleveland survived salacious stories of his illegitimate child. Allegations that Donald Trump sexually assaulted more than a dozen women, and the emergence of a videotape of Trump bragging about sexual assault, failed to derail his political career. In other cases public figures survived a sex scandal—Daniel Sickles, Henry Ward Beecher, and Bill Clinton readily spring to mind—but their reputations were forever diminished.

The outcomes in sex scandals often are fact determinative. Gary Hart had presented himself in the media as a white knight. Although a myth arose that Gary Hart dared the press to follow him—he did not do this—he certainly flaunted convention and appeared to be a hypocrite. Hoisting him on his own petard appeared to be well-deserved comeuppance for an elected official who sometimes appeared arrogant and condescending.

Bob Packwood was a serial predator who preyed on vulnerable young women who feared for their professional careers if they resisted his advances. Had he appeared to be a sympathetic figure or exhibited genuine remorse, as Bill Clinton eventually did, Packwood might have lived to legislate another day. With his self-serving rationalizations and his tone-deaf response to his critics, it was little wonder that Packwood was drummed out of the United States Senate.

Gary Condit presented an unusual case because his affair only surfaced after his lover, young Chandra Levy, went missing. Authorities eventually discovered her dead body. Suspicion that Condit was involved in her disappearance and death doomed his political career. He might have survived a garden-variety sex scandal, assuming such a thing exists, but he could not weather the storm when the young woman was murdered.

Anthony Weiner presented an unusual case of sexual misconduct. Weiner's scandals arose because he transmitted lurid photos of himself in various stages of undress. The overwhelming majority of sex scandals in American history concerns public figures behaving badly and attempting to cover up evidence of their misdeeds. Weiner's misdeeds were perverse because an essential feature of the scandal was his deliberate disclosure of the offending material. The psychology of a public man who would willingly send sexually explicit photographs of himself to third parties is difficult to understand. That he "sexted" multiple times, even after he had been caught and suffered devastating consequences, defies rational explanation. Weiner's career did not survive public disclosure because he insisted that it should not survive. Perhaps he suffered from a severe case of impostor's syndrome. He feared that he was not good enough to hold high office. Rather than waiting for others to discover his innate deficiencies, he telegraphed (or more precisely, transmitted via social media) incontrovertible proof that he was unworthy of the public trust. How else can one explain his self-destructive behavior?

History teaches that powerful men can survive sex scandals through one of two diametrically opposed extremes. At one end of the spectrum, the public figure refuses to comment on the issue or vehemently denies it happened. This strategy only works if there is no definitive proof such as photographs, recordings, or DNA evidence. During his lifetime Thomas Jefferson never publicly commented on or acknowledged the rumors about his sexual relationship with Sally Hemings. It was only 170 years after his death that DNA testing indicated the likelihood that he had engaged in sexual relations with his slave and fathered one or more of her children.

At the other extreme a political figure who seems genuinely remorseful and seeks forgiveness can recover from a sex scandal, especially if he can portray himself as acting nobly. Grover Cleveland refused to hide from allegations that he had fathered an illegitimate son, although he suggested that he might not be the father owing to Maria Halpin's promiscuity. His public stance was that he would do the right thing and support the child. In this instance Cleveland could count on his public reputation as "Grover the Good" to gain the benefit of the doubt from a public that otherwise would have been wary of self-serving statements by a crafty politician.

Political corruption is arguably far more relevant to a public figure's fitness to serve than is his sexual behavior. In fact, this observation has helped many a public figure contest charges of sexual impropriety. Alexander Hamilton's defense in the Maria Reynolds affair was to admit that he had engaged in sexual intercourse outside of his marriage, but he had not embezzled money or otherwise betrayed the public trust. Similarly, Bill Clinton claimed that although his private behavior was reprehensible, it was confined to the private sphere. It was between him and his wife. As president of the United States, he had pursued popular policies that protected Americans and boosted the health of the economy. Every public figure caught in a sex scandal from the Founders to Donald Trump has argued that being an abysmal human being is not the proper standard to evaluate the figure's performance. The question is whether the person's policies and programs benefit the populace, or at least a portion thereof.

Sex scandals have been and unfortunately continue to be a feature of American political life. The personality traits that lead public figures to seek election or otherwise ascend into a prominent position in public life often compel them to take extraordinary risks. It requires no small ambition to seek federal elective office, especially the presidency. The kind of person who believes that he can win high office is a person who believes that the risk-reward calculation that applies to most people does not apply to him.

An "average" person would balk at campaigning for elective office. Traveling constantly, raising millions of dollars in campaign donations, standing in front of television cameras multiple times a day, and surrendering one's private life are unfathomable. Such a person colors inside the lines and plays by societal rules because that is how life is lived. Taking enormous risks with a small likelihood of reward is unthinkable.

An elite who wins high office has beaten enormous odds. He or she has taken many risks, and the payoff has been handsome. The elected official is often surrounded by staffers and peers who seek to fulfill the official's every need. Lavish dinners, private jet travel, ceaseless media attention, and public adoration can lead to grandiose expectations. *If I beat these odds, I must be special. Special people are entitled to things that ordinary people are not.*

Although not every elected official views the world this way, enough public figures believe they are entitled to special consideration that they willingly misbehave. *If I ran for public office and won, I can engage in a sexual affair and no one will ever know. This risk may pay off because the risk of running for office paid off.* Perhaps the analysis is less consciously cerebral and more unthinkingly libidinous, but it stems from the same idea. Prominent public figures are entitled to the "rewards" of their exalted position.[1]

The struggle in American political history is to empower and follow leaders who will perform public service without misbehaving in the process. To a large extent, the men and women who serve as public figures have acted honorably. In those cases where they have fallen short, their human failings often are exposed, and they suffer the consequences. Although sometimes public figures suffer few or no negative repercussions, the desire for a good public reputation and the fear of losing esteem check their behavior. Institutional controls—expulsion, impeachment, or lawsuits—also serve as necessary external constraints. These checks do not always succeed, but they are crucial factors in ensuring that public figures usually place the public good above private gratification.

NOTE

1. See, for example, James D. Griffith, "The Psychology of Risky Behavior: Why Politicians Expose Themselves," in *Sex Scandals in American Politics: A Multidisciplinary Approach to the Construction and Aftermath of Contemporary Political Sex Scandals*, edited by Alison Dagnes (New York: Continuum, 2011), 28–46.

References

"Accuser of Packwood Says Friend of His Pressured Her for Silence." *New York Times*, November 29, 1992, 24.

Alexander, Keith L., and Lynh Bui. "Secret Recordings Emerged and the Chandra Levy Case Rapidly Unraveled." *Washington Post*, July 30, 2016, n.p.

"And Now . . . DC's Dynamic Duo." *Playboy* 23, no. 9 (September 1976): 132.

Anthony, Carl Sferrazza. "The Duchess: First Lady Florence Harding and the Tragedy of Being Ahead of Her Time." *Social Science Journal* 34, no. 4 (October 2000): 503–16.

Anthony, Carl Sferrazza. *Florence Harding: The First Lady, the Jazz Age, and the Death of America's Most Scandalous President*. New York: William Morrow & Company, 1998.

"Anthony Weiner Resigns." *New York Times*, June 17, 2011, A34.

"Anthony Weiner Resigns After No Sex, No Crimes, No Complaints." *New York Times*, June 19, 2011, NJ3.

Applegate, Debby. *The Most Famous Man in America: The Biography of Henry Ward Beecher*. New York: Doubleday, 2006.

Bai, Matt. *All the Truth Is Out: The Week Politics Went Tabloid*. New York: Vintage, 2015.

Baker, Peter. "Test Results Are In: At Last, Secret About Harding Is Out." *New York Times*, August 13, 2015, A12.

Barbaro, Michael. "Tearful Weiner Admits Sending Explicit Picture; Says He Won't Resign; Asserts No Crime Was Committed—Pelosi Calls for Inquiry." *New York Times*, June 7, 2011, A1, A28.

Barbaro, Michael, and Megan Twohey. "Crossing the Line: Trump's Private Conduct with Women." *New York Times*, May 15, 2016, 1.

Barringer, Felicity. "The Lost Privacy of Gary Condit." *New York Times*, July 15, 2001, WK3.

Barron, James. "Gary Condit Strikes Back." *New York Times*, December 17, 2002, B2.

Barton, David. *The Jefferson Lies: Exposing the Myths You've Always Believed About Thomas Jefferson*. Nashville, TN: Thomas Nelson, 2012.

Bauer, Susan Wise. *The Art of Public Grovel: Sexual Sin and Public Confession in America*. Princeton, NJ: Princeton University Press, 2008.

Bay, Mia. "In Search of Sally Hemings in the Post-DNA Era." *Reviews in American History* 34, no. 4 (2006): 407–26.

Bellafante, Ginia. "A Candidate Eclipse." *New York Times*, July 28, 2013, LI1, LI6.

Belz, Herman. "The Legend of Sally Hemings." *Academic Questions* 25, no. 2 (June 2012): 218–27.

Bennett, Brian, Teresa Berenson, Massimo Calabresi, Philip Elliott, W. J. Hennigan, and Susanna Schrobsdorff. "Perfect Storm." *Time* 191, no. 5 (April 23, 2018): 20–25.

Bennett, Jessica. "'Strange Sorority' Bids Farewell to Trump." *New York Times*, January 24, 2021, ST4.

Berman, Daphna. "Live from New York, It's Anthony Weiner." *Moment Magazine* 36, no. 3 (May/June 2011): 28–36.

Bernstein, Robert. "To the Editor." *New York Times*, July 25, 2013, A26.

Blumell, Lindsey E. "She Persisted . . . and So Did He. Gendered Source Use During the Trump Access Hollywood Scandal." *Journalism Studies* 20, no. 2 (February 2019): 267–86.

Blumenthal, Sidney. *The Clinton Wars*. New York: Plume, 2004.

Bonner, Raymond. "Police Focusing on Voluntary Absence or Foul Play in Intern Case." *New York Times*, July 6, 2001, A10.

Brands, H. W. *Andrew Jackson: His Life and Times*. New York: Doubleday, 2005.

Brands, H. W. *Heirs of the Founders: The Epic Rivalry of Henry Clay, John Calhoun and Daniel Webster—the Second Generation of American Giants*. New York: Doubleday, 2018.

Brandt, Nat. *The Congressman Who Got Away with Murder*. Syracuse, NY: Syracuse University Press, 1991.

Brodie, Fawn M. *Thomas Jefferson: An Intimate History*. New York: W. W. Norton, 2010 [1974].

Bromwich, Jonah E. "*Apprentice* Contestant Ends Trump Defamation Lawsuit," *New York Times*, November 14, 2021, A18.

Bromwich, Jonah E. "Legal Setback for Trump as 'Apprentice' Star Suit Is Cleared to Proceed." *New York Times*, March 31, 2021, A19.

Brookhiser, Richard. *Alexander Hamilton: American*. New York: Free Press, 1999.

"The Brooklyn Scandal; The Loader-Price Conspiracy; Examination Before Justice Riley; Mr. Beecher on the Stand; The Case Sent Before the Grand Jury; Price's Affidavit." *New York Times*, July 8, 1875, 2.

Brown, Mary H. "To the Editor." *New York Times*, July 25, 2013, A26.

Bruni, Frank. "The Freak Show as Fable." *New York Times*, August 4, 2013, SR3.

Callender, James Thomson. *The History of the United States for 1796; Including a Variety of Interesting Particulars Relative to the Federal Government Previous to That Period*. Philadelphia, PA: Snowden & McCorkle, 1797.

Carswell, Simon. "US Appoints Gary Hart as Envoy to Northern Ireland." *Irish Times*, October 22, 2014, 7.

Chadwick, Bruce. *Triumvirate: The Story of the Unlikely Alliance That Saved the Constitution and United the Nation*. New York: Fall Rover Press, 2009.

"The Charges Swept Away; A Political Scandal Speedily Settled; Report of a Committee of Independent Republicans, Dwelling in Buffalo, Concerning Accusations Against Gov. Cleveland." *New York Times*, August 12, 1884, 5.

Chase-Riboud, Barbara. *Sally Hemings*. New York: Avon Books, 1980 [1979].

Chen, David W., and Javier C. Hernandez. "Weiner Admits Explicit Texting After House Exit." *New York Times*, July 24, 2013, A1, A21.

Chernow, Ron. *Alexander Hamilton*. New York: Penguin Press, 2004.

Chernow, Ron. *Washington: A Life*. New York: Penguin Press, 2010.

Chokshi, Niraj. "Former Staffer Claims Trump Forced Kiss." *New York Times*, February 26, 2019, A17.

Chozick, Amy, and Patrick Healy. "Weiner's Texts Cast Shadow on Campaign; Wife, Top Clinton Aide, Decides to Separate." *New York Times*, August 30, 2016, A1, A15.

Christianson, Stephen G. "Tilton v. Beecher: 1875." In *Great American Trials: From Salem Witchcraft to Rodney King*. Edited by Edward W. Knappman, 171–74. Detroit, MI: Visible Ink Press, 2003.

Clinton, Bill. *My Life*. New York: Knopf, 2004.

Clinton, Hillary Rodham. *Living History*. New York: Simon & Schuster, 2003.

Cogan, Jacob Katz. "The Reynolds Affair and the Politics of Character." *Journal of the Early Republic* 16, no. 3 (Autumn 1996): 389–417.

Cohen, Jared. *Accidental Presidents: Eight Men Who Changed America*. New York and London: Simon & Schuster, 2019.

Coit, Margaret L. *John C. Calhoun: American Portrait*. Boston: Riverside Press, Houghton Mifflin Company, 1950.

Coleman, Jess. "To the Editor." *New York Times*, July 25, 2013, A26.

"Comrades in Arms Mourn Gen. Sickles; Men Who Fought with Him Hold Simple Memorial Service Over His Coffin; Place Flag and Flowers; To-day They Serve as Pallbearers at Service in Cathedral—Burial in Arlington." *New York Times*, May 8, 1914, 9.

"Condit Settles Suit Against Tabloids." *Oakland Tribune* [Oakland, CA], September 10, 2004, 1.

CQ Press Guide to Congress. 7th ed. Thousand Oaks, CA: Sage, 2013. Vol. 1.

Crewdson, John M. "Mills in Seclusion After Report He Was Intoxicated in Car Stopped by Police: Mills Not at Session." *New York Times*, October 10, 1974, 23.

"Daniel K. Sickles." *New York Times*, May 5, 1914, 10.

Daniels, Stormy. *Full Disclosure*. New York: St. Martin's 2018.

D'Antonio, Michael. *Hunting Hillary: The Forty-Year Campaign to Destroy Hillary Clinton*. New York: Thomas Dunne Books, 2020.

Davis, Lanny J. "Public Candor and Gary Condit." *New York Times*, July 12, 2001, A23.

Dean, John W. *Warren G. Harding*. New York: Times Books, 2004.

Dee, Jim. "Pushing Our Politicians." *Belfast Telegraph*, November 1, 2014, 7.

"Democrat Wins Race in Oregon for Packwood's Seat in Senate." *New York Times*, January 31, 1996, A13.

DeRose, Chris. *Star-Spangled Scandal: Sex, Murder, and the Trial that Changed America*. Washington, DC: Regnery History, 2019.

Dillin, John. "Press Unfair to Hart? Polls Show Public Concern; Experts Back Tough Scrutiny." *Christian Science Monitor*, May 12, 1987, n.p.

Dionne Jr., E. J. "Courting Danger: The Fall of Gary Hart." *New York Times*, May 9, 1987, 1.

Dionne Jr., E. J. "Gary Hart: The Elusive Front-Runner." *New York Times*, May 3, 1987, SM 28.

Dionne Jr., E. J. "Gephardt Is Second; Vice President Jubilant as His Troubled Week Ends in Triumph," *New York Times*, February 17, 1988, A1, B6.

Dionne Jr., E. J. "Hart Unsettles Democrats, Which Pleases Republicans." *New York Times*, December 16, 1987, B7.

"DNA Tests of the Relevant Descendants Shows that Warren Harding Had a Love Child by Nan Britton, a Woman 31 Years His Junior." *National Review* 67, no. 16 (September 7, 2015): 13.

Dowd, Maureen. "Time to Hard-Delete Carlos Danger." *New York Times*, July 28, 2013, SR11.

Doyle, J. E. P. Compiler. *Plymouth Church and Its Pastor, or Henry Ward Beecher and His Accusers*. St. Louis: Bryan, Brand & Company, 1875.

Doyle, Michael. "Baskin-Robbins Found It Hard to Get Scoop on Condit; Trial Transcript Reveals Court Costs, Son's Book." *Modesto Bee* [Modesto, CA], January 3, 2009, B1.

Doyle, Michael. "Condit, Author Settle Lawsuit; Ex-Congressman Avoids Deposition, Gets Apology." *Modesto Bee* [Modesto, CA], March 15, 2005, A1.

"Drawn Out Impeachment Battle Dealt Its Meager Spoils to All Sides." *New York Times*, February 14, 1999, 1, 29.

"Dreadful Tragedy; Shocking Homicide at Washington; Philip Barton Key Shot Dead in Street by Daniel E. Sickles; Sad Story of Domestic Ruin and Bloody Revenge." *New York Times*, February 28, 1859, 1.

Egan, Timothy. "Oregon Now Wonders Who Is Real Packwood." *New York Times*, December 8, 1992, B12.

Egan, Timothy. "Packwood Is Leaving as a Pariah in His State." *New York Times*, September 9, 1995, 8.

Ellefson, Lindsey. "White House Calls Trump Assault Accuser E. Jean Carroll's New Defamation Suit a 'Fraud—Just Like the Author.'" *The Wrap*, November 4, 2019. Accessed on September 3, 2021. www.thewrap.com/white-house-calls-trump-assault-accuser-e-jean-carrolls-new-defamation-suit-a-fraud-just-like-the-author/.

Ellis, Joseph J. *American Sphinx: The Character of Thomas Jefferson*. New York: Vintage, 1998.

Evensen, Bruce J. *God's Man for the Gilded Age: D. L. Moody and the Rise of Modern Evangelism*. New York and Oxford: Oxford University Press, 2003.

"Excerpts from Hart Speech to Convention Exhorting Party for Campaign." *New York Times*, July 19, 1984, A18.

Fallows, James. "Was Gary Hart Set Up?" *The Atlantic* 322, no. 4 (November 2018): 26–29.

"Fanne: Acting 18 and Feeling 50," *Time* 104, no. 25 (December 16, 1974): 23.

Farquhar, Michael. *A Treasury of Great American Scandals: Tantalizing True Tales of Historic Misbehavior by the Founding Fathers and Others Who Let Freedom Swing*. New York: Penguin Books, 2003.

Fermino, Jennifer, Jason Silverstein, and Larry McShane. "Sick Wein and Teen; Girl: He Said Be 'Mine,' and Sent Crotch Pictures; New Low Could Turn Pervert Into Prisoner." *New York Daily News*, September 22, 2016, 4.

Ferrell, Robert H. *The Strange Deaths of President Harding.* Columbia and London: University of Missouri Press, 1996.

Feuer, Alan, and Benjamin Weiser. "Biden's Justice Dept. Backs Trump in Defamation Case." *New York Times*, June 9, 2021, A17.

Foerstel, Herbert N. *From Watergate to Monicagate: Ten Controversies in Modern Journalism and the Media.* Westport, CT: Greenwood Press, 2001.

Fontaine, Felix G. *Trial of the Hon. Daniel E. Sickles for the Shooting of Philip Barton Key, Esq., U.S. District Attorney of Washington, D.C., February 27, 1859.* New York: R. M. De Witt, 1859.

Fox, Richard Wightman. *Trials of Intimacy: Love and Loss in the Beecher-Tilton Scandal.* Chicago: University of Chicago Press, 1999.

Frisken, Amanda. "Sex in Politics: Victoria Woodhull as an American Public Woman, 1870–1876." *Journal of Women's History* 12, no. 1 (Spring 2000): 89–110.

Furgurson, Ernest B. "Moment of Truth: Grover Cleveland's 1884 Presidential Campaign Was Rocked by a Sex Scandal. His Unconventional Response Saved His Political Career—and Offered a Case Study in Public Relations." *American History* 48, no. 4 (October 2013): 64.

Gabriel, Mary. *Notorious Victoria: The Life of Victoria Woodhull, Uncensored.* Chapel Hill, NC: Algonquin Books, 1998.

Gabriel, Trip. "A 10th Woman Accuses Donald Trump of Inappropriate Touching." *New York Times*, October 20, 2016, n.p.

Gates, Anita, and Katharine Q. Seelye. "Linda Tripp, Whose Secret Lewinsky Tape Led to Clinton, Is Dead at 70." *New York Times*, April 9, 2020, B11.

"Gen. Sickles Dies; His Wife at His Bedside; Long Estrangement Ended When Fatal Illness Attacked Veteran; Career a Stirring One; Soldier, Politician, and Diplomat, He Lost a Leg at Gettysburg, and Lived to Be Almost 91." *New York Times*, May 4, 1914, 1, 3.

Goldmacher, Shane. "A Tabloid Publisher Will Pay $187,500 FEC Penalty for Its Trump Hush-Money Payment." *New York Times*, June 1, 2021, n.p.

Gordon-Reed, Annette. *The Hemingses of Monticello: An American Family.* New York: W. W. Norton, 2009.

Gordon-Reed, Annette. *Thomas Jefferson & Sally Hemings: An American Controversy.* Charlottesville: The University of Virginia Press, 1998.

Gormley, Ken. *The Death of American Virtue: Clinton vs. Starr.* New York: Crown, 2010.

Gould, Lewis L. *Grand Old Party: A History of the Republicans.* New York: Random House, 2003.

Graves, Florence, and Charles E. Shepard. "Packwood Accused of Sexual Advances; Alleged Behavior Pattern Counters Image." *Washington Post*, November 22, 1992, A1, A26, A27.

"The Great Pastor Dead; Henry Ward Beecher's Peaceful End; Rest Coming to Him as He Had Wished; The Funeral Services on Friday Morning." *New York Times*, March 9, 1887, 1.

Griffith, James D. "The Psychology of Risky Behavior: Why Politicians Expose Themselves." In *Sex Scandals in American Politics: A Multidisciplinary Approach to the Construction and Aftermath of Contemporary Political Sex Scandals.* Edited by Alison Dagnes, 28–46. New York: Continuum, 2011.

Grigoriadis, Vanessa. "Monica Takes Manhattan." New York (March 19, 2001): n.p.

Grynbaum, Michael M. "A Greek Tragedy with Elements of Danger. Carlos Danger." *New York Times*, October 8, 2013, A20.

Hamilton, Alexander. *Observations on Certain Documents Contained in No. V & VI of "The History of the United States for the Year 1796," in which the Charge of Speculation Against Alexander Hamilton, Late Secretary of the Treasury, Is Fully Refuted, Written by Himself.* Philadelphia, PA: Printed for John Fenno, by John Bioren, 1797.

Harris, Chris. "A Murder Case Crumbles: Who Killed Chandra Levy?" *People* 86, no. 7 (August 15, 2016): 56–57.

Harris, John F. *The Survivor: Bill Clinton in the White House.* New York: Random House, 2005.

Hart, Gary. *The Restoration of the Republic: The Jeffersonian Ideal in 21st Century America.* Oxford and New York: Oxford University Press, 2002.

Heidler, David S., and Jeanne T. Heidler. *Henry Clay: The Essential American.* New York: Random House, 2010.

Heil, Emily. "Anthony Weiner Finishes His Prison Term." *Washington Post*, May 15, 2019, C2.

"Hemings." The Thomas Jefferson Heritage Society. www.tjheritage.org/hemings. Accessed February 5, 2020.

"Henry Ward Beecher." *New York Times*, March 9, 1887, 4.

Hernandez, Javier C., and Michael Barbaro. "Weiner Admits to More Lewd Exchanges but Denies an Addiction." *New York Times*, July 26, 2013, A18.

Hernandez, Raymond. "Despite Plan to Enter Rehab, Weiner Still Faces Calls to Resign." *New York Times*, June 13, 2011, A18.

Hernandez, Raymond. "In Chaotic Scene, Weiner Quits Seat in Scandal's Wake; Vulgar Shouts During Announcement in Brooklyn—Relief for Democrats." *New York Times*, June 17, 2011, A1, A30.

Hevesi, Dennis. "Wilbur Mills, Long a Power in Congress, Is Dead at 82." *New York Times*, May 3, 1992, 54.

"Hey, It's Our Ol' Chum! Weiner Fish Food in *Sharknado 3*." *New York Post*, July 12, 2015, 3.

Higham, Scott, and Sari Horwitz. *Finding Chandra: A True Washington Murder Mystery.* New York: Simon & Schuster, 2010.

Holzer, Harold. *The Presidents vs. the Press: The Endless Battle between the White House and the Media from the Founding Fathers to Fake News.* New York: Dutton, 2020.

Horowitz, Helen Lefkowitz. "Victoria Woodhull, Anthony Comstock, and Conflict Over Sex in the United States in the 1870s." *Journal of American History* 87, no. 2 (September 2000): 403–34.

Horwitz, Sari, and Allan Lengel. "Chandra Levy Ruled a Homicide Victim; D.C. Police Ask FBI Lab's Help in Learning How Ex-Intern Died." *New York Times*, May 29, 2002, A1.

Horwitz, Sari; Scott Higham; and Sylvia Moreno. "Chandra's Secret," *Washington Post*, July 14, 2008, A1.

Horwitz, Sari; Scott Higham; and Sylvia Moreno. "Who Killed Chandra Levy?" *Washington Post*, July 13, 2008, A1.

"Huma Abedin Decides to Withdraw Divorce from Weiner." *News India Times*, January 19, 2018, 8.

Hunter, Marjorie. "Mills Reveals Alcoholism; Plans to Stay in Congress." *New York Times*, December 31, 1974, 45.

The Impeachment and Trial of President Clinton: The Official Transcripts from the House Judiciary Committee Hearings to the Senate Trial. New York: Times Books, 1999.

Isikoff, Michael. *Uncovering Clinton: A Reporter's Story*. New York: Crown, 1999.

"It Gets Worse for Weiner; Embroiled in Sexting Trouble with Teen." *Toronto Sun*, September 22, 2016, A10.

Jeffers, H. P. *An Honest President: The Life and Presidencies of Grover Cleveland*. New York: HarperCollins, 2002.

Jefferson, Thomas. *Notes on the State of Virginia*. New York: Penguin, 1999 [1785].

Jenrette, Rita. *My Capitol Secrets*. New York: Bantam, 1981.

Kane, Joseph Nathan. *Facts About the Presidents*. New York: Ace Books, 1976.

Kantor, Jodi. "Friends Recall Trump Accuser's Claims from 1997." *New York Times*, October 9, 2020, A25.

Kavanaugh, Shane Dixon. "Weiner's Gift to His Mayoral Rivals." *Crain's New York Business* 27, no. 23 (June 6, 2011): 1.

Keegan, John. *The American Civil War*. New York: Knopf, 2009.

Keneally, Meghan. "List of Trump's Accusers and Their Allegations of Sexual Misconduct." ABC News, September 18, 2020. Accessed on September 3, 2021, https://abcnews.go.com/Politics/list-trumps-accusers-allegations-sexual-misconduct/story?id=51956410.

Keneally, Thomas. *American Scoundrel: The Life of the Notorious Civil War General Dan Sickles*. New York: Anchor Books, 2003.

Kennedy, Roger G. *Burr, Hamilton, and Jefferson: A Study in Character*. Oxford and New York: Oxford University Press, 1999.

Kerrigan, Michael. *Dark History of the American Presidents: Power, Corruption, and Scandal at the Heart of the White House*. London: Amber Books, Ltd., 2011.

Kirchmeier, Mark. *Packwood: The Public and Private Life, from Acclaim to Outrage*. New York: HarperCollins, 1995.

Klebanow, Diana. "'Pressed' to Destruction: The Saga of Gary Hart." *USA Today* 143, no. 2838 (March 2015): 56–57.

Knappman, Edward W. "Daniel Sickles Trial: 1859." In *Great American Trials: From Salem Witchcraft to Rodney King*. Edited by Edward W. Knappman, 127–32. Detroit, MI: Visible Ink Press, 2003.

Krauss, Clifford. "Drinking Might Have Prompted Sexual Advances, Senator Says." *New York Times*, November 28, 1992, 9.

Krauss, Clifford. "Senator Enters Alcohol Clinic for Evaluation." *New York Times*, December 1, 1992, A18.

Kulig, Teresa C., Francis T. Cullen, and Murat Haner. "President or Predator? The Social Construction of Donald Trump in a Divided America." *Victims & Offenders* 14, no. 8 (November 2019): 940–64.

Lachman, Charles. *A Secret Life: The Lies and Scandals of President Grover Cleveland*. New York: Skyhorse, 2012.

Leddy, Chuck. "Beecher: Abolitionist, Preacher, Lover; Henry Ward Beecher Was a Legend in His Time, for Both Theology and Scandal." *Christian Science Monitor*, July 11, 2006, 16.

Leonnig, Carol, and Philip Rucker. *I Alone Can Fix It: Donald J. Trump's Catastrophic Final Year*. New York: Penguin Press, 2021.

Leuchtenburg, William E. *The American President: From Theodore Roosevelt to Bill Clinton*. Oxford and New York: Oxford University Press, 2015.

Levine, Barry, and Monique El-Faizy. *All the President's Women: Donald Trump and the Making of a Predator*. New York: Hachette Books, 2019.

Long, Kim. *The Almanac of Political Corruption, Scandals & Dirty Politics*. New York: Delta Paperbacks, 2007.

Lyons, Richard D. "Mills Quits as Chairman; Young Democrats Advance." *New York Times*, December 11, 1974, 1, 27.

Malone, Dumas. *Jefferson the President: First Term, 1801–1805*. Boston: Little, Brown, 1970.

Marion, Nancy E. *The Politics of Disgrace: The Role of Political Scandal in American Politics*. Durham, NC: Carolina Academic Press, 2010.

Marszalek, John F. *The Petticoat Affair: Manners, Mutiny, and Sex in Andrew Jackson's White House*. New York: Free Press, 1997.

"A Maverick Bows Out." *Washington Post*, January 1, 1969, A18.

McFadden, Robert D. "Fanne Fox Who Plunged Into a Reservoir and Emerged Famous, Dies at 84." *New York Times*, February 25, 2021, A21.

Meacham, Jon. *American Lion: Andrew Jackson in the White House*. New York: Random House, 2008.

Meacham, Jon. *Thomas Jefferson: The Art of Power*. New York: Random House, 2012.

Mee Jr., Charles L. *The Ohio Gang: The World of Warren G. Harding*. Lanham, MD: M. Evans, an Imprint of Rowman & Littlefield, 1981.

Miller, John J. "He, Gary Hart." *National Review* 55, no. 9 (May 19, 2003): 34–36.

Miller, Patricia. *Bringing Down the Colonel: A Sex Scandal of the Gilded Age, and the "Powerless" Woman Who Took On Washington*. New York: Sarah Crichton Books, Farrar, Straus, and Giroux, 2018.

"Mills Aide Reports Representative Ill." *New York Times*, October 12, 1974, 62.

"Mills Derided in Congress Over Link to Stripper." *New York Times*, December 3, 1974, 32, 85.

"Mills Quits as Chairman; Young Democrats Advance," *New York Times*, December 11, 1974, 1, 27.

"Mills Says He's 'Still Embarrassed.'" *New York Times*, October 17, 1974, 28.

Mills, Wilbur. "My Life on the Rocks; The Tragic Fall of Wilbur Mills, Once a Candidate for the Presidency, and How He Fought Back to Respectability Is Told to His Friend and Professional Colleague Roger Zion." *Saturday Evening Post* 251, no. 4 (May/June 1979): 28, 30, 32, 114, 116.

Monroe, Jennifer. "Anthony Weiner." In *Our States*. New York: History Reference Center, 2020, 3.

"Monticello Affirms Thomas Jefferson Fathered Children with Sally Hemings: A Statement by the Thomas Jefferson Foundation." The Thomas Jefferson Foundation. Accessed on January 31, 2020. www.monticello.org/thomas-jefferson/jefferson-slavery/thomas-jefferson-and-sally-hemings-a-brief-account/monticello-affirms-thomas-jefferson-fathered-children-with-sally-hemings/.

Morton, Andrew. *Monica's Story*. New York: St. Martin's Paperbacks, 1999.

Nevins, Allan. *Grover Cleveland: A Study in Courage.* New York: Dodd, Mead, and Company, 1932.

"New Morality, New Journalism." *National Review* 39, no. 10 (June 5, 1987): 15.

Nordheimer, Jon. "Donna Rice Aims to Resume Life After Hart." *New York Times,* June 20, 1987, 34.

Orden, Erica, and Nicole Hong. "Anthony Weiner Pleads Guilty Following Sexting Probe; Many Democrats Say the Case Involving the Former Lawmaker Contributed to Hillary Clinton's Defeat." *Wall Street Journal,* May 19, 2017, n.p.

Packer, George. "The Legacy of Donald Trump: His Reign of Lies Poisoned Our Mind and Our Politics, with Effects that Will Long Linger. But Democracy Survived." *The Atlantic* 327, no. 1 (January/February 2021): 9–12.

"Packwood: Behavior Was 'Wrong'; Senator Rejects Calls to Resign." *Washington Post,* December 11, 1992, A1, A16.

"Packwood Diaries: A Rare Look at Washington's Tangled Web." *New York Times,* September 10, 1995, 1.

"The Packwood Problem." *New York Times,* December 11, 1992, A38.

"The Packwood Resignation." *New York Times,* September 8, 1995, A26.

Pager, Tyler. "Weiner Is Out of Prison and Living in Brooklyn." *New York Times,* February 18, 2019, A16.

"Panel Gets a New Complaint on Packwood." *New York Times,* December 3, 1992, A17.

Patton, Venetria K., and Ronald Jemal Stevens. "Narrating Competing Truths in the Thomas Jefferson–Sally Hemings Paternity Debate." *Black Scholar* 29, no. 4 (Winter 1999): 8–15.

Payne, Phillip G. *Dead Last: The Public Memory of Warren G. Harding.* Athens: Ohio University Press, 2009.

Pearson, John. "Gary Hart." In *Our States: Colorado.* Toledo, OH: Great Neck Publishing, August 31, 2020: 1–4.

Perez-Pena, Richard. "Man Accused in Levy Killing Is Cleared of All Charges." *New York Times,* July 29, 2016, A15.

Peterson, Merrill D. *The Jefferson Image in the American Mind.* Charlottesville: University of Virginia Press, 1998 [1960]).

Pianin, Eric. "Senate Inquiry on Packwood Signals Sea Change in Attitude; Conduct No Longer Seen 'Above the Law.'" *Washington Post,* December 7, 1992, A1, A8, A9.

Pierce, J. Kingston. "Andrew Jackson and the Tavern-Keeper's Daughter." *American History* 34, no. 2 (June 1999): 20–26.

Purdum, Todd S. "Condit Denies Any Knowledge of Levy's Fate." *New York Times,* August 24, 2001, A1, A16.

Ramirez, Mark D., and David A. M. Peterson. *Ignored Racism: White Animus Toward Latinos.* Cambridge and New York: Cambridge University Press, 2020.

Randall, Willard Sterne. *Alexander Hamilton: A Life.* New York: Harper Perennial Political Classics, 2014 [2003].

"Recount Confirms Senator Morse Loss." *Washington Post,* December 22, 1968, D2.

Reed, Roy. "Mills Forced to Campaign Hard Following Tidal Basin Incident." *New York Times,* October 19, 1974, 65.

Remini, Robert V. *Henry Clay: Statesman for the Union.* New York: Norton, 1991.

Remini, Robert V. *The Life of Andrew Jackson*. New York: Harper, 2010 [1988].

"Rev. Henry Ward Beecher; Mr. Tilton's Accusation Against the Brooklyn Clergyman; An Extraordinary Story; The Evidence Against Mr. Beecher; Private Letters of the Parties Implicated; Mr. Tilton's Statement in Full." *New York Times*, July 22, 1874, 1.

"The Rise and Decline of Mr. Mills," *New York Times*, December 8, 1974, 252.

Risen, James. "Fourth Condit Interview Is Possible, Washington Police Say." *New York Times*, July 24, 2001, A16.

Robenalt, James David. *The Harding Affair: Love and Espionage During the Great War*. New York: Palgrave MacMillan, 2009.

Robson, Ruthann. "The Sexual Misconduct of Donald J. Trump: Toward a Misogyny Report." *Michigan Journal of Gender & Law* 27, no. 1 (2020): 81–148.

Rucker, Philip, and Carol Leonnig. *A Very Stable Genius: Donald J. Trump's Testing of America*. New York: Penguin Press, 2020.

Russell, Francis. "The Sickles Trial; Arguments and Speeches on Both Sides; Verbatim Reports of the Addresses of Mr. Carlisle and the Prosecution and Mr. Stanton and Mr. Brady for the Defence; The Prayers for Instructions to the Jury; Verdict of the Jury—Mr. Sickles Acquitted; From the Special Reporter of the *N.Y. Times*." *New York Times*, April 27, 1859, 9.

Rutenberg, Jim. "Former Playboy Model Tells of Affair with Trump That Lasted 10 Months." *New York Times*, March 23, 2018, A19.

Sacchetti, Maria, and Keith L. Alexander. "Ex-Suspect in Chandra Levy Slaying Is Deported." *Washington Post*, May 9, 2017, B5.

Sager, Mike. "The Final Days of Gary Condit." *Esquire* 138, no. 3 (September 2002): 180–90.

Schrobsdorff, Susanna. "Provocateur Stormy Daniels Takes an Unexpected Turn in the National Spotlight." *Time* 192, no. 17 (October 29, 2018): 12–13.

Seelye, Katharine Q. "Body of Intern Found in Park in Washington." *New York Times*, May 23, 2002, A1, A28.

Seelye, Katharine Q. "Packwood to Leave in 3 Weeks as Dole Fails to Buy More Time." *New York Times*, September 9, 1995, 1, 8.

"Sen. Morse Concedes Election to Packwood." *Washington Post*, December 31, 1968, A4.

"Sexual Harassment in the Senate." *New York Times*, November 24, 1992, A14.

"'Shadow Life' Stuns Family." *New York Times*, September 11, 1995, B10.

Shapiro, Isidore. "To the Editor." *New York Times*, July 25, 2013, A26.

Shear, Michael D., and Eileen Sullivan. "'Horseface,' 'Lowlife,' 'Fat, Ugly': How President Demeans Women." *New York Times*, October 17, 2018, A1.

"Shocking, Lurid, and True! A Hart-Stopping Campaign." *Biography Magazine* 3, no. 9 (September 1999): 18.

"The Sickles Tragedy; Trial of Daniel E. Sickles for the Murder of Philip Barton Key; Twentieth and Last Day's Proceedings; Verdict of Not Guilty; Extraordinary Scene of Excitement in the Court-room; How the Verdict was Received; Mr. Sickles Carried Off in Triumph by a Friend; Closing Scenes of the Trial." *New York Times*, April 27, 1859, 1; 8.

Siegel, Tatiana. "The Hillary Mystery at the Center of the Anthony Weiner Movie." *Hollywood Reporter* 422, no. 3 (2016): 72.

Smith, Jeff. "Lords (and Ladies) of Misrule: Carnival, Scandal, and Satire in the Age of Andrew Jackson." *Studies in American Humor* 3, no. 12 (2005): 52–82.

Smith, J. Scott. "With a Little Help from My Wife: An Examination of Anthony Weiner's Image Repair Discourse Through Third-Party Defense and a Postcrisis Discourse of Renewal." *Northwest Journal of Communication* 44, no. 1 (Spring 2016): 35–61.

Spencer, Suzette. "Historical Memory, Romantic Narrative, and Sally Hemings." *African American Review* 40, no. 3 (Fall 2006): 507–31.

Stephanopoulos, George. *All Too Human*. Back Bay Books, 2000.

Summers, John H. "What Happened to Sex Scandals? Politics and Peccadilloes, Jefferson to Kennedy." *Journal of American History* 87, no. 3 (December 2000): 825–54.

Summers, Mark Wahlgren. *Rum, Romanism, and Rebellion: The Making of a President*. Chapel Hill: University of North Carolina Press, 2003.

Swint, Kerwin. *Mudslingers: The Top 25 Negative Political Campaigns of All Time, Countdown from No. 25 to 1*. Westport, CT: Praeger, 2005.

Takiff, Michael. *A Complicated Man: The Life of Bill Clinton as Told by Those Who Know Him*. New Haven, CT, and London: Yale University Press, 2010.

Tavernise, Sabrina. "Chandra Levy's Killer Gets 60 Years for Murder, Ending Case That Chilled Capital." *New York Times*, February 12, 2011, A12.

Tavernise, Sabrina. "Salvadoran Convicted of Killing Intern Chandra Levy." *New York Times*, November 23, 2010, A18.

"Testimony Excerpts from the President." *Chicago Tribune*, September 22, 1998, n.p.

Toobin, Jeffrey. *A Vast Conspiracy: The Real Story of the Sex Scandal That Nearly Brought Down a President*. New York: Random House, 1999.

Twohey, Megan, and Michael Barbaro. "Two Women Say Trump Made Unwanted Advances Long Ago." *New York Times*, October 13, 2016, A1.

United States Congress. *Congressional Record*, 106th Congress, 1st Session, 1999. Vol. 145, no. 7.

United States House of Representatives, Committee on the Judiciary. *Report on the Committee on the Judiciary, House of Representatives, Ninety-Eighth Congress, First Session, Identifying Court Proceedings and Actions of Vital Interest to the Congress*. Washington, DC: U.S. Government Printing Office, 1984.

Van Natta Jr., Don, and Richard L. Berke. "Lewinsky Again Faces Jurors as Starr Seeks to Compare Accounts." *New York Times*, August 21, 1998, A1, A20.

Vespa, Mary. "Fanne Foxe, Tidal Basin Bombshell, Writes a Sizzler to Pay the Bills." *People* 4, no. 12 (September 22, 1975): 12.

Wald, Matthew L. "Hart, in Surprise, Resumes Campaign for White House; Democrats in Disarray; Coloradan Cites Dismay That Others Have Not Pressed for Some of His Ideas." *New York Times*, December 16, 1987, A1, B7.

Watson, Jamal E. "Despite Polls, Weiner Looks Ahead." *New York Amsterdam News* 96, no. 32 (August 4–August 10, 2005): 1.

"Weiner Roasted as Capitol Scofflaw King." *New York Post*, March 30, 2011, 2.

Weiser, Benjamin. "Weiner, Teary and Chastened, Is to Serve 21 Months for Lewd Texts." *New York Times*, September 26, 2017, A1.

Westfall, Sandra Sobieraj. "Donna Rice 30 Years After Political Scandal: How the Woman at the Center of Gary Hart's Presidential Campaign Monkey Business

Went from 'Rock Bottom' to Healing." *People* 90, no. 21 (November 12, 2018): 77–80.

"Wilbur's Argentine Firecracker." *Time* 104, no. 17 (October 21, 1974): 21–22.

Witcover, Jules. *Party of the People: A History of the Democrats*. New York: Random House, 2003.

Wolff, Peter. "Fanne Foxe Finally Tells All! Meet the newest member of the 'Cheri' family!" *Cheri* 1, no. 9 (April 1977): 14–15, 91, 96–98.

Wood, Kirsten E. "'One Woman So Dangerous to Public Morals': Gender and Power in the Eaton Affair." *Journal of the Early Republic* 17, no. 2 (Summer 1997): 237–75.

"The Wreckage of Anthony Weiner." *New York Times*, September 26, 2017, A26.

Wright, Ed. *History's Greatest Scandals: Shocking Stories of Powerful People*. San Diego, CA: Thunder Bay Press, 2013 [2006].

Yee, Vivian. "After His Latest Scandal, Weiner Avoids Spotlight." *New York Times*, September 1, 2016, A22.

Yee, Vivian. "Weiner Confirms City Agency Is Investigating How He Treats His 4-Year-Old Son." *New York Times*, September 2, 2016, A17.

Index

About the Author

J. Michael Martinez is the author of more than a dozen books, including *The Greatest Criminal Cases: Changing the Course of American Law* (2014) and *Political Assassinations and Attempts in U.S. History* (2017). He resides in Monroe, Georgia, and teaches political science and public administration courses at Kennesaw State University in Kennesaw, Georgia. Visit him online at www.jmichaelmartinez.com.